Educating the Women of Hainan

Educating the Women of Hainan

The Career of
Margaret Moninger in China
1915–1942

KATHLEEN L. LODWICK

THE UNIVERSITY PRESS OF KENTUCKY

Copyright © 1995 by The University Press of Kentucky

Scholarly publisher for the Commonwealth,
serving Bellarmine College, Berea College, Centre
College of Kentucky, Eastern Kentucky University,
The Filson Club, Georgetown College, Kentucky
Historical Society, Kentucky State University,
Morehead State University, Murray State University,
Northern Kentucky University, Transylvania University,
University of Kentucky, University of Louisville,
and Western Kentucky University.

Editorial and Sales Offices: Lexington, Kentucky 40508-4008

Library of Congress Cataloging-in-Publication Data

Lodwick, Kathleen L.
    Educating the women of Hainan : the career of Margaret Moninger in China, 1915-1942 / Kathleen L. Lodwick.
       p.   cm.
    Includes bibliographical references and index.
    ISBN: 978-0-8131-5630-9
    1. Moninger, Mary Margaret, 1891-1950. 2. Women missionaries—China—Biography. 3. Women missionaries—United States—Biography. 4. Presbyterian Church in the U.S.A. Hainan Mission—History. 5. Presbyterian Church—Education—History. 6. Women—Education—China—History—20th century. I. Title.
BV3427.M516L63   1995
266'.51'092—dc20
[B]
                                                                                         94-29319

*For my mother and father,
Kathryn Elizabeth and Algha C. Lodwick,
for their love and encouragement.*

Contents

Foreword by David D. Buck   ix
Acknowledgments   xiii
Introduction   1
1. Joining the Hainan Mission, 1915   13
2. The Young Missionary, 1916-1921   46
3. Turmoil and Flight, 1922-1927   95
4. Come Rejoicing, 1928-1935   138
5. Warfare, 1936-1942   170
Conclusion   211
Notes   218
Bibliography   244
Index   247

Illustrations follow page 96

Foreword

As a HISTORIAN, Kathleen L. Lodwick, it seems, was inevitably drawn into the huge trove of Mary Margaret Moninger's letters once she discovered their order and clarity in the Presbyterian Mission archives. Miss Moninger's letters record in measured weekly installments her twenty-three years as a missionary on Hainan Island. These letters were written in an open, balanced schoolmarm's hand with a favorite Waterman pen on Sunday afternoons and posted by long stages, overland and overseas, in order to present to her family a seemingly casual, but carefully crafted, portrait of her life as a teacher, a missionary, and a member of a remote and small American mission community. These letters are newsy and intimate in a familial, conversational manner and consequently speak almost as clearly across the years separating us from Margaret Moninger as they did to her family in Iowa. Kathleen carefully edited the letters, supplemented them with forays into other archives, as well as with interviews, and wove these materials into a narrative that follows closely the chronology of Margaret Moninger's service and limits itself to the subjects that Miss Moninger herself raised. Kathleen felt little need to impose an interpretive scheme and skillfully and unobtrusively lets Margaret Moninger speak for herself.

Much of Margaret Moninger's life remains in shadows, but Margaret herself intentionally created those spaces where we cannot see, and rather than speculate about them, Kathleen shows us Margaret's self-portrait in a careful chronological narrative structure built around the stages of Margaret Moninger's missionary service: begun deliberately with understated commitment, established and maintained with determination, punctuated by sabbatical leaves or by political upheavals, and ended not really by World War II but by her own illness. The result is a view through an intended window into Margaret Moninger's life.

The values reflected in these letters and this life are familiar to students of the American missionary movement of the nineteenth and twentieth centuries. Margaret Moninger was part of a community of people dedicated to, indeed often truly absorbed by, their calling. Wherever they went in the twentieth century, they built American-style churches, houses, schools, and hospitals. They taught and preached about Christianity and lived a distinct Protestant American form of their universal religion. They usually retained their American dress, as much of their American food as possible, and their established social practices. Frugality, sobriety, moral uprightness, restraint, devotion to work, cleanliness, and order were evident everywhere in their lives and activities. They maintained a familiar American schedule with its seven-day week, its regular five-and-a-half-day round of work regulated by the clock, a pause for personal matters on Saturday afternoons and evenings, and its enormously busy day of rest each Sunday, with services, special meals, and—for Margaret Moninger—a long family letter to be written.

Kathleen's account preserves for us so clearly that sense of establishing an American order in China, where housing, food, dress, the daily round and indeed the longer schedules of time, and the cycles of work and rest were arranged in completely different ways. She provides some hints of how Miss Moninger and her fellow missionaries—like all teachers—knew that simply establishing and preserving their own order was a key to their endeavor.

A subject that these letters consistently underplays is the role of missionary activity, but here Kathleen has found other sources that reveal to us how sure Margaret Moninger was in her trust that Christianity in its American Protestant practices would fit the lives of the young girls in her school and the women in the villages she visited.

She can tell us little of Margaret Moninger's personal, emotional life. No one is ever named as an object of her affections; even mention of her emotional ties to her family members is deeply muted. To maintain her privacy, Margaret Moninger burned the letters she received from her family and adhered to the mission practice of addressing other missionaries formally, as Miss Skinner or Dr. Morse. Missionaries had different ways of dealing with the emotional isolation of life in a mission station. We have no idea how or when such springs of feeling may have opened for Margaret Moninger, but that is as she intended.

Kathleen is able, however, to provide some truly wonderful insights into Margaret as a person taken from the letters of a fellow missionary, Esther Morse, M.D. Dr. Morse, who shared a house with Miss Moninger for many years, in her letters gives us some sense of the energy, strength, and determination that Margaret successfully dampens in her own letters, as well as a much better measure of Margaret's likes and dislikes than she would ever permit herself to reveal. Clearly, Margaret Moninger was more determined, assertive, and controlling than she revealed to her family.

Recent studies such as William Hutchinson's *Errand to the World* (1987), Jane Hunter's *The Gospel of Gentility: American Women Missionaries in Turn-of-the-Century China* (1984), and Irwin Hyatt's *Our Ordered Lives Confess* (1976) present rich historical interpretations of the missionaries and their roles in Chinese and American life. Pearl S. Buck, in her prize-winning but largely forgotten biographies of her parents, *The Exile* (1936) and *Fighting Angel* (1936), provides well-textured psychological portraits of missionaries and their lives in China. Kathleen is familiar with all of these books and indeed is much more widely read in the literature produced by and about China missionaries than I am, but she does not build her account around any of these interpretations.

Instead, as I have suggested, she lets us see Margaret Moninger through her own words with the added and welcome insights of Esther Morse. As I finished reading this book in manuscript, I was reminded of Jonathan Spence's truly marvelous biography, *The Memory Palace of Matteo Ricci* (1984), in which he dispensed with most elements of chronological narrative. Instead he organized his account of the famous Italian Jesuit missionary to China around the mnemonic system (the "Memory Palace" of the title) and certain key images that embodied Ricci's missionary approach to the Chinese as chapter headings and topics. Consequently, the narrative structure of the biography itself dropped the familiar childhood-to-death chronology and took on the character of Matteo Ricci's own mind. We see him using the mnemonic device of a memory palace to master the spoken and written language of the Court and pursuing his missionary work by introducing key concepts into his exchanges with Chinese. The result is a challenging biography that forces readers to step outside the familiar way of reading about others' lives and to apprehend Ricci's own ways of thinking before they could proceed.

Certainly such an approach would have appealed to Margaret Moninger, for she wrote her letters to create a certain image of her life in China. And indeed, that is what Kathleen has provided in her biography. The care, order, restraint, accuracy, and sense of duty that characterize Margaret are found everywhere in Kathleen's account.

David D. Buck

Acknowledgments

MANY PEOPLE HAVE ASSISTED me in the writing of this book, and without them it would never have been written. My original plan was to write a history of the Presbyterian mission on Hainan, but that now is my next project, since I was waylaid by the intriguing letters of Margaret Moninger, which I first found at the Presbyterian Historical Society in Philadelphia while researching the history of the mission. At the Presbyterian archives there are so many people to thank, including William Miller, formerly director, now retired; Frederick Heuser, formerly archivist, now director; Janet Bishop, former assistant archivist; and Kristin L. Gleeson, archivist. Others who assisted in their own individual ways are William B. Bynum (at the Montreat, North Carolina, office), Julius Coaxum, Glenn Colliver, Gerald W. Gillette, John Haas, Max Kofsky, Mary Plummer, John G. Peters, Boyd T. Reese, Norotha B. Robinson, Kenneth J. Ross, Barbara R. Schnur, Edward Starzi, Martha Thomas, Betty Walker, John Walker, and Pamela (E. for Efficiency) Douglas Webster.

I thank Margaret's niece Dorothy Gill Barnes and her husband, Marshall; Margaret's sister-in-law, Susannah Moninger, and her daughter, Susannah Moninger Dodson, and her family, not only for loaning me their collections of Margaret's papers and photographs but also for providing accommodation to me while I was working on them. I am also grateful to Margaret's niece Mary Teschner for contributing photographs.

Special thanks are due to Evelynn Thomas, who wanted to know more about the mission where her husband, Robert, had grown up and most auspiciously telephoned the Presbyterian Historical Society asking for items on Hainan just months after I began researching the mission. Through the Thomases I came to know the missionaries who served the Hainan mission and their children and grandchildren, all of whom loaned me their families' papers and photographs without which this book could not have been written. The Hainan missionaries are Henry and Louise Bucher, Margaret Burkwall, Evelyn French, and Freda Manus, and I thank all of them for their friendship and cheerful willingness to answer all my questions and to remember things that happened fifty, sixty, and seventy years ago. Special thanks are due to the "miskids," Ruth Tappan Bauer, Nathaniel Bercovitz, Samuel Braden, David Byers, Geneva Steiner Liebsney, Hugh and Marie Melrose and Sylvia Melrose Ryan, Ronald Seaton, and Robert and Daniel Thomas; to Jane L. Gilman, daughter-in-law of Frank P. Gilman, and her daughters, Margaret Checkur and Irene Gilman; and to other missionaries' grandchildren, Donald and Richard Campbell, Carolyn McCandliss and Margaret Seaman, a McCandliss descendant, and Daniel Ray, a Gilman descendant; to all the "miskids'" and grandchildren's family members—for friendship, endless questions answered, hospitality, accommodations, unfailing good cheer, and patience! Thanks are also due to Olivia Mirtz, widow of Orville (Jimmy) Mirtz, for loaning me her husband's papers and photographs, through the courtesy of Dottie Bauer, granddaughter of David and Luella Tappan. Three other people who helped in special ways are included here in grateful remembrance—Stuart Seaton, who served the Hainan mission from 1924 until its end; Laurence Byers, son of George and Clara Byers; and Tirzih McCandliss, daughter-in-law of Olivia and Henry McCandliss.

I am also grateful to Martha Smalley, archivist at the Yale Divinity School Library, and her staff. Christopher McKee assisted me at the Grinnell College archives. Matt Tharp of the Deasey Laboratory, Pennsylvania State University, Department of Geography, made the map of Hainan. The Reverend Thomas Bower and Audrey Rober at the First Presbyterian Church in Marshalltown, Iowa, introduced me to church members who had known Margaret Moninger. Thanks are due to the staff of the University of Oregon Library Special Collections Department and of the Marshalltown, Iowa, Public Library. Thanks also are due Suzanne Wilson Barnett, University of Puget Sound; Daniel Bays, University of Kansas; David D. Buck, University of Wisconsin—Milwaukee; and Lawrence Kessler of the University of North Carolina—Chapel Hill for years of unfailing friendship and collegial support. For careful reading of the manuscript and comments I am grateful to Casimir and Christine Kulikowski, Rutgers University; Judith Liu, University of San Diego; Jessie G. Lutz, now retired from Rutgers University; Sarah Mason of Marine on St. Croix, Minnesota; Murray Rubinstein, Baruch College of City University of New York; Jack S. Service, now retired from the University of California, Berkeley; and the anonymous reviewers contacted by the University Press of Kentucky. Thanks, too, to the Luce Foundation/University of Kansas Christianity in China project headed by Dan Bays for funds to allow me to travel to Hainan and for the beneficial week-long seminar on Christianity in China in the summer of 1990; to the National Endowment for the Humanities for a Travel to Collections grant; and to Jack Royer for Pennsylvania State University, Commonwealth Educational System, Faculty Development Funds. At Pennsylvania State University/Allentown Campus special thanks to John V. Cooney; to Gene Slaski for his encouragement and financial support; and to Nancy Eberle and Sue Snyder for printing and copying the various drafts of the manuscript. Special thanks to the staff of the University Press of Kentucky. Thanks, too, to my teacher, John F. Cady, professor emeritus of history at Ohio University, and his wife, Vivian, who first encouraged my interest in China and who have been dear friends over the years. Thanks are due to my brother, Laurence, for assistance with Margaret's botany projects, and to my brother, Al, and my mother for reading the manuscript with their critical eyes.

Locations of the Hainan Presbyterian Mission, 1885–1942

Introduction

Educating the Women of Hainan is the story of Margaret Moninger, an American woman who spent nearly half her life in China in the early years of the twentieth century. *Brilliant* and *Genius* were the words her colleagues used to describe her. The family that produced her was far from typical. Eldest child of a genteel Iowa farm family, her parents were both college graduates and her four grandparents had pioneered in the state. In China in the 1930s, her colleague Esther Morse, M.D., termed Margaret *bourgeois* in her attitudes. Indeed, that was her background. Not many farmers would spend their yearly vacation as Margaret's father, Will, did, judging cattle at the state fair so that he could spend his salary on Haviland china or sterling silver for his wife. Margaret once wrote from China that one of her college friends said it was at the Moninger home that she was first initiated into the "mysteries" of such fine goods.

Born in 1891, Margaret, like all the women at the Hainan mission, came from a family that could afford education for its daughters. When only about 20 percent of American college graduates were women, Margaret was among that elite, having graduated Phi Beta Kappa from Grinnell College in 1913.[1] But she lived at a time when few careers were available to women of her brilliance. Most usual among the career options was teaching, and that is the one Margaret chose. She taught for two years in New Providence, Iowa, primarily to pay off her debts from college. Caught up in the Student Volunteer Movement for Foreign Missions (SVMFM), which swept college campuses in the early years of the century and had as its slogan "The Evangelization of the World in This

Generation," Margaret signed the SVMFM's pledge to become a missionary during her junior year in college and applied to the Presbyterian Board of Foreign Missions for appointment to China in 1913.[2] She was assigned to Hainan and spent the years 1915–42 on the island, except for three furloughs at home. (Furloughs generally lasted about a year, although Margaret's second one, begun in 1927, lasted two years because of the political unrest in China as well as the needs of her family following her mother's death.) During most of the twenty-three years she lived in Hainan, she taught and served as principal of one of the mission schools.

Margaret's choice to become a missionary was one made by other adventurous American women college graduates of her time. China was the center of missionary activity, although India, the Middle East, Japan, Korea, and Africa also attracted some. How many missionaries served in China is difficult to determine, but total numbers probably approached 50,000, as many stayed only a short time because of illness or an inability to adjust to the country. At the height of the missionary activity in China in the 1920s, it has been estimated that 6,500 individuals, representing hundreds of sending agencies, were on the field.[3] Except at the beginning of the missionary endeavor in the period before the Opium War, the majority of those serving in China were women. Mission boards were reluctant to send single men to the field, thinking that they could not manage without wives, but they commonly sent single women.

When the Hainan missionaries were arguing over the issue of holding station prayers, about which Margaret felt strongly, Esther Morse wrote to her family that she did not believe Margaret was inherently more religious than the other members of the station. This was undoubtedly true, and on a larger scale, missionaries as a group were not inherently more religious than other members of America's churchgoing population. If the traditional view of missionaries has been that they were "holier than thou" individuals, research suggests that this simply was not the case, at least as far as the Presbyterian Church was concerned, and it was not true of the Hainan mission in particular. Many of the Hainan missionaries had borrowed money from the church to finance their college educations, and five years' service to the church canceled the loans. (Margaret had attended the Congregationalist Grinnell College and had borrowed money, but not from the Presbyterian Church.) To be appointed as a Presbyterian missionary, a person had to apply to the Presbyterian Board of Foreign Missions. One did need to belong to a church, but it did not have to be a Presbyterian church. Applications of the Board of

Foreign Missions reveal that those who served the Hainan mission were, at the time of application, Baptists, Congregationalists, Methodists, and one was a Christian Scientist. Evidence suggests the same was true for other mission locations. Few applicants were rejected for any but health reasons, the sole exceptions being men who were draft dodgers at the time of World War I.

Yet, while virtually no healthy applicants were rejected, the criteria for selection of individuals to serve as Presbyterian missionaries changed in the mid-1890s. Prior to that time most of the people who became missionaries, particularly to China, probably felt they were called by God to do so. But in the mid-1890s the job of missionary became more a profession than a calling. Earlier the application to the Board of Foreign Missions had asked if the applicant freely "joined the mission for life, God willing," but that provision was changed after it proved a difficult obstacle when the Board sought to have elderly missionaries retire, accept pensions, and return to the United States. The precise date of the change in the application has not been pinpointed, but it was certainly a part of the growing professionalism of the missionaries. The change came about gradually as the application still asked why one wanted to become a missionary and everyone answered "to teach the Gospel" or some variation of that statement. (One hardly need call attention to the fact that as a teaching of Jesus, and thus a central part of Christianity, the desire to spread the Gospel can hardly be considered a goal unique to those who became missionaries.) With the growing emphasis on professional qualifications for missionaries, individuals who were "called" and would put their hands to anything that needed to be done at the mission stations were no longer sought. Instead, applicants were now assigned specific jobs on the mission field. For Presbyterians in China, the China Council set priorities for the various missions and their list described specific positions they sought to fill. For example, Margaret was recruited to fill the slot, "woman educator for Kachek, Hainan." [4] By the 1930s many Presbyterian missionaries tended to view with skepticism anyone who claimed to have had a "call" on the grounds that they could not explain what a "call" was.[5] With the change, Presbyterian missionaries also became better educated, as only those with college degrees were accepted. Indeed, even the wives of ordained men who wanted to go to the mission were required to apply as missionaries and were expected to meet the same criteria as their husbands and the single women. (In the Hainan mission a few married women who had been educated in Europe and did not hold college degrees were permitted, reluctantly, to join the mission.) As it was expensive to send a person to China, the Board of Foreign Missions still hoped, in the early years of the twentieth century, that the people they sent as missionaries would successfully learn the language, adjust to the culture, and in Hainan the climate, and remain in the service of the Board for many years. However, there were exceptions to this general policy, as two of the missionary daughters, Ruth McCandliss and Janet Gilman, served the Hainan mission with their parents for short terms between graduation from college and marriage. Later in the 1930s when the need for missionaries was great but the Board's finances unsure, some individuals were recruited for short, usually three-year, terms of service, and the Hainan mission had several people who served on that basis.

A career as a missionary offered a salary comparable to what one would earn at home, along with travel to and from the field for furloughs and annual vacations paid by the Board. Housing was provided and new missionaries received allowances for household furnishings and clothing. Missionary families were paid allowances for each child as well as for schooling expenses. All medical expenses were paid by the Board, and each mission station had at least one medical doctor in residence to care for the missionaries. (The mission hospitals used by the local populace were of secondary concern to the Board and were intended to be self-supporting even though that goal was not always achieved.) Missionaries routinely employed local people to do their housekeeping, shopping, gardening, and other tasks, and for many the difficult years were those when they were at home on furlough and were responsible for such jobs. Becoming a missionary offered a great deal of job security, particularly once one had made the adjustment to living in another culture and had learned a foreign language.

In the worst years of the Depression, Margaret noted that her furlough had been postponed a year and that the exchange rate at which her salary was paid was less favorable, but no one in the Hainan mission was released for lack of funds. The Presbyterian Board also provided a retirement pension for those who worked to age seventy or retired early for health reasons. Thus, if one were seeking a very secure job situation with benefits few other positions offered, plus the opportunity to travel to foreign countries, becoming a foreign missionary was an excellent career choice. If mission societies at home stressed the religious commitment and sacrifices missionaries made, they did so to maintain interest in and financial support for their missions. Few missionaries mentioned their sacrifices; Margaret certainly never did, nor did she refer to any particular religious commitment she felt she had. She did remark that she went to church every Sunday, but so did many church members at home.

In many respects Margaret's life followed the pattern described by Jane Hunter in *The Gospel of Gentility,* in that Margaret was the eldest child in her family, came from a rural area, was educated at a small, church-affiliated college, and had taught school before joining the mission.[6] Yet Margaret was also atypical in that her specialty was mathematics, and she proved so adept at the Chinese language that she compiled a two-volume Hainanese-English dictionary. A career as a missionary attracted a disproportionate number of the best and brightest American women in the early years of the twentieth century. By 1942 five years of warfare had greatly depleted the missionary force in China, as the American government had been actively encouraging withdrawal from the field for several years and had prohibited those at home from returning. Yet on her way home Margaret learned that thirteen of the forty members of Phi Beta Kappa aboard the repatriation ship, the SS *Gripsholm,* were women.

To teach in China, particularly in Hainan, was much more an adventure than teaching in a small town in Iowa. Shortly after arriving in Hainan, Margaret became the head of a girls' boarding school, a position she would not have attained so quickly had she stayed at home. She also served as the mission agent and for many years as the treasurer, being responsible for the management of many thousands of dollars in a multiplicity of currencies. As mission secretary, she was responsible for communications with American diplomatic personnel, the Presbyterian China Council, and the Board of Foreign Missions in New York. It was she who arranged for the telegraphing of the news of the murder of her colleague, the Reverend George D. Byers, to the world outside Hainan. Few women of her generation in America held positions of such responsibility. Going to the mission field also provided women of Margaret's time with a chance to see the world, to travel to the far corners of the earth—at someone else's expense—and to incur not criticism but praise and admiration from those who stayed at home. A sense of adventure had to be a part of the makeup of all who engaged in such endeavors, and Margaret admitted to her family that on one of her expeditions into the remote, mountainous land of the aboriginal Miao people she had finally realized one of her life's ambitions—to go where no white woman had ever been before.

The great questions of the foreign mission effort in China, namely whether or not schools and hospitals detracted from the evangelical work that some thought the only proper endeavor for missionaries, had been resolved before Margaret applied to be a missionary. The Hainan mission was established in 1884 as an outstation of the Canton mission, primarily for the purpose of converting the Miao and Loi aborigines who lived in the central part of the island. Among the first letters written to the Presbyterian Board of Foreign Missions about Hainan was one detailing the presence of these people on the island and suggesting that they would be more open to Christianity than were the Han Chinese.[7] The Miao aborigines were more numerous and were visited more often by the missionaries who were stationed at Kachek, where Margaret served most of her time in Hainan. The mission had only three stations—Kiungchow, Kachek, and Nodoa. Kachek and Nodoa, both in the interior, each had missionary residences, a church, a hospital, and elementary schools for boys and girls. The Kiungchow station had property in both Kiungchow, the island's capital, and the adjacent port, Hoihow, for, as Margaret explained in *Isle of Palms*, "The work shifted back and forth between the two places for some years after the beginnings were made." The station hospital was located in Hoihow, where there was also a church, elementary schools for boys and girls, and missionary residences. Three miles from Hoihow were the two Kiungchow properties, across the street from each other. At one was the church, secondary school for boys, and missionary residences, while the other contained the secondary school for girls and a residence for single women missionaries who taught there. Each station had many outlying chapels and preaching places. When Margaret arrived, twenty-four missionaries were serving in Hainan, and they counted about one thousand converts.[8]

Like those who preceded her to the Hainan mission, Margaret came from an America that did not ask questions about cross-cultural exchanges. Americans were convinced of the superiority of their culture and government and did not question their rights of extraterritoriality in China, gained and kept as they were by the gun. Margaret, like many, if not all, missionaries, came from the segment of American society that centered its life around the church and thought it their Christian duty to pass their religion and their lifestyle on to people of less-blessed countries. They thought all Americans shared their church-centered lifestyle. Margaret often referred to American culture as Christian. As a group, the missionaries engaged in the casual cultural imperialism of Americans of their time.

To Margaret, teaching nationalism to the Chinese meant teaching them to sing patriotic songs to the tune of *America*. In maintaining their Western lifestyle, the missionaries taught the Chinese at least as much about how foreigners lived as they did about Christianity. Margaret once wrote her family that she realized how completely one group of people could become absorbed into a larger one and noted that the aboriginal Kak Miao were almost indistinguishable from the Yao, but she never seemed to understand that she was contributing to that same type of cultural alteration, with both aborigines and Chinese, in the school she headed. The Hainan missionaries had another impact on the island, for in their desire to eat as they had at home, they imported many plants, altering the island's ecological balance.

Arriving in China just a few years after the 1911 revolution, Margaret was witness to the May Fourth movement that swept China after World War I. Indeed, with the mission schoolgirls she participated in many of the mass meetings that were a part of the movement. Since the emancipation of Chinese women was one of the goals of the May Fourth movement, Margaret, as head of a girls' school, often spoke at these meetings. Careful to maintain the missionaries' neutrality, Margaret frequently stated that nothing critical of other countries was mentioned at the meetings in which she participated. Highly skilled at both written Chinese and the spoken dialect of Hainan, she apparently never read the secular Chinese literature produced in such quantity in those years. She was directly concerned with the education of Chinese women but never made reference to any Chinese literature on the subject. Indeed, she seems to have confined her readings in Chinese to the Bible and biblical literature.

Margaret's letters, written to her family every Sunday from 1915 to 1942, along with letters to friends and supporters, and her other writings and those of her fellow missionaries, are the primary basis of this work. Three of the surviving members of the mission, the Reverend Henry Bucher, Mrs. Evelyn French, and Stuart Seaton, M.D., attest to the authenticity of Margaret's letters. In Mrs. French's words, "If Margaret wrote it, you can be sure it was accurate."[9] Dr. Seaton remembered Margaret's attention to detail, and the Reverend Mr. Bucher noted that Margaret was the closest the Hainan mission ever came to producing an official historian. Most of her letters were written to family members, and she told them of the China she wanted them to know. She certainly did not tell them everything. Indeed, her selectivity began the first week she was in China. She told the folks at home that on her first day in Hainan she had traveled by sedan chair from Hoihow to Kiungchow when she could not speak even one word to the chair carriers. She assured her family that the older missionaries were confident she would arrive safely. Only years later, in retirement, did Margaret write that the trip included being set down and left for a while by the chair bearers, who went off to smoke opium!

So voluminous are Margaret's writings about her life in Hainan that I have been able to include here only a tiny part of what she wrote. Her beautiful, flowing script, neatly spaced on the page, filled thousands of sheets of paper. In 1937 she inquired of her family, "Does my writing look any different? You remember my beloved Waterman pen that Dad gave me in 1907, when he came back from State Fair? It's one of the old-fashioned unscrew to fill kind, you know. I have never even had a new pen point in it but it got to scratching so badly this fall after I bent it a couple times that I had Mr. [Paul] Melrose take it to Hong Kong for me and get a new pen point. It writes splendidly now." Some of Margaret's letters and most of her reports to the Board of Foreign Missions were typed on what Esther Morse described as "an old, old desk typewriter that sounds like a threshing machine."[10]

Obviously, letters written to one's family contain many references to matters of interest only to them, the concerns and changes of the family and their friends and neighbors. I have omitted nearly all of Margaret's mentions of fashion; as one might expect of a young woman with several sisters, clothing, dressmaking, and fashion were frequent topics of her letters. Thus, from Japan she wrote that she had seen "beautiful silk kimonos, all embroidered, for seven yen fifty or $3.25...and evening coats that would make one successful socially for life in the States."[11] Her family kept her supplied with the necessities, ranging from corsets to comfortable American shoes. Margaret once made an autumnal request that the family send her white shoes to wear home the following summer, apparently sending the family and the Marshalltown shoe merchants into a tizzy. Margaret remarked several months later that she had forgotten that fashions were seasonal at home! I have included a few references to food but have omitted nearly all the detailed descriptions of the missionaries' Thanksgiving and Christmas dinners and Margaret's lavish accounts of the menus of the Chinese wedding feasts she attended. Margaret's great fondness for ice cream could be indulged only on rare trips to Hong Kong or Shanghai or at Hoihow/Kiungchow after the city acquired an ice plant, but the homemade ice cream of Hainan always elicited the comment from her that ice cream made with canned milk was *not* as good as that made with fresh cream.

Margaret also loved writing poetry, particularly about the everyday things she saw about her, and her poems frequently were filled with puns. I have included here only parts of her "Hainan Alphabet for New Recruits," her "Owed to Hainan Fever" sent to the doctor during her first attack of malaria, and the poem she sent to the Board of Foreign Missions as her annual report at the end of her first year in Hainan. Topics of some of her other poems were the furniture of Dr. and Mrs. J. Franklin Kelly, which circulated in the Hainan mission for decades after the Kellys returned to the United States, the curiosity of the Chinese at an inn where she was spending the night, and the Hainanese pigs that were often fellow passengers on the coastal steamers to Hong Kong. Although Margaret published several articles in the *Lingnan Science Journal,* the *Journal of the North China Branch of the Royal Asiatic Society,* and *Woman's Work,* a church magazine, as well as in other church publications, her hometown newspaper, a Hong Kong newspaper, and college alumni publications, very little of her work ever saw print. She served for years as the anonymous editor of the mission's *Hainan News Letter.* Her only book, *Isle of Palms: Sketches of Hainan,* listed her only as "M.M.M. editor." Significantly, this book was republished by Garland Press as part of Ramon H. Myers's series on the modern Chinese economy in 1980; it was the only missionary work in the series and the only one on Hainan. Indeed, *Isle of Palms* is the only book in English about modern Hainan in many major research collections.[12] Margaret's monumental two-volume dictionary of the Hainanese colloquial language and English was never published.

From Margaret's writings one sees an intriguing portrait of a foreigner's life in Hainan, but from the letters of Dr. Esther Morse, who joined the mission in 1930, a different picture of mission life and Margaret emerges. The gossipy, at times even catty, comments from Dr. Morse give glimpses of the personality problems of the Hainan mission, magnified by the isolation and the small number of foreigners at each of the stations. Dr. Morse lived with Margaret for several years, and from the doctor's letters to her own family we see a Margaret perplexed by actions she knows she must take but worried about their impact on the Chinese she hoped would convert to Christianity. For example, the two women once left the relatively isolated Kachek mission compound to sleep in the safety of the street chapel in the market during a time of particular unrest. Although Margaret worried what the Chinese might think, she knew all too well the danger: her colleague, the Reverend Mr. Byers, had been murdered at the compound a few years earlier, precipitating an extraterritoriality case that dragged on for over a year. Likewise, she yearned to have the Chinese accept her religion and participate in the life of the church, even though she felt displaced as the church organist when one of her students replaced her permanently after she had been ill for several weeks.

I have chosen to call Margaret by her Christian name in this work for several reasons. The missionaries in Hainan maintained strict formality among themselves, never referring to each other by their Christian names. Many of the Hainan missionaries formed friendships that lasted a lifetime, but they maintained the formality even in retirement. Katherine Schaeffer, who was older than Margaret's parents, for a brief time called Margaret by the nickname Emsie, but she too soon resumed the formality of "Miss Moninger." Writing in retirement, Margaret addressed this custom: "Personally, I never called my fellow-workers by their first names. A new missionary lady, who was to be my housemate, once said, as we were discussing plans, 'What do you think of calling each other by our first names?' I answered that I hadn't been accustomed to doing that on the field, and she said: 'Good. I've seen too many cases where two people got so intimate and had such a crush on each other it just couldn't last, and any friendship for a third party, either Chinese or foreign, caused violent jealousy and general disruption.' So I felt my policy justified, though it began as shyness toward my seniors rather than as a considered decision, and my co-workers are my very good friends yet, though still Dr., Mr., Mrs., or Miss So-and-So."[13]

Because of this practice, for the twenty-three years Margaret lived on Hainan she was never called by her Christian name by anyone. It was only in her letters to her family, the basis of this book, that she was Margaret. Perhaps the formality of the mission custom was necessary, but she must have longed to hear her Christian name from time to time. Undoubtedly, the intense personal nature of the letters from her friends and family, to whom she was always Margaret, was one of the reasons she anticipated the arrival of the mail with such eagerness. Because it is Margaret's writings that so vividly describe her life, I have chosen to preserve her voice whenever possible, letting her tell the reader about Hainan as she observed it and as she chose to reveal it to others far away. This is Margaret's story, not a history of twentieth-century China or a history of the mission movement in China or in Hainan. Yet in a larger sense

Margaret's story is typical of the lives of those American women college graduates who found their escape from the limitations of American society in the early twentieth century by going to the mission fields that offered them opportunities not available to them at home.[14]

A word must be said about the place-names that appear in the text. I have decided to use the traditional spellings of Hoihow, Kiungchow, Kachek, and Nodoa, which the missionaries used for the places they lived, as well as for the other places in Hainan and on the mainland. A different problem is posed by the places Margaret mentioned when she traveled into the Miao country. Since the Miao were seminomadic people who practiced slash-and-burn agriculture, their settlements were not permanent.[15] Hence, the places Margaret mentioned appear on no maps of Hainan, not even on the ones the missionaries themselves made of the island. Sometimes Margaret drew rough maps of the places she visited, but she always added the note that the locations were only approximations. Since it would have been difficult to find some of the Miao villages only a few years after Margaret visited them, locating them after sixty or seventy years is simply impossible. Therefore, I leave the place-names as they appeared in Margaret's text and make no effort to fix them on a map. Although Margaret tended to hyphenate place-names to facilitate pronunciation by her family, I have decided to omit the hyphens in order to maintain consistency with the names Hainan, Hoihow, etc. I have hyphenated personal names to more easily distinguish them for the reader but again have preserved the romanizations of the Hainanese pronunciations that the missionaries used. In a few cases of well-known people, such as Sun Yat-sen, I have used the more common historic romanizations. Converting everything to the more recent pinyin romanization system would only confuse everyone.

Margaret's story is that of a single woman at a China mission station. In many ways it is the opposite side of the coin of the life portrayed in *Golden Inches: The China Memoir of Grace Service*.[16] Grace Service's story begins nine years earlier than Margaret's and ends five years before Margaret's and takes place in Szechwan and Shanghai, parts of China far removed from Hainan. While the Service story centers around the efforts of a mother to maintain her family in a Chinese environment, Margaret's story tells of a single woman at a mission whose primary concern was school and evangelistic work.

Neither Margaret nor anyone else could have known that her arrival in Hainan in 1915 marked almost the halfway point in the history of the mission. Founded in 1884, the mission ended with the evacuation of the missionaries in 1942, although there was a brief attempt to reestablish it in Hoihow with a reduced staff in the years between the end of World War II and the success of the Communist Revolution.

Upon her return to the United States from China in August 1942, Margaret, who always had a great sense of humor, must certainly have enjoyed the Mark Twainesque opportunity to read the reports of her death that had appeared on 17 and 18 January 1942 in newspapers from coast to coast. The story, which originated with a Nationalist Chinese communiqué from Chungking, Szechwan, headlined that Margaret and the other Hainan missionaries were "Missing in China" and "Slain by the Japanese." The Moninger family refused to believe Margaret was dead but preserved the stories of her death in newspapers from places as far afield as Los Angeles and Washington, Pennsylvania, birthplace of her paternal grandparents.[17] Ironically, at about the same time families at home were reading of the massacre of the missionaries on Hainan, the missionaries were, in fact, entertaining at a farewell tea the Japanese army officers who were being transferred to the Philippines. Margaret died eight years after reports of her death had been front-page news from coast to coast.

CHAPTER ONE

Joining the Hainan Mission
1915

CIRCUS ELEPHANTS WERE unloading at the Marshalltown, Iowa, train station on 22 July 1915, distracting eight-year-old Jack Moninger as his family gathered on the platform to see their eldest daughter, Margaret, off to China and to her new life as a Presbyterian missionary. Travel was one of the exciting elements of the life of a missionary. Before making the decision to go to China, Margaret had never been farther from home than Des Moines, where she had attended the state fair. Once her decision was made, she traveled to Kansas City, Missouri, to a convention of the Student Volunteer Movement for Foreign Missions, where she formally applied to the Presbyterian Board of Foreign Missions. Accepted by the Board, she traveled to St. Paul, Minnesota, in April 1915 to a women's conference, where she was commissioned as a missionary and "adopted" by the Waterloo, Iowa, Presbyterial (her home group), which supported her throughout her years in China. In June she went to New York City to attend a conference for outgoing missionaries, and in July she departed for China.[1]

Journeying westward that summer, Margaret was not only leaving America to spend her adult life as an expatriate in China, but she was also leaving her own family to join the Hainan missionaries, who would now serve as her extended family. To her birth family she would be linked for the next twenty-seven years, save the four years she was home on furloughs, only by letters, which her family carefully preserved. Perhaps because of the isolation of the Hainan mission and the relatively small number of people who served it, the personnel of the mission functioned as a fictive family. They visited one another's blood families while at home on furlough, and some among the generation of missionary children have maintained contact until the present, nearly fifty years after the end of mission work on Hainan.

The family that Margaret left behind was an illustrious one, and she was extremely proud of it. Writing from China in 1917, she asked her mother to "please pay my D.A.R. dues."[2] On her father's side, Margaret was descended from immigrants from Karlsruhe, Germany, who had briefly settled in Maryland and then moved to Washington County, Pennsylvania, in 1800. In 1859 their grandson, Demas Moninger, Margaret's grandfather, married Mary Ringland, a descendant of a veteran of the American Revolution. Mary had journeyed to Iowa in the company of her brothers in 1856 but returned to Pennsylvania to marry Demas before settling with him on newly opened land in Marshall County, Iowa. The eldest of their four sons, William Ringland, the identical twin of John Howard, was Margaret's father. Will and John enrolled at Grinnell College in the fall of 1882, where they met Mary Helen "Minnie" Kellogg. Minnie was the descendant of another pre-Revolutionary War family that had moved west to Iowa, where her grandfather had donated the land on which Grinnell College was built.

Will and Minnie were engaged before they graduated from Grinnell in 1886. (Will later returned to Grinnell, receiving a master's degree in 1889.) Tragedy struck the Moninger family in the summer of 1887, when John and a younger brother, Frank, then eighteen, drowned in the Iowa River, which ran through the Moninger farm. Gloom descended on the household, and their mother mourned her sons until her death in 1919.[3] Despite the family's sadness, Will married Minnie Kellogg on 27 December 1887 in Grinnell. Shortly after their marriage, Will wanted to go to South America to represent the farm equipment company for which he worked. His mother, an extremely strong-willed woman, refused to consider allowing him to venture off, insisting instead that he remain on the farm. Complying with her wishes, Will remained in Iowa and purchased a farm near his father's. Will was active in public life, serving as a regent of the State University of Iowa, as a trustee of Iowa State College, and as superintendent of the local schools for many years. He also helped start the area's telephone company.[4]

Will and Minnie's firstborn child, Mary Margaret, arrived on 23 September 1891. Will kept a diary during Margaret's first months, writing on the day she was born, "A dear little daughter was given to us at half-past nine Wednesday morning. She weighed nine pounds and measures twenty-two inches." The following day he wrote, "We have named our little girl 'Mary Margaret.' The first name being the names of her great-grandmother Ringland, of her grandmother Moninger, and of her mother. The second name is a favorite name of ours, Margaret, 'a pearl,' the symbol of purity. We also think of the French 'Marguerite,' 'a daisy,' the emblem of modesty. We shall call her Margaret."[5]

Joined by her sisters, Dorothy in 1896, Helen in 1898, and Louise in 1904, and her brother, John (sometimes called Jack), in 1907, Margaret's childhood on the farm was a happy one. Writing about it later while under house arrest by the Japanese in Hainan, Margaret called her memoir "Cedarcroft," after the name of the house her parents built in 1902. She wrote that there were "bookcases everywhere," for "we were a reading family."[6] The family library was extremely varied, and Margaret once wrote from Hainan, "If you have any stray pamphlets on tropical plants please send them along."[7]

During Margaret's teenage years, the family at Cedarcroft frequently included Minnie's sister, Harriette Kellogg, who worked in the botanical department of Iowa State College, where she cataloged plants. During the summers Margaret frequently drove the buggy for her aunt on plant-collecting trips and in the process learned much about botany. Harriette was also "an unusually good amateur photographer, and while we were often unwilling and I fear ungracious subjects, she took many pictures we love to see now," Margaret wrote in the 1940s.[8]

Pets were numerous on the farm, and Margaret's special favorite was Jerry, the pony. Writing from China, Margaret compared her horse there with Jerry and was finally told by the family of his death. Years later she wrote, "Mother said when I started to China I hated to leave [Jerry] almost more than I hated to leave the family! And he died before I came home on my first furlough."[9]

Margaret's upbringing was ecumenical. The family attended the Presbyterian church at Albion, which Margaret once described as "very plain."[10] When that church was closed for a few years, the Moningers attended the Congregational Church at LaMoille, as Minnie's family were Congregationalists.[11] Will's youngest brother, Harold, and his family, who lived across the road from Cedarcroft, attended the Friends' meeting, to which, Margaret wrote, "we were always invited...on special days and never felt left out because on Sunday mornings our road led elsewhere."[12]

The Moninger family placed great emphasis on education. Margaret wrote to her brother in 1940, "I remember mother saying once...that she and Dad wouldn't have very much in the way of worldly goods to leave us, but they did at least want to have us get our education, no matter what else we didn't have."[13] When Margaret finished the eighth grade in the country school, she went to Marshalltown to attend high school. "It was during my senior year [1908-9]," she later remembered, "that the Billy Sunday evangelistic meetings were held in Marshalltown for six weeks, I think, and almost every night we went to the big tabernacle with its sawdust trail," but she made no comment about whether or how this experience had influenced her.[14]

Margaret's sole recollection of anything Asian from her childhood was that her Auntie Parks, who lived in Grinnell and provided housing for college students, had at one time housed a Japanese student from Yokohama, who kept in touch with her for several years after returning home.[15]

In the fall of 1909 Margaret enrolled at Grinnell College, her parents' alma mater. If Margaret wrote to her parents while at Grinnell, no letters of that period survive. She excelled at mathematics, history, and Latin and also studied German and French. While in college she lived with her grandmother, two blocks from the campus. Her college years gave little indication of the success Margaret would have in her career. The student newspaper, the *Scarlet and Black,* like small-town newspapers, contained social news of the students, yet Margaret's name never appeared. Indeed, the first mention of her is in her senior year, when she was one of four students elected to Phi Beta Kappa.[16] The only other time Margaret's name appeared in the newspaper was when she graduated.[17]

Margaret's first serious thought of becoming a missionary came, she wrote, during her freshman year in college, when she was influenced by many talks she had with the missionary Dr. George E. White, dean of Anatolia College in Marsovan, Turkey, who was spending a furlough at Grinnell.[18] The concept of a career of service was prevalent at the college during the years that Margaret attended. Although it is impossible to know which activities Margaret participated in, there were talks, specifically on missionary service, at chapel, the YMCA, and the YWCA, and the Grinnell-in-China project took shape during her senior year.[19] Her college yearbook, the *Cyclone,* listed Margaret as belonging to the YWCA and participating in "class hockey" but gave no other indication of her interests and curiously did not include her in the list of YWCA members or in the picture of the group.[20]

During her junior year Margaret took the first step toward her career as a missionary when she joined the Student Volunteer Movement for Foreign Missions. Filling out the SVMFM application in the spring of 1912, Margaret reported that she belonged to the local chapter and attended its meetings, but she had joined "under no particular influence except the ordinary missionary interest of the college." She also noted that she belonged to the YWCA and was planning to do graduate work and to be a teacher. She reported that in Bible classes she studied the life of Christ, the life of Paul, and the history of the early church but that she had reached her decision "without having read any literature on the subject save the Bible, but I have since read and appreciated very much several of the Volunteer pamphlets, 'The Life That Wins,' and 'The Supreme Decision.'"[21]

In answer to a question on the application asking if any of her family members were missionaries, she listed "a cousin, Emily Dickinson, Yokohama, Japan," and noted that she "publishes a paper for women" and "is under Methodist board." It is unlikely that Margaret had ever met this distant relative until she stopped in Yokohama during her first trip to China. Interestingly, Margaret never mentioned in either her application or in any of her letters that one of her Grinnell classmates was a man from Japan.[22]

Although Margaret's college yearbook did not list her as a member of the SVMFM, a picture of her with the group did appear. Of the eighteen members, nine were women, and in later years Margaret wrote home several times about one of the group, Frank Meacham, who became a missionary in Africa.[23]

Following her graduation from Grinnell in June 1913, Margaret taught Latin and mathematics for two years at the New Providence, Iowa, Consolidated Schools, where she earned sixty dollars per month.[24] In the summer following her first year as a teacher, she attended the SVMFM conference in Kansas City, where she made formal application to the Board of Foreign Missions of the Presbyterian Church for appointment as a missionary to China. Asked to state in her application what languages she knew, she replied that she had studied Latin for eight years, German for two years, and French for one year and noted that "languages have always been easy for me." She also wrote that she could play the piano and the organ "enough for hymns and church music" but that she could not lead singing. She also indicated that she had no knowledge of bookkeeping.[25]

The Board was interested in applicants' backgrounds in church work, their personal religious practices, and their knowledge of Christianity. Margaret's replies to questions reveal her upbringing in a Presbyterian family as well as the rather casual attitude she had toward religion until she joined the Christian Endeavor Society. She noted that she followed the Christian Endeavor and Sunday School readings in her daily Bible study and that she was particularly interested in the Epistles of Paul and the Psalms. In response to a question about her personal experience in "bringing others to Christ," she wrote that she had had some experiences through Sunday School, the YWCA, and Christian Endeavor: "I know various people whom I have helped to bring to Christ, but do not know of any one case in which under God I was wholly responsible for the decision made."[26] Perhaps fearing she lacked the qualifications necessary for acceptance, she enclosed a letter to the Board along with her application. She wrote, "From the time I first learned to read I have known something of what the decision for Christ meant....Ever since I can remember I have had regular attendance at church and Sunday School. At the age of fourteen I was supposed to be converted in some revival meeting and joined the church. I said supposed to be advisedly as in looking over my past life I cannot say now that I really was consecrated for Christ at that time. Three years later in the fall of 1908 I joined the Christian Endeavor Society and I believe my Christian life really begins from the night I signed that Christian Endeavor pledge."[27]

She went on to say that she had joined the "Volunteer Band [SVMFM] on 23 January 1912. I would have become a member two years before, but my parents wished me to wait until I was an upperclassman to be sure my decision was final. They have never opposed me in the matter, feeling it was a duty that rests upon me. My motives for seeking foreign missionary work may be briefly stated in this way. I want to be of greatest possible service to Christ. This can best be done by serving others. The greatest need is on the foreign field. I am comparatively free to go and so far as I know physically able." She also noted that she was then attending a Friends' meeting, as it was the only church in the town where she was teaching, and she wrote that while in college she had had a student membership in the Congregational church in Grinnell, since there was no Presbyterian church in that town. "I have been trained to be liberal along denominational lines. China has always been my goal, but should there be a vacancy for a mathematics teacher elsewhere, I believe I could give up the China idea."[28]

The Presbyterian Board accepted her as a missionary in 1914 and asked her to go to Nanking, but she declined, stating that the offer had arrived after she had promised the superintendent of the New Providence schools that she would teach for the coming year and she had been raised not to break her word. The Board acted more quickly the next year, appointing her to Hainan on 18 January 1915. She sailed for China that summer.[29]

Little in Margaret's recollection of her early life suggests the career she was to have in China. It is clear that she was quite scholarly and loved to read. Her knowledge of Latin, German, and French only hinted at the success she was to have with the Chinese language. Church was an integral part of the life of the Moninger family, but the Albion Presbyterian church, which Margaret had attended as a child, had little interest in missions, and she never mentioned meeting any missionaries there when she was young. If any visited the other churches she attended, she never mentioned meeting them. She must have read about mission work in the church publications that she remembered the family having, but she recalled no lasting impressions of them. Even a Billy Sunday campaign rated only a brief mention in her recollection of her childhood.

Margaret's niece Dorothy Gill Barnes recalled that the Moningers were a solemn family.[30] The early years of Will and Minnie's marriage were marked by the memory of the tragic drowning of the two Moninger brothers and by Grandma Moninger's continued mourning for them. Minnie's life was a hard one, and the pictures of her late in life show a solemn woman. Will, holder of a master's degree from Grinnell and pillar of many community organizations, had seen the dream of his youth, a career in South America, crushed by his domineering mother. Likely it was the denial of their own aspirations that led Will and Minnie to allow their beloved Margaret to fulfill her dream in China. Whatever their reasons for agreeing to allow Margaret to go to China, her parents always supported her work. They could scarcely have realized as Margaret departed that July day that she was entering the larger Hainan mission family that in many ways would be as important to her as they were.

Indeed, in her last year in China Margaret was told by her brother that their father was gravely ill, and John requested her immediate return. She responded that she could not leave the mission "short-handed" and "would accept God's will."[31] After the Hainan missionaries were placed under house arrest by the Japanese in July 1941, she received permission from the Board of Foreign Missions to return home; yet again she responded to her brother that the China "Council tells me to leave, but there's been no steamer since their letter came and under the circumstances I can't very well leave Miss [Alice] Skinner alone....But the way will open in due time, I'm sure."[32]

On her way west in the summer of 1915 Margaret's letters home reveal her sharp eye for detail and her keen sense of humor. She reported that the other travelers included "a University of Missouri graduate in electrical engineering" who, "recognizing my Phi Beta Kappa pin, came and talked for a couple hours last night....So there is chance No. 2, for a romance, but you needn't worry."[33]

In San Francisco, Margaret met for the first time Margaret Melrose (called Mother Melrose in later years to distinguish her from her daughter-in-law), one of the pioneers of the Hainan mission who was to accompany her to China. The Reverend and Mrs. George D. Byers and their son Bobby completed the party bound for Hainan. The group embarked on the Pacific Mail line's SS *Manchuria* on 2 August. They were seen off by others of the Hainan mission, the Reverend and Mrs. Paul McClintock and the Reverend and Mrs. Samuel Braden, who were home on furlough. Writing from the ship, Margaret described Mrs. Melrose as "very pleasant indeed. She is a masterful sort of a person, perfectly capable of taking care of herself and those under her. We are having a fine time together." The ship's crew was Chinese, and Margaret wrote that "Mrs. Melrose talks pigeon English and Chinese to our boy and he falls all over himself to do things for her." The Byerses were described as "very nice indeed, and Bobby Byers, aged about three years, is a match for any youngster."[34]

Clara Byers, a secretary at the Shanghai YMCA before her marriage, did not speak Hainanese, so she and Margaret began learning the language together, and Margaret reported to her grandmother that she could say "I, we, you, he and they." Yet it seemed she was not too keen to begin serious language study, since the following week she wrote that "Mrs. Melrose makes tentative remarks about Hainanese but Mrs. Byers and I don't say much and Mr. Byers' books are down in the hold so I guess we are safe for a while." On the ship, bound for Honolulu, Margaret noted "the Hawaiian swimmer [Duke Kahanamoku] who has held the world's championship until just a week or so ago was in the swimming tank today and it was great fun to watch him." On board ship Margaret became a part of the international mission community, which was far more ecumenical in outlook and practice than the individual churches the missionaries represented. Ships bound for China usually carried a mixed group of passengers—missionaries and what Margaret called the "fast crowd," that is, those who drank alcohol.[35]

Arriving in Yokohama, Margaret already realized how far away from home she was and wrote instructing her father how to cable her "should you ever need to." She was also very concerned that the Pacific Mail line had sold five of its steamers, including the SS *Manchuria*: "This new shipping law that doesn't allow Chinese or foreign labor on ships is doing the mischief—all our sailors and cabin boys are Chinese and it is so much cheaper and more satisfactory for the company, as the Chinese are accustomed to the tropical climates. That means twenty less mails a year each way for us, and leaves the passenger traffic across the Pacific in the hands of the Japanese steamers....As the man says, the U.S. has beautifully destroyed her Pacific commerce and given Japan practically full control of the situation."[36]

It was in Yokohama that Margaret learned, in letters from Mae Chapin and Katherine Schaeffer, the Hainan missionaries' plans for her. To her family Margaret related the news that she would stay in Kiungchow until January with Mae Chapin, who was "alone in her work as Miss Skinner and Miss [Henrietta] Montgomery are both home on furlough....I'll begin my language study at once, and go to Kachek as soon as Miss Skinner returns."[37]

When the ship docked in Manila, the Hainan missionaries discovered they were just in time for a mission meeting attended by several Board officers from New York. At a reception Margaret met "a number of Iowa people here and some of them knew people I know." She also reported that the Chinese cabin boy to whom Mrs. Melrose had been speaking Chinese "tried to get her to smuggle in some morphine for him."[38]

Arriving in Hong Kong on 2 September, Margaret and the others were met by Mrs. Wilbur Campbell and Dr. and Mrs. J. Franklin Kelly and their children, who were in Hong Kong for a brief respite from their work on Hainan. The Kellys told Margaret that they would take her to Kachek for a visit as soon as she reached the island, so that she could at least see the place where she would eventually live before settling down to her temporary assignment with Mae Chapin in Kiungchow.[39]

It was customary for Hainan missionaries to purchase most of their necessities in Hong Kong, and Margaret had a long list, so with the other women she went shopping. It was also while in Hong Kong that Margaret first came into contact with the British presence in China and with the British attitude toward the war they were fighting with Germany. After attending a service at the Union church, she wrote she had "heard a very interesting sermon....[The way the preacher]...prayed for the English to win [the war in Europe] took my breath for a minute, since at home we always hear the minister pray that 'war shall cease,' rather than for one side to win." She also noted that the pastor's Scottish "bur-r-r was hardly understandable to me at first, and his wig *would* get awry as the punkahs swung back and forth."[40]

Margaret embarked for Hainan on 5 September aboard the *Kaifong*, accompanied by Mrs. Melrose and the Byers and Kelly families. "The cabins are small, and the foot of the lower berth is right under the head of the upper berth. It was good and hot, and part of the cargo was live chickens and live sheep, and the steerage passengers were playing Chinese fiddles most of the time." The trip from Hong Kong to Hainan took twenty-seven hours. "We had a great time getting our luggage started off on two cargo boats....I had my trunks, suitcase, bag,...hat box,...two small rolls [of] matting, music rack, and four chairs....I held my breath while the coolies put a rope around my big trunk and let it down over the side of the ship with a block and tackle into a little cargo boat bobbing up and down severely on the waves. We have to go in five miles to shore. The last part of that distance is really up a big river, beyond the sand spit. We tacked considerably but got in in an hour....We went past two ruined forts and the Standard Oil buildings and landed at the customs house....we walked on down to the compound—through 'Pig Alley.' Chinese pigs are very nice looking, only swaybacked. Their snouts, legs, lower half of body and tips of tails are white, the rest black, and they are very clean. Bobby Byers wanted to play with every one we met but Mrs. Byers did not see it that way. Then we ended up at the compound."[41] Margaret wrote that she slept well her first night in Hainan "under the mosquito net, a contrast to another new missionary a year or two before, who had a nightmare and ripped the mosquito net to shreds, thinking someone was trying to smother him!"[42]

Her new colleagues had decided that Margaret should go to Kiungchow the next morning, so "we were up at six and...started off. It is about a four-mile trip and they sent me over alone...but...told the coolies where to take me....The chairs are very comfortable, and there were so many things to see I enjoyed my trip very much. We went out through the residence part of Hoihow, and along a crazy winding path through salt marshes and rice fields. Now and then we would cross little Chinese bridges, just about a foot wide. I saw two women swinging a basket from a couple poles and couldn't tell what they were doing until I reached them. They were dipping or scooping water up from a ditch over into the rice field across the road. We went by some temples and inns, now and then seeing a beggar, and finally came into the main road to Kiungchow. There we would meet a horse and carriage occasionally....As you come into Kiungchow about all you see are graves. They are round hummocks, looking more like hay cocks than anything else, and there are acres of them just outside our compound here."[43]

Years later Margaret remembered that the journey had been more exciting than she had admitted to her family. Her chair was carried by "two ragged puny-looking Chinese coolies...[who]...put the chair poles on their shoulders, grunting, groaning, and complaining over my substantial weight. They were opium smokers, as most chair coolies were, and after we had skirted the outer edges of Hoihow and reached a little wooded place...they set the chair down and disappeared!" presumably to smoke opium.[44]

During Margaret's first year in Hainan, her letters centered around three main themes—learning Chinese, descriptions of Hainan and its people, and her life as a member of the mission community. Her initiation into life in China included a celebration at one of the local temples: "Just down [the] street a little way is a big temple of a kitchen god, whose birthday is tomorrow. The celebration has already begun, and Chinese fiddle, tomtoms and singing(?) have been going on all day, with firecrackers popping every little while. Some music!"[45]

A few weeks later she witnessed Chinese theater for the first time: "The stage was just built out on the hillside....There was sort of a husk shelter over it and a little dressing room in back. They use no scenery, and the actors are all men. An old king in big black beard, big wig with two long feathers on sticks that stuck up about four feet, and full Chinese regalia, was holding forth in great style. Two court officers and two soldiers or policemen were scrapping over something, and the orchestra consisted of a man with a huge pair of brass cymbals that he banged incessantly. The audience...mostly stood around. The peddlers were there with sugar water, peanut cakes, salt fish, shrimp, rice, pork, anything you wanted, and two cute little native monkeys were running around the roof of the temples. I must get some films for my Kodak the next time anybody orders anything from Hong Kong."[46]

To her family, Margaret identified the members of the Hainan mission with whom she was to share most of the next three decades. In her first letter from Hainan, she wrote, "I met Mr. [Frank P.] Gilman....We passed Mr. Campbell going to Hong Kong and China Council meeting on our way down. Mrs. Campbell and Dwight and Gertrude are in Hong Kong. Mrs. [Alfred E.] Street and Edith [are] in Kuling for the summer, Mrs. [H.M.] McCandliss, Ruth [and]...Charlie, Mrs. Gilman and Dr. and Mrs. [Nathaniel] Bercovitz will come from America soon. Mrs. [Clarence] Newton is away somewhere, Miss Skinner and Miss Montgomery home on furlough, Mr. and Mrs. McClintock ditto, Mr. [David] Tappan and Miss Schaeffer in Kachek and Mr. [William] Leverett and Dr. and Mrs. [Clarence] Salsbury and baby and Rev. and Mrs. [John F.] Steiner in Nodoa."[47]

A few days after Margaret's arrival the Kellys took her along on the promised trip to Kachek. They traveled by boat and sedan chair and on approaching one village saw "fifteen or twenty people squatted along the roadside. Chinese returning from the South Seas were in chairs ahead of us. As their chairs approached the squatters arose and blocked the road, holding out deformed hands and begging with cowling faces. As we came up they drew back, saying, 'It's the doctor and his wife,' and smiles appeared, as Dr. and Mrs. K. worked faithfully in the leper village near Kachek. By long established custom, lepers could come out and beg on the first and fifteenth of the lunar months, but the calendar slipped a bit when word got around by grapevine that a coolie ship was in and people [were] coming home from Penang, Singapore, Kuala Lumpur."[48]

Travel about the island was always an adventure. When Margaret returned to Kiungchow, the missionaries sent her on the trip accompanied only by Chinese. Of this journey she wrote to her family, "Kia-sang, one of the deacons of the church, is going to carry my road baskets for me, and I will have a chair. The mother of one of Miss Schaeffer's schoolgirls will spend the night with me at Uidiok, and Miss Chapin will send a woman up to Tunggnai who will be with me in the boat. Although I can't talk Chinese very much yet, I am not afraid as I just came down with the Kellys and know what the road is like."[49]

Despite the careful arrangements, George Byers accompanied Margaret to the first stopping place on the road to make sure that the journey was safely begun. After he returned home, Margaret was "left to my own self for two days and two nights and did not hear one single word of English. Naturally, my Chinese is pretty limited, but I can tell when I want to walk, find out what the villages are, get rice and hot water, etc. The people in the inn at Uidiok had not had a foreigner in their place for some time, and every door and crack and hole in the wall was full of eyes while I ate my supper and went to bed. My curly hair particularly causes comments. But the people are so good natured about it all I don't mind, and they never offer to molest anyone who doesn't look afraid. They always guess my age and never yet have missed it more than a year....Kiasang paid all the bills, per Miss Schaeffer's order, and I think my night's lodging cost twenty-five cents Mexican, and it was so much because the woman and I had a room that usually accommodates six people." Margaret also thought the scenery was beautiful and somewhat comparable to the Catskills. She wrote, "Hainan is a wonderful place, anyway and you can see I am thoroughly in love with it and the people."[50]

Chinese Lessons Begin

Once she returned to Kiungchow, Margaret began studying Chinese, and in the letter written to her family on her birthday, 23 September, just fifteen days after arriving on the island, she referred to her lessons as a normal part of her days. She was very interested in her Chinese lessons and would soon become extremely adept at the language: "The study of Chinese is progressing pretty well considering. My teacher comes three hours a day....I can write about thirty characters, read about sixty, and say a few words and sentences so I can be understood. I went to prayer meeting last night and was able to understand at least a few words each person said." To her sister Helen she wrote, "You ought to hear me talk Chinese to the women at church! I say 'I do not understand Chinese yet. I am studying with Mr. Dang, but I have only been in China three weeks. I am an American.'...I certainly have a fine teacher....My, but it is fun, and Miss Schaeffer says I do very well."[51] She also told her family that "all unmarried women out here are *Kuniang* and my name is *Mong Kuniang*. *Mong* is nearly like my name in Chinese and means 'misty.'"[52]

Two months after arriving in Hainan she wrote her family that she could "talk quite a little now and make myself understood pretty well, with the help of voluminous gestures." She outlined her course of study for the first six months as "reading Mateer's *Introduction to the Study of Chinese,* and Brown's *Foreign Missionary* in English, mastering the system of Romanization and handing in ten Romanized sentences a week to the literary committee, studying Hainanese geography, taking thirty lessons in the phrase book, twenty lessons in grammar and idiom in Baller's *Primer,* conversation and tone drill with the teacher, memorize the Lord's Prayer, Creed and Ten Commandments, and learn to write thirty characters a week."[53]

Later, after Dr. and Mrs. Bercovitz arrived, Margaret's first teacher was assigned to them, and she began studying with the teacher who had previously taught Mae Chapin. Margaret continued to describe learning Chinese as "heaps of fun," writing that her new teacher "yells out a sentence at me and I yell it back at him, watching the characters in the book."[54]

Years later Margaret detailed the danger of knowing a little Chinese. Hainanese had nine different verbs, all of which translated into English as "to carry." One of them, *neng,* meant "to carry by a handle fastened on two 'ears' or loops, as a pail." Margaret wrote, "Imagine our secret merriment at a greatly beloved missionary whose Chinese was not too good saying at prayer meeting one night that a carrier 'neng-ed' him across a river! The mental picture of the gentleman dragged along by a rope tied to his ears, his long legs floating behind, was almost too much for our risibles." But she noted, "The inherent politeness of our Chinese listeners keeps us ignorant of our worst errors and enables us to carry on, though jokes may come out long afterwards, as of the minister preaching earnestly from the text, 'I am the light of the world,' and persistently saying, 'I am the *devil* of this world,' to the sad discomfiture of the Chinese elder sitting next to him."[55]

According to Margaret, "Before the first furlough most of us sooner or later have 'the new missionaries' nightmare.' I remember well the night I had it, when I woke up shaking all over and crying as if my heart would break. You think you are at home, sent back because you could not learn the language, and wherever you go—church, street, anywhere, people say, 'Oh, I thought you were in China!' and you dodge behind pillars, slink around corners, feel like a suspected criminal, shadowed by the F.B.I."[56]

Margaret survived her nightmare, but shortly after arriving in Hainan, she suffered eyestrain. The mission doctors thought "the climate and the reading up and down instead of across are necessitating a change of lenses."[57] The New Year brought Margaret continued trouble with her eyes. She spent a week in Hoihow without studying Chinese while Dr. McCandliss checked her eyes carefully. Margaret wrote her father that the trouble could not have been anticipated by her doctor at home since she needed "a change of lenses...due to the effect Chinese characters have on astigmatic eyes." A doctor Margaret wanted to visit in Canton had gone home on furlough, so she consulted a French doctor attached to his country's diplomatic mission in Hoihow who advised her not to study Chinese for three months and then to have her eyes tested again.[58] Forced to concentrate on the spoken language, she continued her studies with a new teacher and wrote, "It is most mighty good drill for me, now that I can talk some, as [my teacher] talks to me just as one Chinese talks to another, and makes me talk to him the same way. He is taking a great deal of interest in his job, and I like him very much." [59]

At the end of six months' study, each of the new missionaries had a language exam conducted by other, more experienced missionaries. In mid-April 1916 Margaret's language exam took place: "Mr. Tappan came up and he and Miss S[chaeffer] proceeded to put me through my paces. There were sentences given me in Chinese to translate into English. Mr. T. started out with the one 'Oh, my, this is hard to do.' and so he was prepared to have some fun, as you can see. There were fifteen of that sort, then fifteen where he gave me English to turn into Chinese. Then Miss S. gave me the questions on Chinese geography, which consisted of the province of Hainan, the provinces of China, the larger rivers, the capitals and the treaty ports, all the names being in the native form. There were also the questions on the Chinese radicals, and a few on the course of study and the English readings required. Then they let me go for that time, as the man with whom they wanted me to have my Chinese conversation had not yet come." On Friday the exam continued, with Margaret talking to Ngou Ngi-tin, who "asked me about my parents, how long I had been in Hainan, how long it took me to come here from home, what countries I visited on the way out, whether I liked Kachek or Kiungchow better, etc. Then Mr. T. told me to question him [Ngou], since that is etiquette in China. I asked about his honorable parents and his wife and family, about his school that he has, and some other things. Mr. T. still was not satisfied and so had me tell about my trip down here from Kiungchow." [60]

Margaret received a grade of ninety-one on her exam, and Miss Schaeffer said that "they had been watching the experiment [of learning the spoken language first] with great interest, and they were almost ready to recommend to the mission that the new people after this give the first six months to this sort of work rather than the old course. I can understand so much more of what is said than if I had put in my time studying to read and write, and that can be gotten later. Hearing, understanding and being able to talk are more essential than the knowledge of character if you are to mix with the people at all."[61]

Margaret's Chinese lessons went on after her examination, and her admiration for her teacher increased: "I do like my Chinese teacher so much. He is so anxious that I learn the language well, and he is so patient with me and all my mistakes....He just has to laugh at me sometimes but I don't care because I know it must sound terrible to him, and I get it back at him when he tries to talk English to me. And I think he is too much of a gentleman to make fun of me to the other boys, though I presume they laugh over some of the things I try to say. However we never would learn to talk if we didn't try to do it."[62]

With her eyes still bothering her, she went to Hong Kong in August 1916 to see a specialist, who told her she had a mild case of trachoma. He "says my eyes easily account for the slight attack of 'nerves' I developed last winter and spring."[63] With new glasses, she resumed her Chinese studies. After Margaret had been studying Chinese a little over a year, she wrote to her sister Helen, who was studying French, that she should "learn Chinese if you want something simple and interesting to while away your time with. It surely is fun."[64]

In response to a request from one of her sisters for information about the girls in the mission school, Margaret wrote, "The schoolhouse is a rather long narrow two-story building of gray brick. Downstairs there are two study halls with double desks, one room for the larger and one for the smaller girls. In the middle of the building are several smaller class rooms, storerooms for books, etc. Upstairs are the dormitories, and I wish you could see them. There are fifteen or sixteen girls in each of the big rooms. Their beds are wide boards on sawhorses, with a piece of matting for a mattress and a red blanket for a cover. The mosquito nets are hung from frames fastened up. The girls simply kick off their shoes and crawl into bed—no undressing to bother about. The girls wear Chinese costume, of course, trousers and coat. If it's a little chilly they put on an extra coat or two."[65]

She described the students as having "long, heavy, blue-black hair, braided in one long braid. They oil their hair and it always lays smooth and shiny on their heads. Some of the girls wear bangs....Of course, these girls are much more fortunate than girls not in school. The other girls either go to their boy husband's homes as slaves for their mothers-in-law, or work in the fields or are *da* women. *Da* women carry heavy loads of anything there is around. They have a pole about five feet long over one shoulder and the loads hanging from either end. They walk along with a peculiar almost trotting movement that makes the load easier to carry. Or sometimes a specially heavy load is fastened from the middle of the pole and two women *ko* it, each with one end of the pole on her shoulders. It looks so funny to see a pig in a wicker basket that just fits him...being *koed* along."[66]

Once on Margaret's evening walk she "met a little girl about ten years old carrying a *da*-load of rice that must have weighed about sixty pounds. She had been to Hoihow and was coming back, making about seven miles altogether and she certainly was almost tired out."[67] When one of her aunts inquired about supporting a girl in the mission school, Margaret estimated that "$25 American money will keep a girl in our school, clothe her and give her everything she needs for the whole year."[68]

The schoolgirls helped in running the mission school: "Every girl in our school has to work. They change work every week. One big girl and two middle-sized ones cook for a week. They cook just rice and vegetables, with a little meat, and they cook for about fifty people. Others sweep the schoolrooms, dust things, keep the yard and garden in order, and inspect the work. Every pupil washes her own dishes, because they only have a bowl and a pair of chopsticks....The girls make their own clothes, too, and they do all their own washing."[69]

All Margaret's letters from her first year in Hainan, and many of those from subsequent years, describe the life of the Chinese she lived among and the lives of the foreigners at the mission stations. She once cautioned her family about publishing her letters, which they sometimes did, relating an incident about Mae Chapin, who "sent a letter home telling about the Canton flood. In it she remarked that the Chinese are dirty—which is perfectly true. Her father published the letter in his paper and the Chinese students in Champaign [Illinois] at the university nearly had a fit right then and there. So please be *very careful* if you ever take the occasion of printing anything I send home."[70]

Margaret wrote that "Kiungchow is a walled city in fact has one of the most beautiful walls in all China, and we are going to walk around the city on top of it some afternoon soon when it isn't too hot." Later when she had walked around the wall, she noted, "It is a wonderful wall—about twenty-five feet high, built of stone, and with dirt walled up on the inside so that in places it is twenty feet wide on top. About every two feet there are stone battlements three feet wide, four feet high and one foot thick with a hole in the center for the cannon to be fired through.

The wall is about two miles and a half long altogether and I presume about three hundred years old, as the Chinese have been here only about that long. Now the battlements are crumbling just a little, and they are overgrown with beautiful ivy and ferns growing in their niches."[71]

In one of her earliest letters, she described a Chinese funeral: "The family were dressed in white with coarse brown coats and big hats. The priest had on white robes. The altar of paper was fixed up on a table, and everybody bowed down before it with paper prayers. The hired musician banged his cymbals constantly and the hired mourner screeched continually. Everybody had something to eat, and then they all went home except the pall bearers who carried the coffin out to the appointed spot and built a little wall of bricks up around it until the appointed time or lucky day to bury it comes. That may not be for years yet. Whenever we walk out back of our compound we see lots of the stone heaps—some that have been there so long the heavy wood coffins have rotted away."[72] There was also a foreign cemetery near Kiungchow. Margaret once inquired of Auntie Parks, "Did you ever come across the fact in your reading that the Jesuits had been in Hainan? There are Jesuit graves in the foreign cemetery here that date back to 1600, they tell me, and we are going out to see them soon. There are several little children belonging to missionaries buried there, and at least one missionary."[73] Eventually she did visit the Jesuits' graves and reported that they "dated 1681 and 1686 and have both Latin and Chinese inscriptions. I translated the Latin without any trouble."[74]

In other letters she mentioned that "not very far up the road are the execution grounds." One afternoon "I was studying away with [Mr.] Dang and I heard a peculiar kind of a reed flute holding forth down [the] street a ways. Miss Chapin was studying with her teacher, too, and she came in and said there was going to be an execution, and we went out to the compound gate to see the procession. The execution grounds adjoin our compound on the north, but there's a thick bamboo hedge so we can't see the performances, fortunately. There were four men condemned. They had been soldiers, and they became leaders of robber bands, and there was no doubt of their guilt apparently. Each man had chains on his feet that we could hear clanking on the stones, and a soldier walked on each side of him. About a dozen soldiers marched along behind with their guns, and the two musicians brought up the rear. A little while after the procession went by we heard nine shots, and the deed was done. I don't care particularly to have such things repeated, but am glad to see how they treated the men—no torture or anything like that. And the men killed are usually guilty beyond doubt. Though I do not believe in capital punishment myself." Margaret clearly knew very little about Chinese justice, but she had been in China only a short time.[75]

She did not tell her family that the mission had difficulty in obtaining land for its quarters in the early years the missionaries were on Hainan, and, finally, they were able to obtain the land adjoining the cemetery and the execution ground through the intervention of officials and then only because no Chinese wanted to live in such an unlucky place. On another occasion, she reported, "One night we went down to the old teachers' temple that is being built over into a feast hall, and also saw the Temple of Horrors, but were not in it. We are going through it some day soon, as it has images of the punishments of wicked men in the next world, as Chinese justice sees it. I am anxious to compare it with Virgil's *Aeneid* and Dante's *Inferno*."[76]

Several weeks later some of the missionaries went to visit the Temple of Horrors, or the Judge Temple, as Margaret literally translated it from Chinese. "It is a model of what they think the next life will be. There are ten divisions, each having a judge, two ministers of state, and imps to carry out the punishments. The models of the judges are life size, the ministers (one black and one white) are about three feet high, the imps, who are black and have horns, and the men and women passing through the place are about a foot and a half high. The Chinese say everybody goes through these ten places, but the good just go on through, and whenever a bad man comes to the place where one of his sins is punished he pays the penalty and then goes on to the next. At the end of the string is the wheel of life that brings the good back to another life, but the bad never get back, apparently. Some were covered with snakes, some had to stand with their tongues out (gossips, I think), some had to drag plows for good people, some were stuck full of knives. One of the most suggestive was a greedy man being pulled through the square hole of a cash by his queue. One man was being ground in a rice mill (synonymous with our sausage grinder) and several were being fried. Some tried to cross a beautiful bridge, but an imp on the bridge pushed them headlong onto the rocks below. One man was being 'sawn asunder' a la Foxes' *Book of Martyrs*. They were hung in stocks by their heads, crucified, and tied in various uncomfortable positions. I am going to have my teacher explain the whys and wherefores as soon as I can understand a little better, but it was most interesting. The old man in charge is so nice. He explained everything to Mr. Gilman, but I couldn't understand much of what he said."[77]

With Mae Chapin, Margaret made a trip to Hoihow one Saturday afternoon: "We rode down on wheelbarrows and were very comfortable.

The wheelbarrows have one big wooden wheel about two inches in thickness and two feet in diameter, protected on top by slats....Then there is one little slat and a bar just behind the wheel, to sit on. [The wheelbarrows] squeak constantly—a peculiar screech of wood on wood that cannot be mistaken." They did some shopping and called on Mrs. Alfred E. Street and Mrs. Ledeboer, whose husband was the manager of the Asiatic Petroleum Company: "Mrs. Ledeboer, who is Dutch, was telling us that the three French sisters...who have an orphanage in Hoihow, had not had one bit of money from France since the war broke out, and are almost at their wits' ends, with their forty youngsters to look after. The sisters do beautiful embroidery and are selling it now for money for the school."[78]

When Margaret was invited to a wedding, she "had the teacher wrap up my present of a dollar this morning and fix it all up in proper style."[79] A week later she attended the wedding of a sixteen-year-old girl who "had been in school a few months. The groom is the mission coolie and a very fine young man. The procession came with the groom in a common sedan chair and the bride in a very fancy red chair, all closed up and fastened so no one could steal her. She went in to Mrs. McC[andliss]'s and was dressed in her wedding clothes. We watched them comb her hair, put in her gold bars and pins; put on her wreaths, earrings, rings, and then her wedding dress, which was a beautiful green silk brocaded suit. She had pretty slippers and a fan to match. Then the procession went over to the church and Mr. Gilman married the couple, but he preached a sermon first! Then we went to the feast. I do wish I could really describe that feast. We foreigners were served first. We sat on benches around the table, and the band of two pairs of cymbals, horns, fiddles, etc., was banging away just outside the door. The table had nuts, candies, black duck eggs, etc., on first. We had our chopsticks, a china ladle and a big bowl of rice to eat other things with. We had birds' nest soup, and it is as good as anything I ever ate. We had chicken with dressing, duck, cuttlefish, native macaroni, native chili sauce, giblet stew, abalone, pork with dressing, chicken soup, sweet soup, steamed cake, tea, anything we could think of, almost. We dipped in with our spoons and put our share on our rice and ate away, or else fished out what we wanted with our own chopsticks. Mrs. McC. very kindly took forks and spoons for us but I didn't use them, as I soon could manage my chopsticks. Everything was so good. The pickled radish and 'sour-sweet' meat sauces are fine. It sounds barbarous, I know, but it isn't, and the people are just as hospitable as any could be. I enjoyed it very much."[80]

China's Political Turmoil

Margaret frequently asked her tutor about political events in China, and in December 1915 she inquired about the restoration of the monarchy by Yuan Shih-k'ai. The 1911 revolution had ended the Ch'ing dynasty, but many Chinese remained monarchists, and there had been some local celebration of the restoration. Margaret asked the teacher "if there would be trouble over it here in Hainan and he said no—Hainan was the tail of the snake and it would only wiggle a little, but there would be trouble in Shanghai and Canton. He said the republicans here would have to keep quiet because they had no place to escape to, but that they would keep petty thievery and rioting going on most of the time. As a matter of fact Hainan will probably be about the quietest part of all China politically. If any trouble should come up we women and children would go to Hong Kong, but there is no likelihood of any necessity for such doings. Only we never commit ourselves to either side."[81]

Margaret's interest in Chinese politics continued, and in April 1916 she wrote that the missionaries were having difficulty deciding "whether our province did or did not revolt from the Yuan Shih-k'ai government. The report came that they had, and all the republicans were so happy that they stood on their heads, figuratively speaking, and meaning those who had their heads still on. Then in a few days came the report that it was a false independence, a trap to catch the republicans, and that heads were going off right and left out in the city. So now we don't know what is the truth, except that conditions are pretty unsettled and that the Chinese think that entire silence in regard to the situation is the only way to be sure they will not be nabbed."[82] A week later she wrote that "Hainan is rather unsettled politically these days. There have been riots and battles in several places down near here and Dr. Kelly has some wounded soldiers in the hospital....but the trouble is really over the taxes that have been levied by the Canton powers who are in sympathy with Yuan Shih-k'ai. A telegram came yesterday saying that the governor at Canton had abdicated and if that is the case things will quiet down at once. Three men have been executed here in Kachek these last few days, one for carrying a bomb. I don't know what the charge was against the other two. The soldiers have been going through the market quite frequently."[83]

At the end of May the island was "still rather disturbed politically. The soldiers loot any where they go. The district city...was attacked last week and looted, and when Mr. Ong was telling Miss S[chaeffer] about it he said when robbers went through a town they used a comb on it but the soldiers used a *din* or a very fine comb that the people use to get lice out of their hair, when they went through a place."[84]

In the summer of 1916 Margaret's teacher arrived in Kiungchow and related to her the difficulties his village had been having with the revolutionaries: "[Elder Li] is terribly anxious about his family. While we were in Nodoa about 800 revolutionists camped near his village for a little while and then went over to Uihong city and fought there. The Uihong magistrate ran away to Kachek and called all the Doaloe (my teacher's village) elders to come to a council with him there. He told them they had to do six things or he would send his soldiers to burn their houses and kill the men, and he gave them several days to answer him. The six things were 1) repair the Uihong city wall, 2) repair the temple of Confucius, 3) repair the school, 4) repair the official's house, 5) catch the 800 revolutionists, and 6) give up all the guns the village owns as protection against robber bands. The elders decided he didn't have men enough to destroy all the houses in a village of 5000 people and to kill all the men, and they knew if they acceded to his demands the revolutionary party would think they were traitors, so they sold all their pigs, turned their cattle loose in the mountains, killed their chickens and ducks to eat, and took all their baggage and went away. The teacher was in Kachek and couldn't get home and has had no word from any of his people for some time. He is so worried about [his] little baby and [his son]."[85]

Then in August Margaret wrote her grandmother, "Things are fairly quiet here now although robbers are pretty bold. I will not go into Kachek alone, probably. Mr. Byers will likely come out to the river to meet me. There is really no danger for foreigners but it is better not to travel alone when things are unsettled. In ordinary times there is no danger whatever."[86]

Missionary Lifestyle

During her first weeks on the island, Margaret became interested in the flora of her new environment. While in Hong Kong she "was lucky enough to find a manual of plants in Kwangtung province and a dictionary of botanical terms and a folding magnifying glass, so I am happy, although my big gray 'Gray's Botany' wouldn't come amiss." She noted that, "as a matter of fact, Hainan is unexplored as regards flowers, birds and insects." Within a month after her arrival on the island, she was able to write to her aunt Harriette, who worked at the herbarium at Iowa State College, that she had found "Lantana Camara, Linn.; Crotolaria Striata D.C.; Cassia occidentalis, Linn.; Floscopa scandeus Lour. or paniculata Beuth; Gymnopetalum cochinchinese Kurz; and a Galactin, the species tenuiflora given in my book not seeming to be the one I want." She noted that she was unable to press any plants because of the rainy weather but hoped to do some later.[87]

By 1916 she was corresponding about plants with Henry Shoemaker Conard, a Grinnell professor who was visiting at Harvard, who told her that she should send him specimens and that "especially rare ones will be paid for!"[88] The following year she wrote that Professor Conard had received his specimens and was "howling for more and the Manila Bureau of Science is howling for specimens. The specimens are right here to get and when school is out I hope to get busy with my botanizing, and put in part at least of my vacation being a scientist(?). I have just been trying to find out what a native seed that the people here use for medicine is. I was pretty sure it was a spice, and Mrs. Kelly told me as soon as she smelled it that it was cardamon seed, and that it must have come from India, but I assured her that it grew wild in Hainan. It is quite valuable I imagine."[89]

Less than two months after her arrival in Hainan, Margaret contracted malaria. She often mentioned in her letters home that the mosquitoes were terrible and frequently bit her. "I have been enjoying another typical Hainan experience this week," she wrote. "That is to say, I've had a slight attack of fever. Now don't get scared—everybody out here has it and no one ever has any serious results except little children. It is malaria, of course....The doctor is always anxious about the first attack in seeing whether the new people can take quinine or not."[90] Margaret always enjoyed writing poems, and while sick she composed "Owed to Hainan Fever," which included the lines

> This tale is told of Hainan fever,
> By one who's met the gay deceiver.
> A little shake, and then a shiver,
> An awful quake, and next a quiver.
> Your backbone is a crawling lizard;
> You're colder than a northwest blizzard.[91]

Mae Chapin had informed Dr. McCandliss at Hoihow that Margaret had malaria, and he requested that she "write a note and tell him how I felt. I enclosed my 'Owed' and let it go at that." The doctor replied that "the patient's physical condition was good...but he wasn't sure of her *mental* condition and would come up! Miss C.'s face got whiter and whiter and her eyes bigger and bigger, as she read the note in my presence, until I made her tell me what was wrong. She had not known what I'd sent Dr. McC. so didn't see the joke until I told her."[92]

Margaret described to her family the house she shared at Kiungchow as having rooms that were "all very large....The ceilings are high upstairs as well as down because of the heat. The outside of the house is gray brick, the inside finished with smooth white plaster. The verandas are arched, both upstairs and down, and there are shutters on all the doors and windows." The women employed three servants: "Tai-mui cooks and waits on table and takes care of the downstairs. She gets $8 Mexican a month. Koan-sio washes, irons, and takes care of the upstairs for $7 Mexican. Then Lim-kit is our coolie. He draws water, runs errands, takes care of the horses, makes garden, kills the snakes, etc., for $6.50 Mexican a month. So the three servants cost the two of us $21.50 Mexican or about $9.50 gold a month and we go halves on the bill."[93]

The end of March was the end of the fiscal year for the mission, and accounts had to be settled then. Margaret, in Kachek on 1 April 1916, wrote her family about her housekeeping expenses, which she shared with Katherine Schaeffer: "Last month our vegetables and meat and wood and charcoal that the woman bought on the street for us amounted to $15.92. There is wood and charcoal on hand for about three months out of what we bought this month. Our bill with Mr. Street amounted to $18.08, [for] brooms, salt, vanilla, lemon extract, several tins of biscuits and a case of ninety-six small tins of condensed milk. Said milk will also last us about three months. Our two women servants cost us $9. So our expenses were less than $50 and there are a lot of staples on hand. The figures are Mexican, of course, and we split even on the bills. We have opened about three tins of biscuits and perhaps six tins of fish and fruit, otherwise we live on native food and enjoy it."[94]

The complexity of the money used in Hainan was demonstrated when Margaret sent one of the servants to the bank to cash a check. When he brought the money back, "there were Kwangtung Province dollars, Mexican dollars, French Indochina dollars, and Japanese yen in the bunch. Some combination. For a $25 Hong Kong check I got $26.70 and some cash."[95]

Few sources survive to explain how the missionaries financed their own contributions to the mission, but one that does exist concerns Katherine Schaeffer's contribution. Although Miss Schaeffer and Margaret shared their home, Margaret was unaware that her senior colleague was also paying her salary. Katherine Schaeffer had written to the Board of Foreign Missions that she wanted to contribute $275 a year for three years to help pay the salary of a woman educator for Kachek, but as this was a contribution to the mission, not to the individual who filled the position, she did "not wish her to know that *I* am paying."[96]

It is likely that other missionaries tithed for the work of the mission, as several mentioned supporting children in the mission school. In the summer of 1916 Margaret wrote to her sisters that she paid off her college debts to Grinnell and "now I can save some money and help more with things out here. I have one girl and one boy in school now both Lois—supported out of my tenth." In another letter she mentioned that she paid $30 Mexican a year for the Loi girl and thought that "$18 gold would provide clothes and everything for a girl. Tuition is a little more in the boys' school."[97]

As Christmas approached, the missionaries made preparations for their celebration. Mae Chapin's sister sent a package with gifts for the sixty girls in the school. Christmas Day began early: "At 3:30 in the morning a dozen boys from the boys' school went around and sang Christmas carols at each of the foreign houses. Miss Chapin and I...went out on the upper veranda and thanked them. Then our girls sang a while, too. Well, it was certainly beautiful and almost cold enough for Christmas at home, too." For the morning services, "the men and boys decorated the church beautifully with palms....Everyone had been asked to make a little box and put in their contribution, to be used for the poor here in Kiungchow and for the Canton flood sufferers. These were all brought and hung on the tree and they looked so very pretty....The contributions ranged from a $5 gold piece (Mexican) from the banker, who is not a Christian, to a hundred cash from a poor blind woman down the street here. And altogether we had over $57 Mexican. I tell you that means a lot to these people out here to give that much. It would hustle a church at home to give the equivalent of that in American money from the same sized audience. $17 came from the eighty-odd schoolgirls and women here on our compound, too."[98]

Most of the missionaries' Christmas packages had not arrived in time for the holiday. In mid-January Margaret told her family that "the bill of lading came from Montgomery Ward, and my box was to be shipped December 20, so it will be coming before long. Here I am almost distracted to know what's in it, and the bill only says 'Personal Effects'! Cruel fate! Never say Monkey Ward has no humor."[99]

The Hainan missionaries worked hard at maintaining a Western lifestyle. Margaret once wrote that at a dinner at the Reverend and Mrs. James Shannon's house "Mr. Campbell had on a dress suit, if you please, and Miss Chapin, Mrs. Campbell and I all had on our evening gowns."[100] Other forms of entertainment included tennis, outings, and picnics. After a picnic with the Shannons, the Bercovitzes, and Mae Chapin at the local pagoda, located about a mile and a half from the mission compound, Margaret described it as having "eight floors or seven stories high, octagonal in shape,...over one hundred feet tall....It is of gray brick with arched doors in every story and little square holes for windows. There are shrubs and vines growing on every projection. The stairway is spiral and inside the wall, but up four stories you have to walk halfway round on the outside ledge to reach the second stairs." When she asked her Chinese teacher about the pagoda, he told her "it was over five hundred years old, and that a former chief official of this province had built it. I asked why it was built, and he said the people gave three reasons in their stories about it. One tale said that so many hard winds and typhoons came from the northeast that the people thought the pagoda northeast of the city would propitiate the devils so the official built it. Another tale says that the streams near the pagoda enclose the fields in the shape of a big fish...and the people were afraid the fish would turn over and destroy all their fields so they built the pagoda on top of him to hold him down. Tale number three says the official who built the pagoda was a bad man and jealous because Hainan had so many scholars, so he built the pagoda as an offering to the evil spirits so no more great men would arise. My teacher remarked at the end that none of these tales were true but that the official really wanted to beautify Hainan. You can take your choice of the tales but I myself am inclined to believe the second one if Hainan ever had earthquakes. It is great fun digging out the folklore and the superstitions and it is a fine way to get the people's way of thinking."[101]

In their concern to maintain their American lifestyle and to ease the loneliness for one another, the Hainan missionaries celebrated everyone's birthday with a party and were careful to observe all American holidays as they would have at home. Margaret celebrated her first birthday in Hainan at the station in Kachek just weeks after her arrival. Her day started with her "usual Chinese lesson from 6:30 to 7:30, and then just before breakfast Miss S[chaeffer] gave me a letter from Mrs. Byers that had a lovely Japanese ornament in it, and there was a lovely lavender enamel on silver necklace from Miss S.—the beautiful Hainanese work. This afternoon we went down to the manse for afternoon tea (where Mr. and Mrs. Byers and Mr. Tappan live), and there was a perfectly huge and glorious birthday cake all covered with fancy frosting."[102]

Like all missionaries in China, Margaret spent a great deal of time maintaining her household. While still in Kiungchow, she began looking for a woman to accompany her to Kachek: "I am engaging my servant to take down to Kachek with me, and I'm having a great time doing it, as very few women are willing to go into the interior."[103] Once she arrived in Kachek, she wrote her sister Dorothy that she was "in full charge of the cooking arrangements here now, so for goodness' sake hurry up the cookbook!" In addition to being in charge of the cooking, Margaret wrote her aunt, "I am housekeeper here now and you ought to see me order the cook around and take accounts with my strings of cash. It certainly is fine."[104] All of the missionaries had gardens to supply their vegetables. In February Margaret's garden in Kachek was "in its prime. We have string beans, tomatoes, lettuce, and sweet corn ready to use, beets and carrots coming on, but I think no peas. By the way, I asked when to have my seeds sent out and Miss S[chaeffer] says we plant about September usually and that about August when new seeds first come out is the best time for people at home to send things to us. Beans, peas, carrots, corn, tomatoes, lettuce, cauliflower, and radishes do well but beets and cabbage are very uncertain. My seeds that Miss Chapin planted [in Kiungchow] did beautifully only I had to leave before I got much of the crop."[105]

Responding to a query from her family about what kind of food she was eating, Margaret wrote, "We...eat a great deal of Chinese food....We [have] rice three times a day, cooked as only Chinese know how to do, and it is fine. We [have] fish every morning for breakfast, and waffles and syrup, which are not Chinese. We [have] native vegetables entirely—one that tastes like celery, one like asparagus, one like sour-dock greens, and then native sauerkraut. We [have] meat cooked with the 'sour sweet' dressing, and meat cooked with native chestnuts. [The chickens are] roasted, stewed, fried or 'pied'—only we have to teach the Chinese how to cook it any way but the first."[106]

As Chinese New Year approached, Margaret informed her family that during the first two weeks in February there would be no mail service in or out of Hainan because of the holiday, "so don't worry if no letters come for some time. I will write as usual but that is all the good it will do." After Chinese New Year Margaret moved inland to the Kachek station. She wrote home that she was settling down to life there, but she added that everyone at the station was saddened by the death of Kiasang, the mission employee who had accompanied Margaret to the river as she returned from her first visit to Kachek the previous autumn. Kiasang had "often gone with Miss Schaeffer on trips and had just recently been out with Mr. Byers on a six weeks' trip....He was such a fine man and we all thought a great deal of him. His wife and three little children are going to come here on the compound to live, and the woman will be trained to go with Miss Schaeffer on country trips." Many years later Margaret recollected the arrival of the widow and her children: "She came, a husky village woman, used to working in the garden and rice field, [who had] never [been] in a foreign-style house before. The day after she moved in, we took her upstairs to show her part of her work, and she crawled up on her hands and knees, fearful of falling."[107] Eventually the woman became accustomed to the foreigners and their strange ways and stayed with them.

Because Margaret disliked being carried in a sedan chair and enjoyed horseback riding, she decided to buy herself a horse. She asked her father to send her a saddle and bridle, suggesting that he "use Jerry, for size, as our ponies here are not very much smaller....Also, a twenty-foot or thirty-foot rope about the size of a trunk rope is necessary to tie the horse with nights, and a riding whip." Since the Chinese at the mission compound knew Margaret wanted a horse, they began looking for one for her. In late April she reported that "one of the men brought a horse around for me to try tonight, but I even refused to ride him because he was so little. I don't want one that I feel as if I ought to walk up every hill for because I am actually bigger than he is. Perhaps when I go to Nodoa to mission meeting I will be able to find one that is fairly good size, though one like that will probably cost me about $60 Mexican or $30 gold. However it is economy to get a good horse to begin with, and a young one."[108]

In July, while at Kiungchow, she wrote, "One of the Chinese brought a nice [horse] around the other day but he had a sore back where the Chinese saddle had rubbed it so I wouldn't try to ride him. Told the man to bring him back when his back was well for me to try him....I would have to pay about $40 Mexican for him, I suppose. He's six or seven years old." By the following April Margaret was still looking for a horse. She reported, "We are to have the masons build a short piece of wall between us and the hospital before long and they are to build us a small horse stable at the same time. Miss Schaeffer already has a small shelter for her horse and I will have to have a place for mine. It is absolutely impossible to keep two Hainanese horses in the same stable. They are terrible fighters." In August she wrote to her brother that she was still looking and had seen an old, skinny horse that she had refused to buy.[109]

Then in October 1917, a year and a half after she first mentioned wanting to buy a horse, she purchased one in Nodoa and sent a servant to get it. It was a five-day trip each way, "but he very likely had days of waiting for river boats or carriers to show him the way from Fahhih into Nodoa," Margaret wrote on 21 October, "so I hardly look for him yet. [I] am anxious to see the horse and really have one of my own. Miss Schaeffer's pony's name is Beastie, so I really ought to call mine Beauty, so we would have Beauty and the Beast,...but I think he will be more likely to be Colonel or Major since he used to belong to an officer in Lung Ci-koang's [Lung Chi-kuang's] army."[110] Yet after all the months of searching for a horse, the problem was still not solved: "I had a letter from Nodoa last week saying my new horse had been stolen. Dr. Salsbury thought he could probably recover it, though. I sure hope so, $60 is not to be sneezed at and I do want a horse so badly." The horse story continued into mid-November: "Dr. Salsbury has not been able to find my horse....I have no idea how much he has spent for search parties and so on." Two weeks later she wrote, "My horse was recovered from the thieves but was so thin and worn out and his feet so tender where they had cut the shoes off that he died on the way between [Nodoa and Kachek], so now I will wait until after my vacation this summer before I get another."[111]

The life of the missionaries in Hainan in the early twentieth century was a rugged one. Many of the missionaries had guns and used them on occasion.[112] Mother Melrose frequently carried a gun while itinerating, and Katherine Schaeffer had one, but Margaret never mentioned owning a gun and probably did not. "We have been having sneak thieves around," she wrote in early 1916, "and they appeared [one] night [this week] as usual, but of course they could not do any mischief, so I simply rolled over and went to sleep again when I heard them. The next night they came again, and Miss Schaeffer got up and fired her shotgun off, just to let them know she had one. They go all around the compound, and woe unto anybody who leaves anything out of the house." Later she told one of her sisters that "there was a rumor that the pirates were going to make a raid on Kachek market. So the theater was called off, the soldiers called out on patrol duty, and the people generally ready for some excitement. The pirates are quite bold lately. They are sea-rovers of course. They usually come over here from Dealan, a salt market about twelve miles away, on the sea-coast. Robbery and kidnapping are their specialties. They kidnapped a Kachek merchant's son. Isn't it romantic to live so near the scenes of piracy? They do not molest the foreigners in any way."[113] Margaret had noted that on one of her first visits to Hoihow, "Dr. McCandliss...[got] up in the middle of the night to take care of a man shot in a fight with the pirates. There are pirates all around here and they make it lively sometimes. When there's no boat to molest, they fish. So you see there is no lack of excitement."[114]

Margaret was known among the missionaries for her skill at mathematics, and she was consulted when her abilities were needed. "I had a lot of fun [with a] problem about Mr. Street's ice plant yesterday," she wrote in May 1916. "The ice is made in a mold the shape of a frustum of a square pyramid, and he wanted to know where to cut the block to make four pieces of equal weight. It is quite a problem and I have had a lot of fun over it. They cut it by guess and hit it pretty well, but I have a rule for him now."[115]

Once a year the Hainan missionaries held their mission meeting to discuss the work they were doing and to plan for the future. In 1916 the meeting was held in Nodoa. There was no direct road from Kachek to Nodoa, so the missionaries traveled first to Hoihow and then to Nodoa. Although this was not Margaret's first trip in Hainan, she used the opportunity to describe the journey to her family: "You just ought to see a Chinese inn. I can't possibly describe one and do it justice. You enter the big wooden door, step over a high threshold onto the dirty dirt floor and there you are. Windows none. One or two big tables where the guests eat, beds all around the edges of the room. The place usually has a...little room fenced off in one corner and we foreigners always get that place. This particular inn has boards laid over the top of the room and people sleep up over our heads. As soon as the people know there is a foreigner in town they come to see the show. I got the usual questions, of course, How old am I? Twenty-odd. Why is my skin so white? Why is my nose so high? (They call Mr. Tappan the teacher with the big, big nose.) Why am I not married? (The title *Kuniang* tells them I am single.) Do we Americans never use oil on our hair? Is my dress hot? (I had on a...gingham dress). Why do I wear two pairs of shoes? (Rubbers), etc. And they scare the kids by trying to make them come up to me. Do I eat rice?...[Finally,] I crawled in under my mosquito net and went to bed. We were all comfortably settled and about asleep when one of the men who was right up over me began to sing theater songs. I only understood a little...[and] by this time the F. Lea, Esq. family that inhabited that room had waked up. I had been asleep a while when the family pig began rooting around my door and squealing at a great rate. The landlady yelled at her husband to know why he hadn't put the pig out in the court before he went to bed....And the man clumped down from over my head and put the pig out with some remarks that I understood the intention of even if the meaning of the single words was lost on me. A rat was running over the top of my mosquito net just then so I didn't hear what the landlady said next."[116]

This was the trip that convinced her she needed to buy a horse, as on this journey she was being carried by chair bearers and the roads were very slippery from the rain: "Twice I thought the coolies were going to drop me, but they are very sure-footed and did not. One time it sure would have been funny—they were crossing a little stream and the front coolie stepped on a stone and it rolled with him. There's nothing to do but sit still, however, and *never* scream. You would lose your face forever....[Later] I saw something I had heard of before but never seen. We came to where another trail crossed ours and there was a straw man spread out and a stick stuck through him. It is supposed to be a very efficacious way of cursing people. I just asked the woman about it but didn't understand all she said except that it was devil-doings." Katherine Schaeffer, who had been out itinerating, met Margaret at Dengang, and the two traveled by boat for about thirty-six hours to Fahhih, where they spent the night. The next night they stayed in an inn that "had three rooms (?) separated by bamboo poles set six inches apart....Miss S. and I had the landlady's private bedroom, with its one bed of bamboo splints, about the size of a three-quarter bed....Miss S. *sat through* the bed when she went to get in (I don't see how it happened that I didn't do it!) and had to move herself very circumspectly. We laughed till we cried."[117]

Margaret wrote her family that at Nodoa the "buildings are different from our houses in Kachek but no nicer. The station is older, though, and the lawns and walks in better shape. And they have an electric light plant on the compound!" The mission meeting began on Friday afternoon with "the Devotional exercises, roll call, report of absentees and election of chairman. Mr. Byers and Dr. Kelly are the only voting members absent but they could not leave their families as Mr. Tappan brought news of a battle at Uihong, only four miles from Kachek, and rumors of an attack on Kachek itself."[118] At mission meeting each of the missionaries had to submit a formal report to the Board in New York detailing work and leisure activities for the past year. Margaret submitted her first report in poetry! It read in part,

> 'Tis sad but true, my eyes went bad,
> And study's fate on the doctors hung;
> But after counsel grave and sad
> I've worked along with lungs and tongue.[119]

After the mission meeting, Margaret returned to Kiungchow, where she spent the Fourth of July. The missionaries always celebrated the holiday with a picnic, and this one included sailing and swimming along with lunch on the spit—a long sandbar that stretched out into the bay. That week also brought a surprise: "When Dr. Mc[Candliss] came over from the hospital to breakfast [on Thursday] he brought a young Englishman over with him and we all nearly collapsed. Foreigners are a *rara avis* here, you know. He was an agent for a Shanghai drug firm, and very pleasant. He had intended to go down to Kachek and Nodoa and back, thinking the trip would take two or three days!" After a short stay in Kiungchow, Margaret went to Hong Kong for the first of her yearly vacations, during which she shopped and saw an eye doctor. Margaret liked Hong Kong and met many missionaries, primarily Baptists and Presbyterians, from Canton there. She noted, however, that "the majority of the people are English and have no use whatever for the Americans."[120]

As her first year on Hainan ended, Margaret was making good progress with her Chinese studies and had adjusted to life on the island. She had been living in Kachek but had spent time at both the Hoihow and Kiungchow compounds, and she had visited Nodoa for mission meeting, seeing all of the mission stations much more quickly than most missionaries did. She did some botanical work and began delving into the traditions and folklore of the island. She also had demonstrated her tremendous gift as an observer of the Chinese scene around her. As she became more skilled in the Chinese language, she was able to learn about the milieu in which she lived directly from the people with whom she dealt. From Nodoa in June she wrote to her family, "If I didn't know so many people at home were praying for me things would not be so easy. I never was happier in my life and I am feeling fine."[121]

CHAPTER TWO

The Young Missionary
1916–1921

AFTER COMPLETING HER first year in Hainan, Margaret could no longer be considered a newcomer. She had acquired enough fluency in the language to carry on simple conversations and had become versed in the work of the mission. Hainan was still an exotic place to her, but it was increasingly becoming her home.

During the next five years, up to the time of her first furlough, Margaret gradually assumed more responsibility within the mission, first serving as principal of the girls' schools in Kachek and then in Kiungchow replacing older missionaries who went home on furloughs. She served as editor of the mission newsletter and of the book the missionaries published about Hainan and as mission treasurer. It was during these years that her letters developed certain themes that show the evolution of her ideas about China and the Chinese and the purpose and work of the Presbyterian mission on the island. She continued her hobby of collecting botanical specimens, which she sent to scientists at home and in the Philippines, and she became interested in the Miao aborigines of Hainan and published the first of her scholarly articles about them. She developed the strong belief that the Chinese needed to be taught patriotism in the American mold and participated in the casual cultural imperialism of the mission without seeming to give it any serious thought. Not only did she think the Chinese needed to be taught to be like Westerners, but she also believed that the Miao girls who came to the mission school needed to be dressed like the Chinese so that they would not look different. During these years Margaret wrote to her family, "We never suffer much from monotony out here."[1]

Warfare wracked China in the years following the 1911 revolution, as northern and southern factions fought for control of the country. Hainan was not spared its share of the unrest. Margaret frequently wrote of the armies that invaded the island but constantly reassured her loved ones that the soldiers did not disturb foreigners. Confident that extraterritoriality protected them, the Hainan missionaries went about their business despite the presence of troops on the island.[2] Often Margaret or other missionaries accompanied the schoolgirls in or out of town as they traveled to and from the mission schools so that the girls would not be stopped, questioned, and/or searched by the soldiers. In an attempt to stay on the good side of the local military authorities, the missionaries frequently visited and entertained the wives of military men, and those members of the military who were Christians were welcome guests at the churches and in the homes of the missionaries. On several occasions, the disturbances sent hundreds of Chinese people fleeing into the mission compounds, as they believed that they would be safe there since the missionaries were protected by treaties. When Chinese Christians became victims of the violence, the Hainan missionaries often tried to aid them, not on the basis of the foreigners' extraterritorial rights, but on the grounds that the Chinese government guaranteed its citizens religious freedom.

Political Turmoil

In Hainan, General Lung Ci-Koang's army caused most of the difficulties. In mid-June 1917 Margaret wrote of the departure of the troops and her opinion about the chances for a republic in China, noting that the Chinese said General Lung had gone north "to try to set up a monarchy again, with the northern parties to help him....China is not yet ready for a republic. She is too big and unwieldy and undeveloped, communication is too difficult, and so many illiterate people...make even a republic anything but representative of the masses of the people. But we shall see what comes of it. The southern provinces are quiet this time. They are usually the ones that kick up the rumpus when there is any thing going on."[3]

Shortly thereafter, she wrote, "China is pretty well stirred up over the fact that the old emperor has been reinstated and the president has made himself rather scarce. But the papers say that the emperor will be out of the way inside of three weeks. The southern provinces will not stand for an empire again, so of course they have declared their independence. It remains to be seen what finally comes of the affair, but I imagine that it will be peacefully settled." If Margaret were concerned with the nature of China's government, she was also concerned with more mundane matters. She had asked her Chinese teacher "if he thought they would have to go back to wearing queues and he said he did not think that even the emperor could ever rule China again as regards such nonessential things. There is some danger though that Confucianism will now be made the state religion again, as it used to be."[4]

Margaret clearly thought that the political difficulties would not affect the work of the mission. She also believed, however, that the 1911 revolution had produced political conditions similar to those found in the United States, making the mistake of many missionaries in China who confused the Chinese revolution with the American one: "China is very much unsettled these days...[but] the trouble is not very likely to affect us or our work here. But the people in various places are having trouble with the officials over the revolt of last summer, and a number of our Christian men are in hiding. What they did was to exercise their right of free speech and free thought in a so-called republic that is still ruled by officials of the old type, rather than anything that was a crime."[5]

Margaret had a cynical attitude toward the hostilities. Traveling from Kiungchow back to Kachek, she wrote her family that there were rumors of the "people's army" revolting against General Lung's. After reaching Kachek, she heard "that the business men of Kachek market had put out money to buy off the soldiers so that no trouble would be made here and I think that quite likely that is the case....Most likely nothing will be done except a few people caught and forced to pay over money to get off. I see that usually the ones accused of being implicated are ones who have money enough to get free, or else men who have personal enemies that want to pay off old scores."[6]

During the last six months of 1918 there was constant fighting in Hainan. Margaret missed the worst of the fighting, which occurred while she was vacationing in Hong Kong, but she quickly wearied of it after returning to the island. At the end of September she still insisted to her family that the missionaries' only fear was of stray bullets. Forgetting that she was a foreigner and a guest in China, she wrote her family that the hostilities continued but that "all we want is for them to hurry up and settle the trouble and get out so Hainan can be let alone in peace. Don't worry about us—everyone agrees—that all we need worry over is stray bullets and we can escape those by being careful to stay behind our heavy brick walls. We are on perfectly good terms with both sides and have soldiers of both sides as patients in the hospital, yet we are perfectly neutral and both sides know it and respect our neutrality." She did mention, though, that the mission compound was very near the fort. "Bullets will get over on our side occasionally, as the three small holes in our roof and one in the hospital roof made during the previous forty-eight-hour bombardment testify....If it gets *too* hot here we can go to nearby villages until the fighting is over, but there are about eight chances in ten that there will be no fighting here....There—I have told you the truth, the whole truth and nothing but the truth."[7]

The missionaries' attitudes toward the armies were quite different from those of the Chinese, as was demonstrated when the armies needed help in transporting their goods. The Chinese, all too knowledgeable about the nature of armies, wanted to avoid any contact with them, while the missionaries thought cooperation was a better tactic. Although Margaret was quite cynical about attempting to bribe the armies or seizing rich individuals to obtain money and conversely about the rich paying what was demanded, she naively believed that the soldiers would repay the money they took from the people. Through all the difficulties Margaret's chief concern was that the work of the mission not be interrupted by the fighting. As the Cantonese and Lung's men fought back and forth, Margaret reported, "They caught men and forced them to carry loads. The men who know how to carry ran away and so they caught anybody they could, and the people complained terribly. We scolded them (the people) roundly for not getting the regular carriers out to carry without any fuss, as they knew the soldiers would need men, but they can't see it that way. The soldiers had had no pay so took the son of the head man of the market as hostage and made the market pay $700 cash as ransom, though they promise to send the money back when they reach Hoihow. They are gone—and the Cantonese from the south are already entering the market. We had an occupation and evacuation, or vice versa, again without a shot being fired. The Lord has certainly protected us and our schools. We haven't missed a day, but all the native schools here and down south are entirely disbanded." She also wrote that one of the missionaries, the Reverend Clarence Newton, and the British consul "were negotiating peace, or trying to, [with] Lung promising to leave Hainan."[8]

But the Reverend Mr. Newton and the British consul were not successful in their negotiations, and the fighting went on. Yet it is evident from Margaret's accounts of the armies that they were not inclined to tangle with foreigners and respected her insistence that they not trespass on the property of the girls' school. When the Cantonese arrived in Kachek, she noted they were more likely to loot than were the Hainanese troops. She reported that they entered the school compound "by tens and twenties to look around....I go out and politely but firmly inform them that this is a girls' school where no men are allowed, but they can go to the boys' school grounds if they wish. It's funny how ten or a dozen big fellows with their guns move when I speak but Mrs. Byers teases me a lot about 'the determination expressed in every line of my figure.' Of course they go out for a foreigner, without any trouble, but they won't listen to a Chinese servant. I keep the front gate locked most of the time though I hate to do that when people who have a right to come are coming and going. The soldiers will all be gone by another week, likely. I suppose the final fight will be at Kiungchow, if there is one. Money talks so loud out here that I imagine the two sides will settle financially."[9]

Teaching the Chinese Patriotism

Although the fighting in Hainan came to an end about the same time World War I was ending, China's problems continued. Margaret's proposed solution to those problems reflected her traditional view of nationalism. But nationalism as it manifested itself in China was a combination of its traditional elements—sense of pride in country, shared history, language, customs, culture—and anti-foreignism. It was also decidedly anti-Christian, since Christianity was a foreign religion.[10]

As the Chinese worked at sorting out the political problems of their country, Margaret, like many missionaries, felt that the model of the United States was the only one the Chinese should follow if they desired a democratic government. Indeed, one of the recurring themes of Margaret's letters is her desire to teach the Chinese nationalism. She first mentioned this as one of her goals in China just thirteen months after she arrived in Hainan. She felt that the Chinese were not yet ready to function under a republican form of government but that the missionaries might help China develop into one, if only the Chinese were willing. Margaret frequently wrote to her family and to various church organizations comparing Chinese Double Ten Day, the anniversary of the 1911 revolution, with the Fourth of July. But it was in her descriptions of China's difficulties that she most often revealed her pride in being an

American and her belief that the Chinese were unfortunate people because of their nationality. In October 1916 Margaret observed, "Tuesday was the anniversary of the founding of the Chinese republic and [we celebrated] with a special patriotic meeting...in the chapel....There were speeches by the two head teachers and by several of the boys. China surely does need to educate her young men in the spirit of patriotism for its own sake and not for personal advantage."[11]

A year later, in a letter to a church group, she revealed how much the celebration of Double Ten Day in the mission schools resembled an American patriotic celebration: "Yesterday was the tenth of October, the birthday of the Chinese republic or as we might say the 'Chinese Fourth of July.' The Chinese themselves call it the 'Twin Ten Festival,' because it comes on the tenth of the tenth month. It is customary in our schools here to close on that day....the church was decorated...[with] the two school flags, one with the boys' school name and the other with the girls' school name, and had draped red cloth around in various places....The Chinese flag was fastened to the end of a long bamboo pole and tied to the top of a tall tree, so that it waved bravely over the top of the court....We marched the girls down to the court of the chapel and...the boys marched up...with their flags and drums and horns, formed a double circle around the flag and we all saluted three times. Then the boys sang four of their native songs....We sang a Chinese national hymn to the tune of 'America,' and then the leader read two passages of Scripture....Then one of the young men led in prayer for China and her people...and...gave a fine talk on the need for the Gospel of Jesus Christ in China if the country were ever to be strong. Then we had a second hymn, the Lord's Prayer, the benediction, and then the firecrackers, without which no Chinese feast or celebration is ever complete....[At] prayer meeting...the subject was of course a patriotic one and a number of the young men talked on what they as students and as young men could do to make China the country that she ought to be."[12]

Yet the desire of the missionaries to make the Chinese patriotic had its limits, particularly when Double Ten Day fell on Sunday. When this happened in 1920, the missionaries clearly indicated that it was their view that Christianity came before any type of patriotism. Margaret told her family, "This is Chinese Independence Day and our poor schoolboys feel very much aggrieved because it falls on Sunday and firecrackers and drums have been forbidden until tomorrow. They haven't generations of Sabbath-keeping ancestors back of them as we have and they are sure everyone in Kachek market will think they did not know how to read the calendar right if they wait until tomorrow to celebrate. We have told them they can have a patriotic meeting in the chapel this afternoon if they are quiet about it. I do not know what they will do—some more adventurous and non-Christian boys seem to want firecrackers anyway, but I believe [the Reverend David H.] Thomas put the quietus on that by saying the school was so crowded he could easily dispense with a few pupils. It is hard on the boys, as I said—but we are supposed to have a Christian compound here and we will have to be patient with the boys. Friday was Confucius' birthday so we have had holidays Friday and yesterday....It is hard to know what to do about celebrating his birthday—so many Chinese have worshipped him....In reality he was a wonderful man, one of the very few China can honor as we honor Washington or Lincoln, and personally, I think it all right to celebrate his birthday if Christian teachers and students make the speeches." The following week she wrote her family that there had been no difficulties on the Sunday of Independence Day.[13]

In 1918, as World War I was ending, Margaret wrote, "I wish now that the European struggle is becoming settled that America could help China out of her troubles. She needs a lot before she can be a real republic."[14] Less than a year later, after commenting on China's inability to get her "just dues" at the Paris Peace Conference, Margaret offered a more drastic solution to China's problems: "Poor old China—she surely is in bad shape. I'm beginning to think there is not much hope for her unless some foreign power—preferably the U.S.A. takes a ten-year protectorate over her and does away with all these military governors who are so concerned about their own gain they ravish the country of everything she possesses."[15]

Participating in the May Fourth Movement

The May Fourth movement, which transformed China culturally, began at Peking University on 4 May 1919, when students demonstrated against their country's treatment at the Versailles Peace Conference. When the movement reached Hainan, the students at the Presbyterian mission schools participated actively in it, even though the Americans were initially reluctant to allow the students at the girls' school to join in the meetings: "Friday was a big day the students' unions all over China are having such great meetings. There are about seven hundred members in the Kiungchow association, of which our boys are only a small number....they sent an invitation to us and our girls to attend the first day. You know boys and girls do not mingle at all in China yet but the schools will have to be the opening wedge....[We felt] we should accept, so I said I would take the sixty girls in the high school and higher primary." As they marched to the meeting, Margaret and her students were joined by the principal and the girls of the government primary school. The meeting began with everyone marching "out to the courtyard to salute the Chinese flag three times. The hosts and guests saluted each other and we marched back in. The young man from the government school who was chairman of the meeting certainly made a good speech, [then] he announced the other speakers simply by writing their names and titles on the blackboard....I had to take my turn. I had protested before that I did not want to speak but it seemed the only thing to do. I thought just standing up in my seat and saying a few words might be sufficient, but the chairman came down with a very low bow to escort me up to the platform so I couldn't help myself. I only said a few words of congratulations and thanks and urged the establishment of girls' schools, if China were ever to be a real true republic....Altogether it was a very pleasant experience and the boys deserve a great deal of credit for the orderly way in which things were carried out." Six months later, after attending many more such meetings, she remarked, "I really am glad for the girls to have a share in the thing. The boys certainly treat us with every courtesy and it is a good thing to show them we appreciate their efforts to advance the cause of womanhood in China, by recognizing the school girls."[16]

When the boycotts against Japan that accompanied the May Fourth movement reached Hainan, Margaret reported that she "was amused at my old coolie a day or two ago. I told him to go to the Japanese medicine shop out in the market and buy me a bottle of Horlick's Malted Milk, but he refused, saying there was a boycott on Japanese goods. I informed him that Horlick's was *not* 'made in Japan' but of course told him he need not go there to get it if he didn't want to." On a more serious note, she wrote a week later, "Everywhere boycotts are being proclaimed on Japanese goods....The school boys go out and make speeches in the market, and even Japanese money is taboo. A great many yen are in circulation in China. For a while the Chinese were not willing to use their own dollars with Yuan Shih-k'ai's head on them but now they take those and only refuse Japanese yen and Straits Settlements dollars." The boycotts in Hainan continued for many months. In November Margaret wrote home that "the students are still searching stores to see whether any of them are selling Japanese goods."[17]

Hostilities resumed in Hainan in mid-April 1920, when military men from Yunnan arrived on the island. The missionaries would see a great deal of fighting between various factions in the years to come, and what Margaret described to her father was to become all too typical: "There are so many new soldiers here in Hoihow and Kiungchow this last week or so that the place is just full. They are Yunnan men, most of them. A number of them are just young fellows from the military school in Yunnan and they are quite decent looking....There has been fighting around Kachek as the commander there refused to obey his orders to go to Canton. Miss Schaeffer said there was firing all along the road past the compound and considerable looting in the market, but no one molested our people."[18]

Some of the soldiers who arrived in Hainan were Christians, and the missionaries wanted them to feel welcome in the Christian community. In the spring of 1920 Margaret reported, "Just as I left Hoihow the cannon were fired to welcome the new military commander who...is a graduate of a Japanese military college and has a military school [for] his troops preparing some of the men [to be] infantry, artillery, and cavalry officers. About thirty of these men in the training school are Christians. As many as can come to church on Sunday. Fourteen were there this morning and after service two of the elders and two of the schoolboys brought them over to call." Despite the fact that the men spoke various dialects, Margaret learned they were "Baptists, Presbyterians and Methodists, from various parts of China, [and] a very nice set of men. We served tea and little cookies. They sang some hymns for us in Mandarin and one of them prayed. It must be terribly hard to live a decent life in a Chinese army and if Miss Skinner and I can help these men any by being at home to them we are mighty glad to do it."[19]

Katherine Schaeffer at Kachek wrote to Margaret at Kiungchow apprising her of the continued fighting in the interior. Her letter was much more graphic about the nature of the hostilities the Chinese armies engaged in, yet Margaret enclosed this letter when she wrote her family. One can only guess at their reaction to Katherine Schaeffer's letter, since it differed so markedly from the reassuring ones Margaret always wrote. "Sin Ki-zi left day before yesterday. We heard that the market people were to come out to meet the new army with firecrackers and assurances of food and no soldiers in the market. At 7 A.M. I heard firecrackers and called the girls out to see the welcome. Nobody came and soon we heard firing out toward Denglangfo. Some few soldiers came back on the run and several of Sin Ki-zi's wounded came to hospital....The new soldiers arrived—wet, tired and hungry. There were eight or ten wounded among them. The vanguard fired all the way from the bridge to the market and it echoed fearfully from our buildings. The girls were a little [upset] but we soon went on with...regular class work. The soldiers created terror in the market looting everywhere. Then they began catching carriers and how frightened everybody was. Our girls are all here and a few extra ones. Tonight the new army wounded begged [the doctor] to take them into the hospital [as] they fear they will be killed....Last night the new army executed one of Sin Ki-zi's men after making him kneel by the coffin of the [official whom] Sin shot. They poured kerosene over the poor victim and set fire to him then shot him. Most of the new soldiers have gone to Vangtsiu and the report is that there is a battle on down there now. Tonight Sin is expected to come back to the market and refugees are coming out. Men are sleeping in the school dining room and women on the floor of the Kiangdokia. The other places—boys' school, servants' quarters and hospital are overflowing. The [doctor] will put patients in the chapel. Two pigs have been put into our pig pen with ours. The worst is we are short of rice all round. I think a pig is to be killed tomorrow and our papaya trees are being stripped. Today I had the old white cock and the yellow hen killed for the girls. We are so glad we had Big Sunday when we did. Lucky we did not plan to go to the City now. I am fearful of the wisdom of my leaving such a big school without a foreigner present so I will not go out until July after I've closed school. I asked Hai-so [Margaret's language teacher] whether he did not think it best to bring his wife and children here, that I would have room for them. He feels pretty confident that it is all right so far." Katherine Schaeffer continued, "I've been to market to buy rice. One's purchases have to be personally conducted to home from town so that the soldiers will not seize our necessary food and take the rice carriers to carry for them." [20]

Later in the year as Margaret was returning to Kiungchow from a trip to Kachek, she "heard rumors all along the way of people fleeing from Hoihow and Kiungchow and met some refugees going to the villages. I could not figure out what was the trouble as no one seemed to know exactly. I found out when I got here that the soldiers had all been sent away and the people were sure robbers from [Luichow] or else from the interior, nobody seemed to know quite which, were to attack and loot the city. Our compound was full of refugees, and business generally pretty much suspended. There is no sign even yet of anybody attempting any looting and most of the people are gradually returning to their homes."[21]

Margaret's Religious Beliefs

The violence, of course, interrupted the main work of the mission, which was to convert the Chinese to Christianity. Whether an individual missionary was an evangelist, a medical doctor, a mission agent, an architect, or a teacher in a mission school, he or she had had to answer the question on the Board's application form "Why do you wish to become a missionary?" Uniformly, whatever job the missionary was to fulfill, the answer to this question was "to convert the Chinese to Christianity" or some variation, such as "to spread the Gospel" or "to win others to Christ." Despite this and responses to other questions about religion on the application, it is very difficult to determine exactly what the personal religious beliefs of individual missionaries were. This is particularly true of the women, who left no sermons to suggest their theological thinking. Margaret rarely mentioned her religious beliefs in her writings; after all, her own family probably knew of her beliefs, so there was no need to reiterate them. Among her rare references to religion was one that appeared in 1917. She wrote, "All the papers we see out here say that the world is facing famine. America will have to make extra efforts to have grain enough to feed the other people that are suffering as well as her own men and women, too. Many of the people out here feel that the prophecies of the Bible are being fulfilled and that the second coming of Christ must be coming very near. It is a wonderful thought that those of us who are living now may never see death, but be caught up in the clouds to meet the Saviour....Many preachers at home never seem to think it worth while to preach about the second coming. This is one doctrine that our Chinese have seemed to love especially."[22]

Writing in retirement, Margaret gave another hint of her beliefs when she recalled that she had once visited Kyoto, Japan, in the company of several other missionaries. Although the Japanese removed their shoes when entering Buddhist temples, foreigners were asked to cover their shoes with grass sandals. The missionaries did this, and as they entered the temple "the men removed their hats as if in church, and we walked quietly around examining the statues and other furnishings. It has struck me often as the proper thing to do, of course it was a heathen temple, an idol temple, but should we not respect the feelings of those whose belief is different from ours, and who, perhaps through our collective negligence, have never learned the best and only way?"[23]

Like many missionaries, Margaret was overwhelmed by the thought that the whole Chinese population needed to be told the Gospel of Christ: "I have been to church and taught my two Sunday school classes, had a long talk with a former patient in the hospital who wants to have a poor woman come to school here, etc. I love the work, and it is wonderful to think that this day by actual count I have had the privilege of giving the message to forty-five girls and women, but in many ways I feel so helpless in the face of their tremendous need."[24]

Margaret was always interested in biblical studies, and one of her colleagues, the Reverend Henry Bucher, believed that she was more knowledgeable about the Bible than any of the ordained men of the mission.[25] In 1918 Margaret wrote her family that she had received a copy of *Walker's Comprehensive Concordance,* which she hoped to use a lot, adding, "There is a comprehensive New Testament Concordance in Chinese here but I am not so familiar with my Chinese that I can use it very advantageously yet."[26]

Another hint of her beliefs came in 1919, when, returning to Kachek from a trip to the Miao country, Margaret learned that her Grandmother Moninger had died in Iowa. To her family she wrote, "Grandma was really quite reconciled to my coming to China, I think, though she said you know that she wished I would wait until after she died, as she knew she would never see me again on earth. But I was her 'tenth' to the Lord, I guess, of the ten grandchildren....And we will see her again and then there will be no more partings."[27]

Whatever the personal religious beliefs of the missionaries and however much they might have wanted to convert the Chinese to Christianity, once in China the emphasis of the individual missionary was changed, depending upon the task the person was assigned. Margaret's job in Hainan, once she learned Chinese, was to teach in the girls' school, but she occasionally went on itinerating trips to the interior, particularly to the Miao country. Along with the other Hainan missionaries, Margaret took her turn in telling about Christianity to the large groups of people who visited the mission on special occasions.

Chinese Christians

Before a Chinese person was allowed to join the church, he or she had to undergo strenuous questioning about Christian doctrines. In Hainan, individuals joined the church on Communion Sunday, called in Chinese "Big Sunday," with the examination period taking place on the Saturday before. In October 1916 Margaret attended one of these sessions and reported, "I was very glad to be there and to get some idea of the sort of things that were asked, so that next year...I will know better how to prepare the girls for the examination. I know this much—it would hurry most of us at home to answer the questions that were put up to those girls. They covered the Trinity, the Virgin Birth, the meaning of the ordinances, the evidences of Christianity and the commandments, creed and so on. It took them two hours to examine five people—four of our girls and one of Mrs. Byers' women. All of our girls were accepted, and I am so glad for their sakes, as they would have been very much disappointed. They are all from my Sunday school class, one of them being Zih-fong, the little Loi girl. As far as we know she is the first Loi of these tribes to be baptized. Of course, there are Limko and Damtsiu and Khengtoa Loi Christians, but those Lois are different tribes and of a later date of arrival in the island than the Lengtui Lois."[28]

Big Sundays were important occasions at the Hainan mission, and many Chinese undoubtedly viewed them as the Christian version of temple celebrations, with the added attraction that they could visit the houses in which the foreigners lived. In describing one such occasion in Kachek, Margaret reported that people began arriving as early as Tuesday. To keep everyone occupied, the missionaries held evening meetings: one night they had a prayer meeting, and other meetings included talks about the Miao, malaria, hookworm, consumption, and the dangers of opium use. The Reverend Frank P. Gilman arrived to conduct the service. "He had the preparatory service at seven this morning. We hardly had room for people then. The place was simply packed at ten o'clock when we had service. There must have been at least twelve hundred people here. The market seemed to turn out en masse (the official had called off the big idol festival and they had no where else to go). There were about four hundred and fifty women."[29]

Sometimes it was an idol festival, not the cancellation of one, that brought great crowds of people into the mission compound. "It is the time for a great big idol festival in Kachek market and crowds and crowds of women and men come to see the theaters and then simply stop in here to look over the foreign houses, etc.," Margaret wrote. "They are a terribly unsatisfactory lot to do work with because they come solely out of curiosity, but we can't let the opportunity go by." For the occasion Katherine Schaeffer played the baby organ in the chapel, and both women talked to their visitors in "bunches of fifty or a hundred." As they knew the Chinese were curious about their house, Margaret said they "kept the house up here shut as the rooms are so small but let the women wander around and peer in windows and go through the school rooms." Margaret said she did not mind being stared at but "was so amused at the comment the cook made last night. She said, 'I hardly have any strength left tonight. It has taken all my strength to answer the questions those women asked about how you cook your rice!'"[30]

It was not only the homes of the foreigners that the Chinese found interesting. On one occasion, Margaret wrote, "one of the Christian women asked if I had any old clothes to give away—said a neighbor of hers wanted some. I inquired a little closer into the matter. It seems that the mother is to have a baby soon and wants a piece of the foreigners' clothes to keep the baby well! I refused as I told the woman my clothes had no power of that sort, and as I said, if the mother should have *twin girls* or if anything should go wrong all the blame would come on me and of course on the Christians in general. Poor superstitious people."[31]

Like missionaries elsewhere in China, those in Hainan were most successful at converting their household servants, the mission employees, their Chinese language teachers, and the children in the mission schools. Margaret even observed that boarding students were more interested in Christianity than were the day students who came in from the market. Margaret's personal teacher had been educated in the mission school and employed by the missionaries for a number of years but was still not a Christian. Margaret was very fond of Li Hai-so and wrote often to her family about his situation: "Much to my disappointment my teacher cannot see his way clear to join the church yet. I hope before many years he can do so. I believe as soon as he really gets the deeper vision he will take the step."[32]

On another occasion she wrote more details about the difficulties Li Hai-so was having with his family concerning his conversion. She reported that his five-month-old son "had been quite sick with malaria and [he] has taken quinine...home to him regularly. But the last time the father of my teacher, who of course is the head of the whole family according to Chinese custom, decided that the devil was doing the child and they must have a native priest in to find out about it. So he called the priest and they did a lot of monkey work and pasted up paper prayers all over the house. Then the old father sent for my teacher to come home and have some more devil business. [Mr. Li] told me he had to go home and said he was afraid they were going to do devil. He went, and found the prayers stuck up on the house. He tore them down and when his father told him the devils would get him he stood up and called on all the devils to come and strike him if they wanted to—he was not afraid of their power. Then his father struck him, and then got a rope and proceeded to [try to] commit suicide right before the boy's eyes. So [Mr. Li] said all he could do was to bow before his father and tell him to have his way, but he himself refused to have anything to do with the devil business." Margaret said that her teacher cried when he told the story. After Li Hai-so had a long talk with the Reverend David Tappan, the two men decided it was best for him not "to join the church just now and arouse even greater opposition in his family, but the teacher himself is fully decided in his own mind, I think, and so does Mr. Tappan."[33]

When her teacher graduated from the mission school, he and another man decided to continue their education at the Christian college in Hangchow. Margaret, after much consideration, finally gave her teacher "a self-filling Waterman pen" as a gift. Unfortunately, the two men did not stay long in Hangchow. Margaret guessed that the problem was homesickness: "We are all disappointed that they did not have backbone enough to stick it out for a year at least." Despite the missionaries' disappointment, both men rejoined the mission staff. Margaret's former teacher was assigned to teach Mrs. Byers Chinese and to teach at the boys' school. The other man took up an assignment in one of the country schools.[34]

During the summer of 1919 Margaret wrote, "I am so pleased this summer to see the progress [Mr. Li] is making toward Christianity. He is getting braver and braver about witnessing at home and I think he will come out in full and open confession soon. If the weather is fair next Sunday his mother has promised to come to see us and to go to church, to see what it is like."[35] Eventually her teacher decided to become a Christian, taking the step rather quickly: "We are all rejoicing this week....Wednesday afternoon while we were studying [Mr. Li] said, 'Mr. Tappan said I could be baptized tonight but I haven't quite decided yet what to do.'...Then one of the deacons came up to see Miss Schaeffer [who] told him how my teacher was still hesitating....After only a few words [from the deacon] my teacher agreed to be baptized that night."

The Reverend Tappan baptized him. Margaret noted that this was "fitting as he had been his teacher for four years and loves him like a younger brother. Mr. Li went home yesterday to attend the business meeting of his clan and the discussion of the ancestral funds for school fees. He was to be up against the question of eating meat offered to idols, as Friday was a great day for ancestral worship. We are wondering what he did about it. Of course, Paul says if a man eat in faith knowing that the idols are nothing, he is not condemned but personally I hope he didn't eat of it....Just such things as these make the Bible a new book out here. 'Meat offered to idols' didn't mean much to me at home but it's a very vital question out here." Several months later Margaret reported that her beloved teacher had decided to go into the ministry.[36]

In April 1921 Margaret wrote that Li's wife and daughter had come to visit her. "She is a very nice woman, just about my age. She is intelligent, too—[Mr. Li] is very fortunate. It often happens that a marriage may be anything but pleasant when the match was made in babyhood. The mathematics teacher in the boys' school has a wife who is simply incurably stupid, and she has been in school here for several years."[37]

Margaret was concerned about the Chinese women and girls who were either students in the mission school or employed by the mission. Education for women was still not accepted by all Chinese, and Margaret wrote home that when asked about the subject, many Chinese men "say the women are stupid and can't learn, but usually that isn't true." Of course, many of the Chinese women in the mission schools, and in the Chinese schools, learned a great deal. The mission had only elementary schools at Nodoa and Kachek, so women wanting to continue their education had to go to Kiungchow to attend high school. After the death of her grandmother, Margaret reported to her family, "When I go out to the city next fall I am planning to take one of the girls with me and to pay her school expenses through the high school course, as the best remembrance of grandma that I can think of. The girl is to be Bang Hinzong, little Miss 'Heavenly Glory.' She is the daughter of our Elder Bang and is not engaged. I think she will make a fine teacher. Her father cannot afford to send her and her brother both out to school in the city."[38]

On Christmas Day 1917 when Margaret wrote to Stanley White of the Board of Foreign Missions, she mentioned that her letter "doesn't sound properly missionary" but then revealed "in confidence...the vision of work I have." Her plan was to educate the schoolgirls who were married so that when they returned home they would be able to establish "a chain of Christian schools for the young womanhood of Hainan...[throughout the island, and] in the Loi strongholds and the Miao [country]. Think what that will be able to do! And with God's help that is what I am going to set myself to accomplish." She hoped to take the girls through higher primary and perhaps one or two years of high school at Kachek and then send the more capable ones to Kiungchow to the high school that Mae Chapin headed. She also wrote that she thought the Canton Union Normal School was the "ideal higher education center" and consequently believed that the mission schools should teach Mandarin. "For my girls here, I do not advocate the study of English, at least, for years yet."[39]

Other Chinese women also concerned Margaret, particularly those who were employed by the mission. On the way to Kiungchow in 1918, Katherine Schaeffer and Margaret met "a man [who] recognized our cook and declared she was a runaway daughter-in-law, and was going to take her. She is, but we would not consent to have her taken that way so Miss Schaeffer persuaded the men to take her to Miss Skinner's school and her husband is to come tomorrow to settle for her board,...[which] she had paid Miss Skinner, before he can have her. The husband is an old wretch and not likely even to come so I suppose she will go back to Kachek with me. Miss Schaeffer and Miss Skinner are running the affair....She is really the property of her husband and when she went to Kachek she insisted she had no affairs. But I would rather hate to have her husband beat her."[40]

Sometimes disreputable men tried to interfere with the work of the mission schools, as Margaret discovered in September 1920 when she returned from a brief vacation in Hong Kong and began to prepare for the start of the new school term: "I had heard that one of my schoolgirls, the twice-widowed one, was not going to be able to return to school, so I was anxious to see her and hear what the trouble was. It all came from some malicious rumors and posters fixed by the good-for-nothing gambling husband of Mrs. Byers' amah. He has put these posters up saying Miss Schaeffer or Miss Skinner (their Chinese names are somewhat alike and he has used a name which sounds like either) steals wives and sells them for $120." Despite such bad publicity, Margaret succeeded in convincing the girl to return to school.[41]

Bible women, who were employed by the mission to work with Chinese women, were also of special concern to Margaret. In May 1920 the mission held a conference for evangelistic workers at Kiungchow. Margaret mentioned that two Bible women had come from Nodoa but that

Katherine Schaeffer at Kachek had sent none of the women from that station: "The [Chinese] women cannot get very much from the [evangelistic] talks sometimes as they are hardly educated....We find it strange—at least I do—that when we want to talk about school work or anything like that with the Chinese, it has to be with the Chinese men, as ordinarily speaking the women, aside from those educated in our schools, know nothing of such subjects." She concluded with her opinion of Chinese women and the influence she felt Christianity was making on them: "I'd hate to be a Chinese woman, with no outside knowledge or interests whatever. Christianity though is making big changes in that respect as well as in others." Some of the Kiungchow schoolgirls wanted to attend the evangelistic conference, and Margaret allowed them to go, although "it makes the school rather unsettled."[42]

It was not only the women who worked for the mission who interested Margaret. She once went to a nearby village at the invitation of the mission's porters. Margaret wrote that the people were "poor, and they didn't attempt to disguise it. [The porter's] wife cooked dinner for us and it was very nice. Rice of course and vegetables and liver and pork, and she served her meal with the rule grandma always said to me, 'Don't apologize for what you give your guests.' And she said something that pleased me very much when we left and were thanking her. She said, 'I was afraid almost to ask you but my husband said you and the *Tin-taes* [Mr. Byers and Mr. Tappan] knew the difference between high and low and we would just give you what we have and you would receive it.'" Margaret concluded, "I do love this work with the women and children."[43]

Just after Chinese New Year in 1917, Margaret accompanied Katherine Schaeffer to a neighboring village to visit one of their former pupils, the daughter of a man named Ngou, who had been the head teacher at the boys' school for ten years but was then teaching in a government school. They guessed that the girl could not afford to return to school and so "arranged it so we could have her teach four classes of beginners and so pay her board and tuition in school, and we went over to see if she was willing. She certainly was, and we think her father will be. I am very glad she is to come back....We are very anxious that he should accept the Gospel but his heart seems to be pretty well hardened, though he certainly has always been most friendly to all the work of the church. So we are especially glad to have a chance to do a favor to him and to Ziau-hoa, hoping that it may help to reach them both."[44]

But making the decision to become a Christian was not easy for many

Chinese, as Margaret and the others discovered in October of the next year. Margaret wrote home that the Double Ten Day celebration had been a good one, but "the saddest part of the day came for several of us in the evening. Mr. Ngou, the head teacher whom I mentioned before, is not a Christian. His oldest daughter Ziau-hoa, a girl about nineteen, is a student up here in our school. She has finally decided to be a Christian, much to our joy, and that evening she asked her father's permission to join the church, and he said 'no' much to the surprise and disappointment of us all. He added that he would come and see me about the matter, but I haven't seen him come yet. Mr. Tappan says he thinks that very likely when [the father] got permission from the family where the girl is engaged to send her to school and unbind her feet he promised that she should not join the church. I don't know what the girl will do. I'd really like to see her come out anyway and yet the fifth commandment comes in also." Ziau-hoa did not worship the tablets of her husband's family when she married, and she eventually became a Christian.[45]

When Katherine Schaeffer went home on furlough in 1918, the school in Kachek was turned over to Margaret. After three weeks of the school term she reported, "Three new scholars have come this week. One is the wife of a Singapore man, one the bride of one of the schoolboys, who is weeping continuously at present because she is homesick, and one the bride-to-be of another schoolboy. The homesick one will soon be all right again—she won't weep more than a week. At least the other little girl did not take longer than that to get over her tears." The next week Margaret reported that her "homesick pupil put in almost all the time begging me to let her start home tomorrow. She only got here last Monday night and she doesn't know her husband has arranged with me to have her stay here all through the summer vacation! She says she can't learn, but she will be all right in a few days more I think. She is a mighty nice little girl." The following week the Moninger family learned that "my homesick little bride still continues to be homesick. Her husband came this week to tell her goodby before he went to Singapore. He will not let her go home any more than I will, and he did have the heart to say to me that she was making my life very bitter at present but that he hoped she would be all right. I do too. She eats her meals all right though so I do not think she will pine away and dry up right quick. I have done everything but spank her. If she were not almost as large and as old as I, I would be tempted to do that. She is a spoiled only daughter and has never been away from home before."[46]

Not all of the girls attending the mission school lived there, and the day students frequently had problems with trying to live at home and attend a school run by foreigners. Margaret told her family about a conversation she had had with the mother of one of the day students from Kachek. Although the girl was only ten years old, she had "been gambling on the street instead of coming to school." Margaret insisted that if the girl was "to amount to anything in school she'd have to live here and have regular study hours, etc. The family can afford it, all right, but I don't know whether they will." She concluded her account, "You have no idea how gambling plays havoc with all classes and ages of people." Margaret also detailed the problems of another woman, who was "a second wife who can't get along with the first wife [and] wants to come here to school....I told her she must have her husband bring her and then I'd know it was all right. This is not a home for runaway wives."[47]

Education for women was still relatively new to Hainan at the time Margaret began teaching there. In January 1918 she reported that both mission schools "have had our diplomas made out and sent over to the official and stamped, and [we] are very glad that he stamped them, because that gives our graduates the same standing as they would have by graduating from a government school. Our girls' diplomas are stamped, too! A decided victory for the cause of female education. Commencement comes Wednesday and I hope it will be a great day."[48]

While in Hainan, Margaret maintained her certification as a teacher in Iowa in case she ever wanted to return home to teach or if "the Chinese school inspector here should ever want to see my credentials." In February 1918 she asked her father to send a five-dollar check to the state superintendent of public instruction to have her teaching certificate validated for life, and at the same time she revealed something about the financial status of the missionaries in Hainan: "Just now I am pretty badly strapped out here. Settling up accounts with Miss Schaeffer and buying her half of the stores we owned in common and paying the Bible women and going itinerating and going to mission meeting have taken about all my ready cash, though most of that comes back to me at the end of the quarter from the station funds....We are all hard up in this station just now—I do not believe any of us could scrape up twenty dollars of our own money if we had to."[49]

Missionaries living in Hainan occasionally had to deal with Chinese officials. In 1917, while Katherine Schaeffer, the senior member of the

Kachek station, was itinerating in the Miao country, the wife of a Chinese official came to call, so Margaret and Mrs. Lillian Kelly entertained her. "The lady is quite nice appearing. Her husband is the colonel in charge of the Lung Ci-koang soldiers in Kachek. She is a Hunanese woman and of course speaks no Hainanese. So she brought her interpreter with her, and we had to speak through him, though now and then we could understand a word or two of what she said. She was dressed in a light blue silk suit, with her hair done in very fancy braided style, part Japanese, I think, as the Chinese never braid their hair up on top of their heads. She had her woman servant with her and a guard of six soldiers in full uniform, with their guns. We talked a while, and then Mrs. Kelly took her all through the new hospital building and then I brought her up here to see the girls' school. She herself has never been to school at all. She is a young woman just about my age, and I think the 'big wife,' as I have been told that the colonel has two wives. She has no children....It was the day that the girls were having sewing class and she seemed to be especially interested in that. I was sorry that Miss Schaeffer was not here to do the honors, yet I know that she hates these official calls and as this was my first attempt I really enjoyed it." Margaret and Mrs. Kelly returned the call the following day, as was Chinese custom, visiting the woman at the temple where she lived. "She received us out in the courtyard of the temple....She had a table and chairs out there and everything looked very nice. She served tea and Chinese cakes and a dish that she had made herself—sweetened water with a little almond flavor in it and popped rice on the top. It was not half bad. The servant offered us all cigarettes, which of course we declined, and she did too. I do not know why she should have done that unless the women in the trading posts where she has lived were the kind who would smoke. We had quite a pleasant time, though it is hard to know what to say. I had my teacher coach me for about an hour in the morning what was the proper thing to do and not to do, and what were proper subjects of conversation."[50]

Mission Schools

Running boarding schools presented the missionaries with many problems, not the least of which was maintaining the health of their students. Each of the Hainan mission stations had a medical doctor on the compound who took care of the students as well as the missionaries. Since virtually everyone in the tropics had malaria and intestinal parasites, when school started Margaret reported that "every girl had two quinine and one tonic pills" for several days and those with intestinal parasites were given worm medicine: "I line the girls up and dose them all around, poor things, but I am sorry for them." The missionaries also had to cope with Spanish influenza, which arrived in Kachek just before Christmas 1918. Margaret wrote that the doctors thought it had been brought in by some Lengtui Lois who had caught it from Cantonese soldiers.[51]

To improve the health and stamina of their students, the missionaries introduced athletic meets to the island, although at first they were limited only to the boys' schools. Margaret thought these meets were a good idea since they taught the boys "fair play and sportsmanship and so many of the ideals that the Chinese seem to lack." From Margaret's comment about the Chinese lacking a Western sense of fair play and sportsmanship and from the subjects taught in the mission schools, it is clear that the Hainan missionaries had no qualms about cultural imperialism. They were clearly teaching Western civilization to the Chinese in the mission schools, and many of Margaret's letters from the 1921 school year demonstrate this. To her sister Louise she wrote, "Our school began about ten days ago and we are pretty well started with our work now. I am teaching *Pilgrim's Progress* to my eighth grade girls and enjoying it immensely. Then I have one class in the Gospel of Mark, two arithmetic classes, and a class in the native science primers."[52]

Frequently, the missionaries entertained their students at social gatherings to teach them Western etiquette. Invitations to these events were generally reciprocated. Margaret related that on one such occasion the students "got several of us foreigners up to the blackboard at a contest writing Chinese characters and enjoyed our blunders. They were so lenient as to give me first place, but I am rather more in practice than some of the other people." She also said they had told funny stories at the get-together. "I have my old standby of the two men who were going to steal something to eat and they decided to pretend they were cats, so when the first one was discovered he said 'meow, meow' and got off all right, but the second one said 'I'm the cat, what's the matter with you' and of course was caught. It goes very well in Chinese and the boys saw the joke without any difficulty. The boys are nice fellows and I enjoy being with them. They served tea and five or six different kinds of Chinese cakes." On another occasion she wrote to her brother, "One stunt the boys did for us was to play on their native musical instruments. They have flutes, a kind of violin, and a kind of banjo-mandolin instrument. There is one rather like a ukelele yet not quite. I do wish we could manage to get the high school a set of real band instruments. They surely would enjoy them."[53]

The schoolboys did not have "real band instruments," but the church did have an organ, and Margaret gave music lessons to the schoolgirls. At the party given for Margaret when she departed for the United States for her first furlough, "one of the girls that I have given music lessons to played the organ very well."[54]

Along with the desire to impart Western literature and music, the missionaries' rejection of Chinese traditional customs was evident in Margaret's comments about the arrival of a new student. "Her father is a 'captain' in the Chinese 'army' here and before I realized what he was saying he had told the girl to kneel to me and she was down thumping her head on the bricks before me as a sign of subjection to my authority! I do feel so strange when anything like that happens. Of course, I told her to get up as it was not our custom to do anything like that. Her father was going to give her her water pipe too, but I objected to that. She has been to the native school and read the Confucian classics, but I doubt if she knows the meaning of anything she has read. It is a sort of a gamble, this taking in of new pupils sight unseen. Her father came to see me about her before he brought her, but that is all I knew about her." She was also concerned that the girl students at the mission schools not worship their husbands' ancestral tablets when they married. She reported that one of her former students had not done so as she hoped soon to join the church. "We need some encouragement along that line as another one of our girls in whom we had had lots of confidence did worship the ancestors when she was married ten days ago."[55]

Some Chinese customs bothered the missionaries as they tried to make the mission schools conform to a Western sense of time. In 1920, while serving as principal of the Kiungchow school, Margaret admitted that it "annoys me exceedingly that...things cannot be made to start off on time. Here it is two days since school was to open, and only sixty of my supposed to be ninety-odd pupils are here, and I'm just making arrangements for a part-time teacher for the high school Chinese literature." Part of the problem was that one of the teachers at the boys' school had "backed out entirely and another has not yet appeared. Among the Chinese a verbal contract is often no more than a 'scrap of paper' was to some people, and yet many many of our Chinese are as loyal to their spoken word as anyone ever could be." The problem of finding a suitable teacher got even worse. Margaret reported to her mother, "We were going to share a teacher in the two schools and thought we had one all ready when we found out he was a fortune-teller on the side. So he wouldn't do. And the second one proved to have two wives." Margaret finally located a Chinese teacher but then had to pay him much more than she thought the school could afford.[56]

Although the missionaries hoped to convert the students in their schools, most of the students were not Christians and thus the missionaries had to comply with some non-Christian customs. The mission schools closed their term as the last month of the Chinese year began, even though the missionaries forbade their converts to participate in the traditional Chinese New Year festivities. "Tomorrow is the first of the twelfth month, according to the Chinese calendar," Margaret wrote on 20 January 1920, "and people are already beginning to get ready for the Chinese New Year. The white chickens will soon be painted red, the red and gold paper charms be pasted up on the doors and altars and on all the plows and wheelbarrows and other implements, and the supply of incense sticks laid in." Margaret knew it was a difficult time for Chinese Christians. "It takes considerable courage to be the only family in a clan not to worship the ancestors, or even more to be the only person in the village who does not do it. That is what my personal teacher who was baptized last summer is facing. He said then if the Lord would only let him be sick those few days then he wouldn't have to attend the clan meeting and there would be no question of worshipping. I am sure though that he will be given the strength he needs to resist."[57]

The missionaries customarily held their annual mission meeting at Chinese New Year to occupy their time while their Chinese students and employees were at home with their families. When she did have free time at the Chinese New Year, Margaret did not go visiting because she was knowledgeable enough about Chinese customs to know her presence might not be welcome: "I should like to visit around in the villages near here but the heathen families are liable to think it brings bad luck to have a foreigner around New Year's time so I do not think I will visit around. It would make it all the harder for our Christians perhaps."[58]

The Work of the Mission

Beginning in 1912 the Hainan missionaries published the *Hainan News Letter* on an irregular basis to keep their friends and supporters at home informed about their work. While attending the 1917 mission meeting, Margaret wrote home, "The new *News Letters* are out. I will send you a copy very soon after I reach Kachek, as mine are down there. Mrs. Kelly was editor, but she is away, of course. Dr. McCandliss told me last night the executive committee had given me the job, but I don't know yet whether to believe him or not, he is such a tease." But Dr. McCandliss was not teasing, and Margaret became the editor of the newsletter: "There are only three issues a year so it is no especial job except that the material has to be collected and arranged and worked over. I am not especially gifted along that line, I fear, but the man said it was up to me. Mrs. Byers is really the one that should have had it but she simply does not have the physical strength to do more than take care of her family. She just barely manages to drag around and that is all."[59]

In addition to the annual mission meeting, the stations each held quarterly meetings at which the missionaries discussed their work, settled financial accounts, and reported their activities to the Board of Foreign Missions in New York. At the end of September 1917 Margaret wrote home: "This has been rather a busy week as it was the end of the quarter and there were station meetings and quarterly accounts to settle, and I was appointed to write the station Quarterly Letter to Dr. White [secretary of the Board]. Such is life. I am station secretary now so have to keep the record book. Am also station organist! since the Kellys and Bercovitzes are not here and Miss Schaeffer plays only when there is no one else to do it, as she does not like to. And as I am editor of the *News Letter* now, I will have to get at that in about two weeks. Such is life. However, I do not mind, and am glad to be able to help a little with the work, when there is so much to do."[60] So that her family would know what she had written in the *News Letters*, she told them in March 1919, "As regards the *News Letter* whatever appears on the front page is mine unless signed otherwise. And in this February number that I just mailed this week the translation of the sermon by Elder Bang is mine."[61] Margaret noted that for the July 1919 issue of the *News Letter,* she had written the Personals, the Locals, and the Kachek Notes, along with the articles she had signed.[62]

Margaret continued as editor of the *News Letter* for several years and was also given the task of editing a handbook about the island and the work of the Hainan missionaries. The book, *Isle of Palms,* was being published in Shanghai, and in March 1920 Margaret complained that it "had not come yet and I do not understand why—only you cannot hustle the

East!" The following week she wrote, "The two sample copies of the Hainan Handbook arrived from the Press. I was almost afraid to unwrap them for fear they would not be satisfactory but they are really pretty decently printed and bound and the cuts show up pretty well....I'd rather like to see the bill, too, as I haven't any idea how much it will be—$800 or $900, probably, altogether." In April she reported, "The Handbooks must be really done. Twenty-five copies came by mail this week and I suppose the rest will come by freight soon now. I want to send you a copy today but am afraid I'll have to wait until the others come, as these are not mine, really. I've sent one to each family or single person in the mission, either here or at home, and still have a few of the twenty-five left. The people in the mission seem quite pleased with it and I surely did enjoy working at it last summer."[63]

Later Margaret received a letter from A.W. Halsey, then secretary of the Board of Foreign Missions, congratulating her on the *Isle of Palms*, which Dr. McCandliss, who was home on furlough, had told him that Margaret had done: "I have read no publication of any one of our Missions which to my mind gives more fully and satisfactorily the things the home church desires to know and should know about its missions in foreign lands than this little booklet....I wish to congratulate you on the fine bit of work you have done and to express my grateful appreciation of the valuable material you have put in such excellent form for use by all those who are interested in the work in Hainan. It gives the speaker the data he wishes. It gives the pastor interesting and valuable information and with all it is so well put together that it makes a most attractive and illuminating bit of literature on the Presbyterian work in Hainan and the great responsibility resting upon us to prosecute that work more vigorously than ever before. I trust you will make wide use of this booklet as it seems to me of great value to the work. I congratulate you on your task."[64]

In addition to these editorial duties, Margaret wrote articles about Hainan for *Woman's Work,* a church publication. The editor had responded to her with a personal note asking for more articles. "I never was much good with a pen," she told her family, "but there is so much to tell about out here that I am glad to do all I can to help interest people in the work, even though it is such a poor...paper usually." She also regularly published letters in the *Marshalltown (Iowa) Times-Republican,* which, curiously, once identified her as a missionary to the Ainus, the aborigines of Hokkaido, Japan. And sometimes she submitted articles to other church publications, such as *Forward,* which ran an illustrated, three-part article of hers in 1922, called "Picturesque Hainan."⁶⁵

The Hainan mission was one of the smallest missions in China, and although Margaret said, "Why anyone should want to leave Hainan, except where health reasons demand it, is more than I can see," the isolation from American culture did wear on all the foreigners. The intensity of the isolation was evident when Margaret mentioned in August 1917 that she had been to the McCandliss home to visit, along with the Bercovitzes and the Kellys: "We had an English church service. Mr. Street preached, and it seemed good to hear a sermon in English. It has been almost a year since I heard one." She observed that the interior stations were frequently staffed only by a few people and that it was essential for the missionaries to get along with one another. Mission compounds were frequently the stage for intense human dramas as the missionaries, thrown together by chance and isolated as they were, took out their frustrations on their fellow missionaries. In the autumn of 1917, Margaret noted that the recently arrived Dr. Nathaniel Bercovitz had left Kachek for Hoihow and that she and David Tappan and Katherine Schaeffer were again the only ones at the station: "It is fortunate that we are so congenial, or it would be pretty lonesome. However, I have too much to do to get very lonesome." One of the reasons the missionaries at the Kachek station got along was that Margaret, at least, had learned not to discuss controversial topics. As she wrote to her family concerning the United States entering World War I, "I never say much about [the war] out here as Miss Schaeffer of course takes the other side more or less although she is a most loyal American." Margaret clearly had learned what not to discuss with Katherine Schaeffer, but she had a real affection for the older missionary and was most anxious that she visit the Moninger family in Iowa while home on furlough: "It may make Hainan seem a little nearer to you to see someone that has actually been here for over twenty years. I remember mamma said she felt much easier about my coming out here after she met Mr. Tappan's sister at Ames."⁶⁶

As a young missionary, Margaret continued the Chinese lessons that had started as soon as she arrived in Hainan. In October 1917 she had her second-year examination, with David Tappan and Katherine Schaeffer again serving as examiners. A mission employee named Foa and Margaret "had quite a conversation about the different tribes of Lois and about the government troubles of China and so on. I was really sorry when Miss Schaeffer told me to stop, because I was enjoying it very much."

She was also asked questions about the Bible. She wrote to a church group, "I am very glad that the examination is over, even though it was not very hard. Chinese is not so very easy to learn, but I have enjoyed my study of it very much." To her family Margaret gave more details of her Chinese test. The man with whom she had spoken for the test "does not speak quite the same dialect my teacher does but more like the Kiungchow lingo, but he speaks very distinctly."[67]

At the beginning of 1918, after she had been in China less than two and a half years, Margaret had "nearly finished the third year course of reading and done some extra." At this time she was put in charge of the girls' school at Kachek when Katherine Schaeffer went home on furlough to attend to some family business. Margaret continued to study, and from time to time she had hints about her abilities in Chinese. She wrote to her family, "Hum—this morning I told a small boy to bring me a dust-cloth to dust the organ and he brought me a monkey wrench. The inference is that my Chinese is still rather faulty." Despite her language skill, she wrote her family in 1920 that she had two sets of papers to grade and noted, "It takes longer to read papers written in Chinese character, for some reason or other!"[68]

In 1920 Margaret wrote of working on a phrase book for the first time. It is likely that the work she mentioned was the project she would continue for many years that would eventually become a two-volume dictionary of Hainanese and English, which she compiled with the help of one of her teachers: "School work goes along as usual and my part of the Hainanese Phrasebook my teacher and I are working on is about done."[69]

Money Matters

The missionaries at the interior stations had constant difficulty with money. There were no banks at either Nodoa or Kachek, so the missionaries customarily carried Mexican silver dollars with them when they journeyed inland from the port. (The Mexican silver dollar was commonly used in early twentieth-century China because of its purity.) Although the silver was divided up among the road baskets the servants carried, it was generally known, in Hainan as throughout China, that foreigners carried large amounts of cash. Margaret wrote home in 1918, "Mr. Tappan came in Friday, keeping with his carriers who had $300 silver in the road baskets." The shortage of cash at the interior station seemed to be a chronic problem, since several years later Margaret wrote that the Reverend David Thomas planned "to bring $1000 in silver down for the safe. Actually we can't get money in the market. I have only $11.00 and a few stamps in the safe this minute. So many coolies have come back from Singapore because of the scarcity of work there and have left their money in the shops in Hoihow, getting orders on the shops in the market here, that every dollar the merchants take in has to be used to redeem the orders."[70]

Margaret was mission treasurer in 1920, when she wrote to her family about some of the financial dealings of the mission: "We always keep about a thousand dollars in the safe, getting it from merchants in the market and giving them orders on the mission treasurer in Canton. They cash the orders in Hoihow with the doctor there or with the mission agent."[71]

Many types of currencies were in use in China in the early twentieth century, and the Moninger family in Iowa had written asking for some explanation of the various monies Margaret wrote about. Her explanation probably did not clarify things very much for her Iowa readers. "I don't wonder Mexican currency bothers you. So does it bother us!...Formerly gold was at a premium and now silver is. So the only way you can tell how much a certain amount of gold (American money) will bring out here is to ask the bank to figure it for you at the current rate of exchange. We are paid our salaries at a 2 to 1 rate (the old standard, when a Mexican dollar was supposed to contain one-half as much silver as an American silver dollar) and are mighty glad we are, or else our checks would only amount to about $41 per month. Japanese yen, Philippine pesos, French Indo-China dollars, Hong Kong dollars, Chinese dollars and Mexican dollars are the same in value, as is what is known as the Bland dollar or American Trade dollar. The Straits Settlements dollars are a little smaller and at a discount. The Shanghai tael is still another affair and we don't have much to do with it except that it makes exchange between Hong Kong and Shanghai a matter of several dollars on a hundred dollar cheque. As I wrote you before,...bank drafts are a convenient way of sending money. Do not use the international money order made out to Hong Kong. I just heard lately about a funny kink in that deal. Hong Kong Postal currency is not based on current rate of exchange and is so set that the post office gains a certain per cent on every order. It's legitimate pay for their trouble but we can avoid the extra loss by using bank drafts, or else postal orders on the *American* Post Office, Shanghai."[72]

Partly because of the large amounts of silver they frequently had, but also because their standard of living was far above that of the Chinese among whom they lived, the missionaries were frequently the target of thieves. "We had a sneak thief around last Sunday night. He stole some clothes the girls had drying on the veranda, came into my room and stole my glasses and aluminum case off the bureau and knocked down a powder can, which must have scared him out, and I never heard a sound. I don't mind about the glasses much as I will likely get new lenses in Hong Kong but I do hate to lose the nose piece, gold chain and ear guard....The thief called at the Bercovitzes and Gilmans the next night but did not get anything. Funny I did not lose more as my jewel box was right on the bureau, too. My watch of course was under my pillow. Spectacles are favorite prey with thieves out here—but mine won't do them much good as no Chinese can wear that nose piece. Am going to have inquiries made at the pawn shop to see if they were taken there."[73]

Thieves plagued the towns as well as the mission compounds. In the summer of 1920 Margaret noted that the area around Kiungchow was a target. "Thieves are bad here lately. Ten days or so ago a Chinese house near our compound was robbed of practically everything. Then Monday night a thief got upstairs in the girls' dormitory, but they screamed and scared him out. We asked the official then for police to patrol the compound (outside the wall) and they did patrol for a night or two. I do not know whether they are still at it or not. Last night the thieves were over on the other compound, the servants said."[74]

Visiting the Miao People

During her first term of service in Hainan, Margaret became interested in the Miao people. Katherine Schaeffer had been making trips into the Miao country for nearly twenty years, when the Reverend George Byers was specifically assigned the task of converting the aborigines and began regular visits to them. It is clear from the accounts of Margaret and others of the mission that the Miao people were practicing some form of Christo-paganism as they learned something of Christianity from the missionaries and grafted it on to their traditional beliefs. The Christo-paganism among the Miao was first reported in mid-1917 by Katherine Schaeffer, and Margaret, in turn, wrote her family about it. "Some of the people actually seem to have demon possession. They have very peculiar customs and they have learned a little of Christianity and have a most peculiar mixture of it and paganism."[75] The missionaries persisted in their attempts to convert the Miao, with little success, but itinerating into the hinterland was one of the most exciting aspects of being a missionary at the Kachek station.

Margaret's accounts of the Miao, both of her visits to them and of their visits to the Kachek station, are among the most interesting things she wrote. In February 1917 the first Miao people Margaret ever saw appeared at the Kachek station: "We had a surprise....I think I have written you about the Miao people. They are a tribe of nomad aborigines that live in the mountains....The chief had a vision of light flooding his house some time about a year ago and came down here to beg that we send some one there to bring them the Gospel....Then last fall Mr. Byers and [Mr.] Li went into the Miao country for a couple of weeks, and the younger brother of the chief came out here to the boys' school. They have a language of their own but most of the men can speak Hainanese, as they do business with the other people." Margaret continued that the Miao chief and his wife and another woman had arrived in Kachek "to see the sights and [the women] plan to enter school in a few weeks when they have harvested or planted or done something else about their farming that they have to do now. The chief's wife could speak some Hainanese, the other girl none." Although the Miao people were only in Kachek a few days, Margaret, ever hopeful that she might make converts, was able to report that "the chief's wife is a very bright woman and very interesting to talk with. She is eager to learn, too, and...she learned almost all the characters in the Lord's Prayer. We do hope that she will come back to school and learn enough so that she can go home and teach her own people. Our girls were very good about not making fun of them and using every opportunity to make them feel at home. We feel that we are having wonderful opportunities for the spread of the Gospel here, with the Lois first and now the Miaos, literally begging for the message." The missionaries had decided to send one of their Chinese assistants to the Miao country to teach them about Christianity. Margaret wrote that she believed that "the Miaos are connected with the Miaos of South China who have become very much interested in the Gospel up there and I think some literature has been gotten out in a Romanized form of their language. They are primitive people with no written tongue of their own, as the Lois are."[76]

Margaret would later make a study of the symbolism in Miao embroidery patterns, which clearly interested her the first time she saw Miao people. "They dress quite differently from the Hainanese or from the Lois. The men do not—just the women. Their dress consisted of a long coat reaching to the knee, made of dark blue goods and trimmed with bright red at the waist and the neck. Then a very short skirt arrangement that did not pretend to come to the knees, dark blue puttees tied with red strings, no shoes, and a peculiar-shaped hood that seemed to be made of a straight piece of goods with one side sewed up as if they had started to make a bag and left one side open. This of course left a corner sticking out over the back of the head, and a bright red cord is fastened up on the top of the head and draped around the corner of the head dress, hanging down the back. The chief's wife had a beautifully embroidered square kerchief over the top of her hood, with one point coming down over her forehead. The embroidery is cross stitch, in a sort of gray and white combination. They brought one as a present to Mrs. Byers, as Mr. Byers had said when he was at their home that he would like to have one for his wife."[77]

Age-old antagonisms between the Loi and the Miao continued throughout the early twentieth century, and Margaret described these troubles from time to time. In 1917 one of the evangelists returned from the Miao country and reported that "a tribe of Lois have come out and have taken a Miao man and bound him and carried him off because as they say, there has been sickness in the Loi villages, and the Miaos have built their chapel in a place that disturbs the grave of a Loi ancestor. Did you ever hear of such affairs?" Despite this comment, Margaret realized the importance of graves in China and continued: "Graves out here make us more trouble than any other one thing. When we buy land we always have to let the people leave the graves there and when any building is to be done the graves have to be bought and then the people will move them. There are four or five graves on the place where our new house is to be built."[78]

On a trip to the Miao country in 1918, Margaret reported that about one hundred people attended chapel every morning and that the missionaries spent the day and night teaching the people about Christianity. She also mentioned that "this was the first communion ever held in the Miao country." A week later Margaret wrote that about sixty Miao people had arrived at the Kachek station for a communion service. They included twenty women, "among them three of the dearest girls, in their teens, about fourteen or fifteen, I think, to enter school....They are such lovable-looking, quaint little ladies. They are to wear Chinese clothes and tomorrow I must see about buying their clothes, shoes, stocking, rice bowls, chopsticks, etc. It's a wonderful opportunity and I hope we can make the most of it."[79]

Margaret worked diligently at getting the Miao girls ready for school: "All day Monday I was busy...with getting the Hainanese clothes fixed for my Miao girls, etc....We bought goods for two suits of...clothes apiece for them, and each of the higher primary girls made a garment. We bought each [Miao] girl a pair of shoes, a pair of stockings, a handkerchief,...a wash basin apiece, a blanket apiece for two of them as one had a blanket of her own, bowls, chopsticks, slates and pencils, and fans. They seemed to be very much pleased. I want them to wear Chinese clothes as their own costume is so different that it makes them too conspicuous. They have been homesick a few times this week but are getting acquainted now and are much happier. They are bright as they can be. I have given each girl a teacher from the older girls and they are just chasing along with their primers." Despite all Margaret's work and her attempts to make the Miao girls into Chinese, after the girls had been at the mission school just over a month the parents of the oldest came to take her out of school and the two other girls went home too.[80]

On an itinerating trip to the Miao country in 1919, Margaret wrote her family on native rice paper, using a pencil. "I had a long-wished-for accomplishment. I went where no white woman has ever been and even where none of the men of our mission have been as yet. It was a perfectly lovely road over a nice steep mountain, where we had to pull the poor pony up,...and it took us about four hours of pretty steady walking to reach our destination....Early the next morning we prepared for a five or six mile walk to the village of Zongsaubae. Everybody said the leeches would be plentiful, and they surely were. The women had little bags of salt and betelnut flowers tied on sharp bamboo sticks to scrape the creatures with, but I relied on my heavy boots and a bamboo splinter. About every five or six steps we would stop to scrape the animals off, and they were on every blade of grass and stick and stone feeling after whom they might devour. We didn't dare sit down anywhere to rest, or scarcely even stand still. And we climbed the steepest mountain of our whole trip. We had six Miao men with us, with their murderous looking knives, to open the trail and to relieve our carriers. Where we crossed a deep ravine on three slender poles lashed together with bamboo, they had to cut a road for Ajax [the pony] and coming down the mountain he fell several times but fortunately didn't break any of his precious bones. I only got one leech bite where one got down inside my collar. It didn't hurt but bled quite a little." She also reported that on the trip they had visited a Cantonese village "which is widely reputed to be a depository for stolen goods, and just as we left a man greeted me as 'uncle' which has tickled my Chinese company ever since. Miss Schaeffer has a better name, though—they called her 'red-haired uncle' once. And we passed by one village which was prohibiting people from entering [because of cholera]....I haven't heard a word of English for two weeks, but had a perfectly lovely time."[81]

During the Chinese New Year break from school in February 1920 Margaret once more took advantage of her free time to make a trip with Alice Skinner. Writing again on extremely thin Chinese rice paper from a village three days' journey from Kachek, Margaret told her mother that upon arrival in the village "soldiers came to search [our baskets] for arms and ammunition. They were very decent about it, and we gave them our cards to take to the...lieutenant in charge." About two weeks earlier some six hundred robbers had attacked the village, and the soldiers, who numbered only about one hundred, had killed twenty of the brigands. The lieutenant, who was "Cantonese-speaking...was most courteous but...urged us not to go to the Miao country." Despite the warning, the missionaries were determined to continue. And so "we sent our cards saying we were going to start early the next morning, he sent us six packages of Chinese macaroni, and said he still was not easy in his mind about our going. We sent back a tin of baked beans and a tin of sardines and some quinine pills, returned three of the packages of macaroni as too magnificent a gift, and said we were not afraid. Later in the evening he sent again to see if we did not want a guard of soldiers, which we refused with thanks."[82]

In the same letter she mentioned that the Roman Catholics had had a mission near the town of Liamui for about a hundred years but the priests no longer came to see the people and there were only two Catholic families left in the area. "Many of the market women remembered Miss Schaeffer and Miss Montgomery from their visit about twenty years ago. The mission once thought of locating a station at Liamui but later decided in favor of Kachek, which is a much more central location for Hainanese work and fully as convenient for Miao and Loi work."[83]

Margaret next visited Tinsui, "where the Miao people first began to believe the Gospel" but where there were now problems. She related that

"I verily believe that the chief is a consummate rascal. He certainly was the instrument used of the Lord to open the work here, but he apparently did his share with the desire to get glory for himself. Now that the people are learning the truth and not following his false ways he is trying in every way to work against the church by all sorts of tricks and yet to Mr. Byers or any of the rest of us he talks like a saint. He set the date for the Second Coming of Christ a year ago last spring....He is continually telling the people not to study their Bibles as the Holy Spirit will reveal all truth to the unlearned and ignorant, and so on. But he is gradually losing influence in every village except his own. There he still keeps up the jumping, singing manifestations of the Holy Spirit, as he says, much like the Holy Roller sects at home. There are a number of problems connected with the work because of his attitude that would not otherwise occur. Of course, our greatest need is for earnest, consecrated Bible women and evangelists who could come up here and stay one or two months at a time in each village."[84]

Margaret, who was already skilled in the Kachek dialect, was determined to learn the Miao language if the mission returned her to Kachek the following year, as "the [Miao] women do not know enough Hainanese and not having a written language at all, I would have to make a phrase book and syllabary and all."[85] Margaret eventually learned enough of the Miao language to say the Lord's Prayer and the parables of the Good Samaritan and the Prodigal Son.[86] Of the rest of the journey Margaret wrote, "Kialiakha...is a Miao village but very unwilling to let anyone in. We were not at all sure they would let us in and we were pretty sure it would be hard to get anything to eat so we took rice with us. They did let us in at last and we spent the night in a native house." The missionaries cooked over open fires and slept in an alcove in one of the houses. "We were supposed to be asleep when the men began to talk doctrine to the men in the other room and we helped them sing. Then at three o'clock our cook started getting breakfast and at five-thirty we were ready to start. The sun wasn't up yet but the moon was big and bright so off we went. It was a queer experience. Our procession moved along through the woods, which were dripping with dew, and now and then we would go into the jungle so dark and deep we would have to have the coolie go ahead with the lantern so I could see where the pony could go."[87]

On itinerating trips to the Miao country, Margaret knew she was the center of attention and so "carefully chose the foamiest kind of toothpaste available. As I would clean my teeth in full view of villagers, large and small, there were squeals of 'most strange, most strange' so why not give them as good a show as possible?"[88]

When Katherine Schaeffer made a trip into the interior to preach to the aborigines, her letter to Margaret, written on the same type of thin rice paper that Margaret had used earlier, was in turn sent to the Moninger family in Iowa. It offers a vivid description of the work the missionaries did among the aborigines. After noting that she had sold only one book in two days, Katherine Schaeffer wrote, "It would be hard to give you an idea in few words of our crowds yesterday. As soon as we opened doors after we had eaten breakfast, people came in droves and I mounted a bench and held up the picture roll and preached a sermon on each and every one. Then one after another the local brethren mounted the bench. The boys from the Namfo school came in and room was made near the organ. They sang a lot of hymns and were nearly smothered by the crowd surging in."[89] Margaret knew that the crowds came "out of curiosity to see the foreigner, usually, but the seed could be sown just the same."[90]

In 1921 Margaret again went to the Miao country. Writing her regular Sunday letter home, she said, "There are so many people standing around watching me write that I feel like the elephant in the circus. We are having a wonderfully interesting trip....We have Miss Schaeffer's baby organ with us and it sure is proving a great attraction. These people are so fond of singing that they are extra pleased to hear the organ." The missionaries spent the night in the open chapel with a fire for warmth and protection. "The wild antelope were screaming in the mountains back of us (they scream in a manner all out of proportion to their size and timid dispositions)." The following day they walked through a jungle with "climbing vines and creepers arched over the top so thick it was just like a tunnel, across rivers where the tree ferns were magnificent, and incidentally over a mountain or two....Even if it is Sunday I have bought two Miao headkerchiefs and a Loi skirt, and am to have the Loi coat in the spring when the girl gets it done." Margaret thought the mountains were "especially beautiful" and described a river "not very far away where they use hollowed-out tree trunk boats but we did not have a chance to try them out." The church session was attended by six to seven hundred people with fifty-eight being examined for baptism and church membership. Of these, twenty-six men and one woman were baptized.[91]

The following Sunday Margaret wrote more of the trip and included her hand-drawn map of the twenty-one Miao villages she had visited. "These poor people certainly do live awfully bitter lives. When Miss

Schaeffer was down in the Loi country the Chinese elder with her said, 'Even a poor man in America is better off than a rich man in China, but a rich Loi is not even as well fixed as a poor Chinese,' and the same thing could be said with equal truth of these poor Miao people. They suffer so in cold weather although they do have the blessing of plenty of wood and fires in their dark bamboo houses, so they can keep either their faces or their backs warm but not both at the same time. The cold weather here is usually rainy too which doesn't add to their comfort as their villages get so muddy and slippery....I would have liked my picture in my Chinese costume and grass shoes over my other shoes as I fed Buster [the pony] cold rice from a big banana leaf." They went into a Loi village at the invitation of the chief: "These are long-skirted Lois. The women wear skirts coming almost to the ankles beautifully woven in stripes of colored thread. We saw a woman weaving a skirt. She uses a primitive hand loom, with her thread in three layers. The red, yellow and green silk thread they buy from traders, the blue and white cotton thread they spin from their own tree cotton and dye with their own indigo. I took a picture of the woman as she wove and I do hope it is good. I'd love to have two pieces...but I just didn't have the nerve to ask for it because I knew they would refuse pay for it and I couldn't bear to have them do so much work for nothing." She also wrote that she had probably eaten rat, as many of them were being cooked in the villages she had visited.[92]

Margaret had more than a passing interest in the Miao people. In July 1920, while vacationing in Hong Kong, she wrote "The Hainanese Miao" for the *Journal of the North China Branch of the Royal Asiatic Society* and sent it to them.[93] The eleven-page article appeared in 1921,[94] and in it Margaret noted that the Chinese could not distinguish between the Loi and the Miao tribes, "classing them all indiscriminately as Loi robbers."[95] She reported that the Miao "are not native to Hainan. They themselves say that they came from Kwangsi five or six generations ago."[96] The Miao were nomads who practiced slash-and-burn agriculture, and their temporary villages, consisting of six to fifty houses, were all built in deep valleys accessible only by "narrow, precipitous foot-path[s]." She reported that the villages had two or three head men, one who was responsible for taxes and rents for fields and one who entertained guests and strangers: "These men seem to be chosen by common consent when a village is built and apparently hold office as long as the village remains in that location, barring unusual conditions."[97]

Her article continued with a lengthy description of how the Miao built their houses. Concerning their farming, she reported that the Miao, unlike the Chinese, did not grow paddy rice and knew nothing of fertilizing their fields except with wood ashes. They did plant "upland glutinous rice, of which they have ten or eleven varieties, most of them white," along with maize and sweet potatoes. Their simple farm implements and utensils were purchased from the Hainanese. The clothing of the Miao women was decorated with a great variety of embroidered patterns, which included the swastika and "birds, butterflies, silkworm moths, trees, flowers, horses, dogs, dragons, tortoises, [and] Loi children and Hainanese children (two very different figures—and never a figure of a Miao child)."[98] The article was the first scholarly one on the Miao people of Hainan. In years to come Margaret was to write several other articles about life on the island.

Collecting Botanical Specimens

During her trips to the Miao country Margaret was also able to indulge her hobby of collecting botanical specimens, which she sent to Professor Henry Shoemaker Conard at Grinnell College and to Professor E.D. Merrill of the Bureau of Science at the University of the Philippines in Manila. While in Kachek in 1917 she wrote that she "went out botanizing the other morning and got some very pretty specimens of ferns....There is one kind that I have been watching for some time. It grows on the stones of the big bridge here near our compound, and can be seen over the top. The spores seemed to be about right the other day so I went down early in the morning so there would not be any Chinese likely to see what I was doing, and reached over the edge of the bridge and got some of the plants. I told Professor Conard in my letter to the Nature Study club...that if it was not the kind of a fern that was interesting I would be provoked, after all the time I had to get it."[99]

Katherine Schaeffer told Margaret about tree ferns she had seen in a primeval forest that were fifteen feet high, and Margaret was anxious to see them, so in June they took a trip to the rain forest on the edge of the Miao country to collect plants. The trip began with an overnight boat ride up the river, followed by a three-mile walk through vegetation quite similar to that near Kachek, then "the change became quite evident....there were the most beautiful selaginellas and ferns all along. The trees also had peculiar basket-like growths on the trunks and crotches, which I thought at first must be orchids of some sort, but which soon turned out to be spore-bearing, so must be ferns. The climbing vines are simply rampant in their glory, especially the coarse Raphidophora Merrillii, which is no respecter of trees and throws its ugly stems around everything, although it in itself is rather a pleasant sight. The large rather coarse plant of the orchid [family] which the Chinese call *goeh* or 'snake medicine' was very much in evidence. The Chinese say that when men go to catch pythons they strike the snake with this plant to make it quiet. I do not know what there is about the plant to produce this effect, but that is the tale they tell." Eventually, they reached the tree ferns that Katherine Schaeffer had seen and cut down a medium-sized one that was twenty-three inches around the bottom. Margaret noted that the largest one was thirty-four inches around the bottom. "They stand from eighteen to twenty feet high, with the leaves branching out of the top of the stalk or trunk, as in the palm family. The fronds were some of them six or seven feet long, with fifty or more pinnae, which are again pinnately divided."[100]

She reported that it was "not the season for the most flowers, as many of the vines and trees were fruiting. Ferns, however, were in their glory, as the spores were well-developed. In just the varieties that I looked at I saw seven or eight different arrangements of spores. There were climbing ferns, brakes, rock ferns, tree ferns and ferns growing on trees, though I think really air-ferns, ferns with fruiting fronds different from sterile fronds and ferns with fertile and sterile fronds alike. There were four varieties of selaginella that even I, an amateur among amateurs, could not help but notice. There were several varieties of what I think must be orchids, though I am waiting for confirmation of that statement."[101]

After the two-day collecting trip, Margaret sent specimens to Professors Merrill and Conard, as she was anxious to have the specimens compared with the flora of the Philippines: "It would seem as if Hainan had a mixture of the flora of the mainland of China, and of the islands of the Philippines and the Malay Archipelago, and perhaps with some specimens peculiar to itself." Several months later she wrote, "I had a letter from Manila...three of the specimens that I sent had been reported only from Hainan, and one was the second specimen ever sent anywhere for identification, so now it will go pretty hard with me if I can't send the first specimen of something to them....There are not so many things in blossom just now—it is too late in the fall—but the ferns are sporing, and that is the time when one wants to get ferns."[102]

The following year, while on another itinerating trip, Margaret reported that she had "gotten a lot of botanical specimens to press—ferns, orchids, selaginella, etc." Also on this trip Margaret obtained a flying fox from some men who had "shot [it] with a poisoned arrow. It is such a funny thing—has wings like a glorified bat, about a foot and a half long and six inches wide, with the claws at the corners and a bushy tail over a foot long. The skin is about square except for the head and tail when flattened out." By the summer of 1918 Margaret was able to report that she had received "a letter from Mr. Merrill in the Philippines saying there were several new species in the plants I sent him last time and he has named one of them for me. They want more specimens." In 1921 she again wrote that Professor Merrill had named a "new variety" of plant for her.[103]

The Bureau of Science in Manila was also important to the Hainan missionaries, as none of them relied totally on local crops or the local market for food. To grow vegetables they were accustomed to eating at home, many of the missionaries imported seeds, particularly in the years before the mission agricultural stations on the Chinese mainland provided them for foreigners. In addition to sending plant specimens to the Bureau of Science in Manila, Margaret sometimes asked for seeds: "I wrote to Manila not long ago and asked a whole string of questions and sent for some chico seeds, which came yesterday. Chico is a little fruit that I had while in Manila and was very fond of. It had a flavor something like maple sugar, and is on the order of a plum or peach, somewhat—has one pit only. I have planted the seeds in a box and do hope that they grow."[104]

Maintaining a Western Lifestyle

The missionaries also had their families in the United States send them seeds for their gardens. Margaret requested not only seeds but also kitchen utensils! Having been unable to anticipate everything she might require before leaving home, Margaret sometimes found herself in need of rather mundane pieces of equipment that were unavailable locally. Margaret's family kept her well supplied with the necessities of life, and she once told them, "One thing I very much need and can't get out here is a fruit-can funnel. If the ten-cent store has them, stick one in my box of clothes when you send them, and likewise a little individual one-cup flour sifter...would be very convenient, too. Isn't it nice to have a person out here everlastingly tell you what she wants? I must stop it."[105]

But sometimes Margaret found unexpected items in the local market. In 1918 she reported that she had seen Pear's Soap in the market for thirty-five cents a cake and that once she had purchased Colgate's Cashmere Bouquet in the market: "There are quite a number of things that one can get here if one takes time to hunt." Soap was also on Margaret's mind when she wrote a testimonial for Ivory soap, which appeared in one of the company's advertisements in the January 1921 issues of the *Ladies' Home Journal* and the *American Magazine*. Superimposed on a drawing of a building with a Chinese-style roof, the people in the advertisement appear more biblical than Chinese, but one is clearly receiving a gift, presumably of soap, from a Western woman. Margaret wrote, "We try to inculcate an idea of personal cleanliness into our pupils," and went on to relate how one of her former pupils had left school and later had a baby in the mission hospital: "To her great sorrow, [her] old grandmother insisted that it would kill the baby to bathe him. The young mother appealed to us, and we solved the difficulty by sending her half a cake of Ivory, and telling her to assure the grandmother that this fine soap, coming all the way from America, was the soap used in many lands to bathe the babies and never injured *one*. It worked, and yesterday the young father came to me begging me to sell him another cake 'of that nice white soap that was so good for the baby' and went off very pleased with the cake I gave him." As was typical of many things Margaret wrote, she signed the letter to Procter and Gamble "M.M. Moninger," leaving her gender unclear. When her family inquired about the advertisement, she replied, "You were quite right about the Ivory Soap money—they paid me $25 for it and I used it to keep a girl in school a year." Unfortunately, "the Ivory Soap Co. sent me a draft for American gold, but it was at a time when exchange was not favorable and it did not amount to much more than the same amount Mexican."[106]

Margaret left Kachek in the fall of 1919, when she was assigned to the station at Kiungchow. Most of the Hainan missionaries served all three stations at one time or another in their careers, and as Margaret packed her belongings to go to the city, she wrote to her family about the arrangement her colleagues had about furniture: "I'm taking my own little bed because it is so comfortable and not much other furniture, as Miss Chapin's things are all there—wardrobe, bureau, etc. You see we try not to move heavy furniture back and forth between the stations any more than we can help, and it is a standing joke in the mission about the ownership of certain articles of furniture such as heavy wardrobes, dining tables, desks, etc. There is usually a set price on them and whoever is using them pays the last owner and then sells them to the next. This desk that I am using sells back and forth for five dollars. It was originally Dr. [Sidney] Lasell's. I bought it from Miss Schaeffer and she has taken it again to sell to Mr. [Paul] Melrose with the understanding that I take it back when I come back to Kachek." [107]

The missionaries endeavored to maintain all their own customs for birthdays and holidays, which meant improvising and planning months ahead. Even at that, the ordered items, be they food for a holiday dinner or Christmas presents for members of the mission, frequently did not arrive on time, or substitutions were sent. The birthdays of all the missionaries and their children were celebrated with great festivities. Following her birthday in 1920 Margaret reported that Mrs. Shannon's cook had made a birthday cake for her that had "the five station candles on top. Those poor candles do duty for Christmas, birthdays, and all sorts of things." [108]

In early November 1920 Margaret wrote to her sister Helen that she was to entertain the other members of the Kachek station and had ordered food from Hong Kong for Thanksgiving dinner: "My menu is about planned—clear beef soup with salted wafers, creamed crab on the shell, roast duck with stuffing, mashed potatoes with giblet gravy, escalloped tomatoes, peas in patties, pear pickles and olives, either asparagus salad and 'heavenly hash' with fresh grated coconut, or else fruit salad and lemon pudding, and after dinner coffee. I have sent to Hong Kong for walnuts, pecans, Brazil nuts, oranges, lemons, stick candy, layer raisins and fresh cranberries if they can be gotten. We don't usually spend so much on fancy eats but Thanksgiving and Christmas are the times when one likes to have things as much like home as possible. It seems rather awful when you stop to think of the starving people in North China and yet we do without home things most of the time (that really isn't sacrifice, as we have plenty of good food) and it seems good to have something a little bit like a home dinner once in a while." After receiving her shipment from Hong Kong, Margaret sent some of these things, along with candies she had received from her family in Iowa, to Katherine Schaeffer, who was in the Miao country on an itinerating trip. She wrote to Margaret, "Last night I investigated the box of luxuries you sent me. Began at the raisins, went to the stick candy and nuts, down to the gum yum yum and to the little box labeled 'Miss Schaeffer from Dad.' I can't describe all the thrills I felt. They increased in number and force as I went down and that last little box was about the finish. I'm glad I'm 'American, white' and belong to the race which knows how to do such nice things."[109]

Food also was the subject of many of Margaret's other letters. Once, to her mother, she described the best method of eating ripe mangoes: "The only way to eat them in comfort is to stand over a wash basin or a bathtub and let the juice drip wherever it will while you bite off the flesh from the big seeds. They are worse than cling-stone peaches because the seeds are covered with long tough fibers that you can't eat and yet you want to suck the juice out of the fibers."[110]

After her third Christmas in China, Margaret reported to her family that she had received from Katherine Schaeffer "a book in Chinese called *New Terms for New Ideas* that is simply splendid. I am working on it with the teacher. It teaches the new terms that are used in the newspapers and one of my ambitions is to be able to read the Chinese newspapers and get my knowledge of governmental affairs first hand." David Tappan gave Margaret a set of Chinese chess men, which she noted was "a little different from common chess and is said to be a fine game. The Chinese do not gamble with chess so I can learn to play it with perfect propriety. Mr. Gilman plays it very well."[111]

Near holidays, particularly Thanksgiving and Christmas, or on other special occasions, Margaret sometimes admitted to being homesick: "Christmas seems to be the time of year when I get homesick," she wrote home in 1917. "Salted my pillow down last night, but hope I won't be such a baby again for a while." She had the same feelings the following year, writing, "Thanksgiving and Christmas make me homesick. I cried myself to sleep one night this week." In 1918 she told her family, "Wish I could come home for a little visit, in my airplane and get back here for my work. Not much over three more years until I am due for furlough. Doesn't time fly?" After an English church service at which David Byers and Elizabeth Bercovitz were baptized, Margaret wrote, "I am rather tired and, if truth be told, homesick and lonesome. So there you are. Usually I have too much to do to get either way but special occasions are always harder."[112]

Margaret devised a unique custom in her effort to stay close to her family. Once she had invited the members of the mission to dinner, including Bobby Byers, "because he does not have many excitements and his mother wants him to learn how to behave in company, too." Then she asked the Chinese girl who cooked for her, "Who of my family shall I invite to dinner? As I always get out some of my home pictures when I have company. She answered without the least hesitation 'A-fo' [Margaret's grandmother]....I have the little framed picture of Grandma Kellogg on the mantle all the time as the cockroaches cannot eat it but I have the rest of you securely shut up in my zinc box lest any hungry bug get at you." [113]

Margaret's aunt Harriette was a good amateur photographer, and as a result the Moninger family had plenty of pictures of themselves, as well as of Jerry, the pony, and their various dogs and cats. It was some of these pictures that had been sent to Margaret that elicited some of her most interesting comments about the cultural differences between Chinese and Americans. Although such differences must have been daily evident to the missionaries, Margaret rarely commented about the Chinese attitudes toward Americans. One of these rare occurrences happened when the Chinese schoolgirls who belonged to the Christian Endeavor group visited her house one evening for a meeting and afterward looked at some of the pictures of her family she had recently received. Margaret showed the Chinese girls a picture of her father using a wheelbarrow: "The girls do enjoy looking at pictures, although I had to laugh at the rather disgusted look and tone one girl had over my pet picture of daddy, where he is wheeling a basket of corn to the hogs. Out here wheelbarrow men are a low class. So I further remarked that the Ford in the other picture was father's and not a hack like the ones here, so she is still more puzzled. Her own father is a teacher, who has been a personal Chinese teacher for people in the mission ever since Mr. and Mrs. [John] Melrose came out in 1890." [114]

Letter-writing also kept Margaret in touch with her family, and at one time she mentioned to her mother that she had "about nineteen unanswered letters in my desk drawer and I ought to hustle at them today, but we had a big American mail this morning and I've been reading *Heralds*, [*Times-Republicans*], and a *Forward* when I should have been writing." During World War I censors cut out parts of Margaret's letters from home and occasionally parts of letters she wrote: "It does not make any difference to me, of course, whether my letters are opened or not, but the way in which mail is delayed is unpleasant." To her sister Helen, Margaret suggested, "I suspect the neighbors at home would be thunderstruck at the amount of money the Moninger family, collectively, spends for postage in one year, but I don't consider it an unwise expenditure, do you? I know I enjoy getting letters and writing letters as much as any one thing I do, I think—and it ought to be one way to help keep up interest in missionary work if one is any good at describing all the wonderful things one sees."115

Hainan, far from the centers of power in China, was nonetheless on the regular route of the coastal steamers that plied the waters of the South China Sea between Hong Kong, Manila, Haiphong, and Hoihow. Thus the missionaries in Hainan received mail several times a week and were quick to complain if any issue of their home newspapers went astray or if they failed to receive a letter from home. In a letter written in early January 1920, Margaret commented that the Chinese had reported one of the coastal steamers had sunk but noted she had read nothing about it in the Hong Kong newspapers. She informed her mother that "the big mail is on the *Hoiping*, a little tub which runs between Hong Kong and Haiphong. The Customs men say her engine has broken down and she is somewhere between Hong Kong and Hoihow. She hasn't sunk, apparently, and she's probably been towed back to Hong Kong by now....So we will just have to possess our souls in patience." Near the end of the year one of the Chinese steamers, the *Namhoang*, went down off Hainan Head, the northernmost point of the island. Margaret wrote, "The crew were saved but the mail was lost." And she once received a letter from one of her relatives that was "stamped 'Seattle Victoria Seaplane Mail' and I saw in the *North China Herald* that the first mail ever carried in that way between Seattle and Victoria had come across on the Empress boat due about the time to bring my letter, so I judge I received one of the first batch."116

Vignettes from the lives of the Hainan missionaries appear throughout Margaret's letters. A bit of excitement occurred from time to time: "Yesterday afternoon it just rained torrents so Miss Schaeffer and I sat upstairs and sewed, a rare thing for us to do. When we went back upstairs after supper Miss Schaeffer saw a snake crawl across the floor and under her desk. We had quite a little excitement catching it. I suppose the rain 'drowned it out' and it crawled up the vines to the veranda. It was a little fellow only about fourteen inches long, and not very poisonous. It is the kind called the scale-star snake because the marks on its body look just like the stars or division marks on the native scales. We do not usually have snakes in the house although we frequently see them outside. [Yesterday] our kitten was playing with one...that he had caught."117

Responding to a comment from her family that the missionaries in Kachek seemed to them to be very isolated from other foreigners, Margaret compared the missionaries to pioneers, writing that they had no telephone and thought if they tried to "run a line between Kachek and Hoihow, for instance, it would be like the telegraph line they used to have between the two places. It worked only a little while and then went all to smash. The ants eat the poles, the insulation on the wires cannot withstand this climate for any length of time, and so on ad infinitum. The thought of being so far from other Americans seems worse to you at home than it does to us down here. As a matter of fact, when you come to think about it, we are not one bit worse off than grandfather and grandmother were when they came to Iowa, and not one tenth as badly off as the real pioneers were." Margaret realized just how much her life in Hainan resembled that of her grandmother on the American prairie when she tried baking. After several unsuccessful attempts, she finally wrote for information about a brick oven she knew her grandmother had used. "We do all our baking now in a round oven made from kerosene tins, set over a charcoal fire and with hot coals spread over the top. It is almost impossible to bake things properly, as a charcoal fire is so terribly hot when it is hot and no good at all when it is not hot, so the bread burns on the bottom and the top and the middle is dough. About all I can manage to bake well in the thing is cookies, which want a hot oven and bake through quickly." Katherine Schaeffer and Margaret had decided to build an oven "as soon as we can get a workable plan," and Margaret inquired how her grandmother got the top of the oven hot. Unfortunately, we do not know her grandmother's response, but Margaret went on baking, so she solved the problem somehow.[118]

The missionaries customarily took a short vacation during the summer after the close of their schools. Because of their location on the shipping routes between China and Southeast Asia, it was most convenient for them to go to Hong Kong on these vacations. Hong Kong was also very hot in summer, so most of the Hainan missionaries would have preferred to visit a cooler location in the north where missionaries had several resorts, but the expenses of the journey northward were prohibitive and the distance meant that little time would be spent at the resorts. Departing Hainan was always an adventure, as the port at Hoihow was one of the worst in China. At low tide there was a huge expanse of mud to cross between the dock and ships in port. To avoid the mess, passengers wishing to embark or disembark at low tide customarily took a small boat out to the open water to await their steamers. In the spring of 1920 Margaret and Mother Melrose decided to spend their vacation together and after discovering the high cost of traveling to North China, settled on Hong Kong again. They planned to take the French steamer *Hanoi*. Margaret noted, "We are not very fond of taking her, but the one redeeming feature about her is her regularity, as she comes down one Friday on her way to Haiphong and goes back the next Friday to Hong Kong."[119]

Luckily, on this occasion the two women had not waited for the *Hanoi* because they had completed their work and their packing by Monday evening and decided to sail on Tuesday on the *Jade,* which was due in then. As it turned out, that week the *Hanoi,* which like all ships was subject to the perils of the sea, went aground between Hoihow and Hong Kong, and the crew had to wait for high tide to refloat the steamer. Then the *Hanoi* got caught in a typhoon and finally arrived in Hong Kong nearly forty-eight hours behind schedule.[120] Although the summer interlude in Hong Kong was supposed to be a vacation, the missionaries also used the occasion to visit the eye doctor and the dentist, since Hainan had neither.

Planning the First Furlough

Immediately after returning from her 1920 vacation, Margaret began planning for her furlough. Presbyterian missionaries in Hainan were due a one-year furlough after six years on the field, and Margaret had written earlier that going home was on her mind as soon as she passed the halfway mark in her term of service: "Do you realize, I wonder, just all it means when I say that it was just three years ago today that I landed in Hoihow?...They have been three of the happiest years of my life, even if I have been away from you all and even if I had been putting in most of my time learning the language. From now on I can begin to look forward to going home, which is a luxury we do not permit ourselves until after the half-way mark is past, and even now I don't dare to think of it very much for fear I'll neglect other things. You have all been so good to write to me—but there have been so many changes that it must be very different at home."[121]

Margaret's furlough was due to start on 1 July 1921, and many of her letters in late 1920 contained accounts of her plans—possible routes, ship schedules, train schedules, and finally a precise time when she would arrive in Marshalltown.[122] She began the actual planning for her furlough by seeking information about steamers, both to get her to Hong Kong and to take her across the Pacific: "Steamer connections are so fearfully uncertain between here and Hong Kong that you almost have to allow two weeks to get there and then sit on the beach and take the first tub that pokes its nose in the harbor. There are a number of small steamers that call here but they have no license to carry European passengers."[123]

Finally, in December 1920, she wrote that she had reserved passage on "the *Empress of Asia* sailing from Hong Kong on July 22nd for Vancouver....I want to go the northern route one time or the other anyway and it might as well be going home as coming back....I'll send you a schedule for letters later so that you can write me at Hong Kong, Shanghai, Yokohama and Vancouver, but don't plan to get any letters to Hainan for me later than July 1st and allow six weeks for them to come from home here. I'm actually beginning to feel the thrills of getting ready." Once she received confirmation of her itinerary, she wrote home that she was to leave Hong Kong on 22 July, be in Shanghai on the 23rd, Nagasaki and Moji on the 25th, Kobe on the 27th, Yokohama on the 30th, and Vancouver on 8 August. She planned to take the first Pullman out of Vancouver and be home in time for her sister Dot's birthday.[124]

From other missionaries Margaret had learned that carrying all sorts of identification was a good idea: "In these days it is said to be a good plan to carry identifying paper besides passports along, especially in passing through an island kingdom between here and home. I have my teacher's certificates, D.A.R. membership card, Royal Asiatic Society membership card, two old passports and smallpox-typhoid-plague vaccination certificate, all of which I plan to take along with me." Margaret wrote that she was getting ready for the trip home and was "getting some few little Hainanese silver pins, and coconut shell ware....Only don't get your hearts set for anything great, much as I would like to bring you all Hong Kong!"[125]

As she planned her furlough, the Chinese at the Kachek compound were also making plans for a farewell party for her, where they gave her "some solid gold medals." David Thomas and Margaret departed Kachek together as she started home, and "Chinese friends escorted [them] out with firecrackers." Trying to leave Hoihow for home, Margaret was delayed by a typhoon but finally caught the *Hanoi*. Her departure provided a typical example of the transportation problems Hainan residents faced: "Anyone who wants to take [the *Hanoi*] has to be out in the harbor when she comes in. The agent thought she would come Saturday, so I set the alarm clock for 2:30 A.M. got up and took my various possessions to a little open boat that came to our hospital wharf for me and we poled out to the bigger cargo boat outside the spit. We waited until noon with no sign of the *Hanoi* and then I had the boatman take me over to the *Kaifong* which was lying in the harbor, and I asked them to give me some lunch (the officers were just eating). They absolutely refused to accept any pay for the meal." Two hours later the Campbells' servant "came out in another boat and brought me some lunch!" At 6:00 P.M. the *Hanoi* still had not arrived, so Margaret went back to shore for the night. The following morning she "got up at 3:30 A.M. came out in the little boat again to the cargo boat, and the *Hanoi* actually came in sight about 6:30 and I got aboard about 9:00." She hoped to go to Canton because "one of our boys who has just gone to Canton Christian College wants me to come and see him and I am also very anxious to see Canton."[126]

Margaret spent a few weeks in Hong Kong and then embarked for the journey across the Pacific toward home. She would spend ten weeks of her furlough at the Biblical Seminary in New York, a month speaking in Wisconsin, and frequent weekends speaking at churches in Iowa. She would also receive an M.A. degree from Grinnell College.[127] But first there was the reunion with her family, whom she had not seen for six years. Her homecoming must certainly have been joyous, but all the Moningers, as well as all of Margaret's friends, knew that the year at home was simply a furlough. Margaret loved Hainan and her work there, and at the end of her year she returned to the tropical isle of palms.

CHAPTER THREE

Turmoil and Flight
1922–1927

VIOLENCE MARKED MARGARET'S second term in Hainan, culminating in the murder of the Reverend George D. Byers at Kachek in 1924. Unrest, so widespread in China in the 1920s, reached the island as various factions competed for control, as in the absence of a strong central government, no one exercised real authority on Hainan. Brigandage plagued the island, and in turn one after another of the missionaries fell victim to bandits or to mobs who ransacked mission property. Death also came to the mission in the form of a sawmill accident that took the life of the Reverend William Stinson.

Margaret in these years assumed increasing responsibility for the work of the mission, serving as treasurer and, for a time, as mission agent. She also represented Hainan in Shanghai at the meetings of the China Council, which decided policy matters for all the Presbyterian missions in China. She virtually gave up her botanical investigations, either having found all the plants her amateur eye could identify as new or having discovered other interests to take the place of that hobby. Her interest in the Miao continued, and she began studying their language, but curiously she did not write home as often about them. Probably because of the unrest in the countryside, she did not make long trips into the Miao country. Immediately after her furlough, her letters resumed, much as before, giving the details of the schoolgirls and the missionaries' lifestyle, with occasional references to growing nationalism and the military factions controlling the island. It was with the death of the Reverend Mr. Byers and the exile of the missionaries first to Hoihow/Kiungchow and then to

Haiphong, French Indochina, that Margaret's letters took a decided turn, as she began writing about China's militant nationalism and the boycotts that paralyzed China's cities as well as Hainan.

These difficulties and interests still lay in the future as Margaret returned from her first furlough aboard the *President Madison* from Vancouver. None of the Hainan missionaries accompanied her on the trip, but her sailing companions included many members of the Presbyterian missions in Korea and on the Chinese mainland. Arriving in Hong Kong in August 1922, she was met by Mae Chapin and Grace Macdonald. She wrote, "It surely did seem good to see them." She was delayed in Hong Kong, because of the lack of steamers for Hainan, but finally secured passage so that she would reach Hoihow in time to take the regular boat for Kackek and reach there the day school was scheduled to start. She calculated that by the time she reached Kackek she would have been traveling for thirty-seven days.[1]

Back at her island home, some aspects of life seemed familiar. She reported that on the riverboat to Kachek, her pony, Buster, "got tired about 7:00 and jumped out into the river so the coolies took him the rest of the way by road. I slept in an inn that night and at daylight started out for Kachek, determined to reach there that night if possible. I rode right with the carriers...all day....Just at dusk I was still about twelve miles from Kachek, but the moon was almost full, so I hired a new carrier and came on down by moonlight, getting in here about quarter to eleven. I have always wanted a moonlight horseback ride out here and this is the first time it was ever really proper to have one."[2]

During her furlough and in Hong Kong on her return trip, Margaret acquired more possessions for her household in Kachek. She purchased a sewing machine in Hong Kong and a new mattress, which "came in perfect condition. So did the baby organ, which is a perfect beauty and admired by every one. It has been put right to work being used at school prayers. The Victrola case was cracked in a few places but the motor was absolutely safe and the records ditto, and we have enjoyed it a lot already. The Chinese girls come running whenever I tune it up."[3] Unfortunately, her sewing machine would soon be lost to brigands. Before leaving for home on another furlough, she gave the Victrola and records to some Chinese friends for a wedding present, lest these items also be stolen.

Margaret Moninger, age one month, is held by her great grandmother Phoebe Farnham Parks. Her grandmother Maria Parks Kellogg is seated at right, and her mother, Mary Helen "Minnie" Kellogg Moninger, is standing. The photograph was taken in Grinnell, Iowa, October 1891. From the collection of Mary Teschner.

Margaret Moninger, ca. 1896. From the collection of Susannah Moninger Dodson.

Moninger family, 1905. *Left to right*, Minnie, Louise, Dorothy, Helen, Margaret, Will. From the collection of Susannah Moninger Dodson.

Moninger sisters, 1915. *Standing, left to right*, Helen, Dorothy, and Margaret; *seated*, Louise. This photograph, like the one of Will, John, and Minnie, was taken just before Margaret's departure for China. From the collection of Susannah Moninger Dodson.

Will, John, and Minnie Moninger, 1915. From the collection of Susannah Moninger Dodson.

Hainan Mission Meeting, Hoihow, 1918. *Back row, left to right*: Mrs. Madeline Steiner holding Geneva, Rev. John Steiner, Miss Alice Skinner, Rev. David Tappan, Mrs. Grace Shannon, Mrs. Cora Salsbury, Rev. James Shannon holding Mary Elizabeth, Dr. Clarence Salsbury, Mrs. Elva Bercovitz, Rev. George Byers, Dr. Nathaniel Bercovitz holding Elizabeth, Rev. William Stinson, Miss Margaret Moninger, Miss Mae Chapin. *Seated*: Rev. Clarence Newton, Mrs. Inetta Campbell, Rev. Wilbur Campbell, Mrs. Olivia McCandliss, Dr. H.M. McCandliss, Mrs. Margaret Melrose, Rev. Frank Gilman, Miss Katherine Schaeffer. *Seated on ground*: Chalmers Salsbury, Miss Ruth McCandliss, Mrs. Esther Melrose holding Jack, Rev. Paul Melrose, Miss Janet Gilman.

Hainan Mission Meeting, Kiungchow, April 1934. *Standing, left to right*: Dr. Esther Morse, Jean Thomas, Mrs. Madeline Steiner, Elizabeth Steiner, Mrs. Esther Melrose, Rev. Paul Melrose, Mrs. Meta Thomas, Rev. David Thomas, Miss Margaret Burkwall, Miss Caroline McCreeery, Dr. Nathaniel Bercovitz, Miss Mae Chapin, Mrs. Elva Bercovitz, Miss Mary Taylor, Miss Margaret Moninger, Dr. Stuart Seaton, Mrs. Myrle Seaton, Mrs. Evelyn French, Rev. Orville (Jimmy) Mirtz, Rev. Arthur French. *Seated*: Miss Grace Macdonald, Rev. John Steiner, Miss Alice Skinner, Rev. David Tappan, Mrs. Luella Tappan, Mrs. Geneva Burkwall holding Yola, Dr. Herman Burkwall. *Seated on ground*: Sylvia Melrose, Wallace Seaton, Robert Thomas, Richard Thomas, Peter Bercovitz, Ronald Seaton, David Tappan.

Chinese Bride.
From the collection of the
McCandliss family through the
courtesy of Nathaniel Bercovitz, Jr.

Hainan pagoda.
From the collection of
Orville Mirtz.

Kites. From the collection of Orville Mirtz.

Three generations of Miao. From the collection of the McCandliss family through the courtesy of Nathaniel Bercovitz, Jr.

Girls of the Pitkin School, Kiungchow.
From the collection of the Department of History, Presbyterian Church in the U.S.A.

Above, Miao Christian women. Photograph by Katherine Schaeffer, from the collection of Sylvia Melrose Ryan.

Two Loi women. From the collection of Nathaniel Bercovitz, Jr.

Loi woman with earrings. From the collection of Nathaniel Bercovitz, Jr.

Hoihow Church. From the collection of Nathaniel Bercovitz, Jr.

Standing, left to right: Miss Margaret Burkwall, Miss Margaret Moninger. *Seated*: Mrs. Elva Bercovitz; Lt. Col. Matsuo, commander of the Japanese forces in Hainan; Dr. Nathaniel Bercovitz; Lt. Nakamura, the second; Miss Alice Skinner. Photograph taken after the missionaries entertained the Japanese officers at afternoon tea, Christmas Day, 1941. Note decorated tree.

Margaret Moninger, ca. 1942. From the collection of Dorothy Gill Barnes.

Teaching Again

Upon her return Margaret immediately resumed her duties at the mission school, which had sixty-three pupils. Thirty had been turned away "for lack of room, which hurts me terribly, but we simply can't take in any more until we do have more space. I do not know when that time will come....There is a good-sized temple right next door to us which is being remodelled just now for an agricultural and industrial school. We rather doubt whether they will get many pupils and Miss Schaeffer says she is trying to have faith to believe we will be able to rent it before long. If we do it will help considerably although I wouldn't want to put any girls over there to sleep. We could use it for class rooms and use part of the downstairs of this building for sleeping quarters."[4] The mission boys' school at Kachek also had to turn away students for lack of room.

The agricultural and industrial school began, and the missionaries had to build a wall between it and the mission compound. But a more serious problem arose, as "the man in charge is definitely antagonistic to Christianity." The school's entrance examination had prospective scholars writing on the topic "The church says men were made from dust; do you believe it?" Margaret attributed this question to the principal's "Bolshevist-atheist...French training." Yet less than two years later the missionaries had worked out a congenial relationship with the neighboring school, and Margaret was teaching English there. After giving an English examination to her class there in June 1924, she wrote, "The boys were up to all sorts of tricks trying to cheat. Their whole standard of ethics in such cases is very different from ours. I have really enjoyed the work there and the seventy dollars they paid me this spring has more than made up the amount of the cut in appropriations for the [mission] school."[5]

At about the same time the agricultural and industrial school started, a new girls' school, with twenty-five students, opened in the market at Kachek, and one of the graduates from Margaret's school taught there: "She makes the fifth one of our girls to be teaching right near here, with five more who are teaching for me here, one who is a Bible woman, and five who are in high school. There are a few other eighth grade graduates, most of whom are teaching near their own homes. Altogether it makes a pretty good record for our school."[6]

As always, Margaret took a personal interest in the students at the mission school, and she mentioned how Chinese wedding customs affected the schools when students had to discontinue their studies to be married, sometimes in the middle of the term. At the end of 1923 Margaret noted that the year was the last of the twelve-year Chinese cycle and so was a lucky one for weddings. The following year was supposed to be unlucky, so three of her students had left school to be married before the new year.[7]

In all her years in Hainan, Margaret made few references to serious disciplinary problems with the school's students. Early in 1925 she wrote, "For the first time since I've been in China I saw a Chinese father thrash his son. The youngster is about twelve years old and bright enough, but so mischievous that he didn't pass his grade last term at school, and he was so angry about it he declared he would not study....So his father was sent for, and he thrashed the youngster good, wearing out three bamboo sticks on him. He did it in our Chinese guest room, too, but we didn't interfere except to say that he must not strike the boy on the head. Zikeng has been a model youngster ever since." Later the same year she reported to her mother, "Friday night at our teachers' meeting,...we called eight or ten of our small boys over, scolded them well, and then I strapped some of them with my leather belt—it stings and makes a noise but doesn't do any serious damage. Then yesterday morning I had to punish the three or four day pupils in the class. The youngsters aren't really bad, just mischievous and inclined to scrap among themselves. Perhaps now they'll calm down a bit."[8]

The general lawlessness of China in the early twentieth century had repercussions that frequently caused the missionaries uncertainty about whether or not classes would be held at their schools. In 1923 Margaret wrote, "Soldiers are still quite numerous down here. They aren't accomplishing much apparently as our Christian village in Tintai is still in fear of robbers every night and many of the people are afraid to sleep in their own homes." As a result of the unrest, several men asked Margaret to take their wives into her school. She wrote, "I've a pretty good idea their sudden zeal for the education of their wives was due to the trouble in Lengtui and they considered this a safer place."[9]

In the atmosphere of uncertainty, thieves were common, but the schoolgirls devised methods of coping: "The market is wide open now as far as gambling is concerned and so petty thieving is going on continually. Sneak thieves were around here the other night and we waked up the whole compound with our excitement. The thieves were scared away before they got anything and you would laugh to see the collection of sticks and stones the girls have up in the dormitories now for use the next time a thief comes around."[10]

Miao Interests

During her second term in Hainan, Margaret continued her interest in the Miao people of the island and began studying their language, with a student from her school as her teacher. Margaret wrote in September 1922 that she was "very much interested in [the language]....They have very peculiar sounds, different from Chinese entirely....I hope to get enough so I can at least talk to the women in their own tongue as so many of them do not understand Hainanese." A month later she wrote that the "study of Miao is getting tremendously interesting. The girl who is teaching me is getting onto the job very well and we are getting somewhere, I think. I have a classified vocabulary now of between three and four hundred words, but I am not speaking as much as I should. I'll welcome my first chance to get to the Miao country and try out my newly acquired knowledge." In November she wrote that she studied an hour before breakfast each day and had a vocabulary of six hundred words.[11]

She was also interested in acquiring some Miao clothing and finally succeeded in buying "a Kak Miao head kerchief and coat and girdle...[from] the head man of one of our Christian villages." She noted, "These Miao do not wear skirts like the others, but wear ordinary Chinese trousers. Their head kerchief is oblong, as wide as the other kind but almost twice as long and practically covered with embroidery but in a plain striped pattern of dull colors. None of the folks in the station, not even Miss Schaeffer, had ever seen one before."[12]

Of the Kak Miao, Margaret later wrote that she "realized as I never had before how a tribe and, of course, on a larger scale a race can be so absorbed by another race as to lose its own identity entirely. There are a few scattered villages of Kak Miao which seem to be really Yao. They do not wear their distinctive clothing any more and the children speak only Hainanese. The next older generation knows only a little of their original language and it will be only a matter of one more generation until they will be indistinguishable from regular Hainanese."[13]

When Margaret journeyed again to the Miao country in August 1923, she met some of the Miao who had converted to Christianity: "This afternoon I had an interesting talk with some of our Miao Christians who used to be Buddhist priests, and to do the spirit or devil worship for their people. They certainly feel freed from a great burden since they have accepted Christianity." Writing about this trip, Margaret made one of her now rare references to her botanical collection, reporting that "among the...specimens I picked up in the Miao country was a bean pod...thirty-seven inches long." [14]

By Christmas of that year, conditions in the Miao country were again dangerous. Mr. de Rautenfeld, who had been with the Chinese Imperial Maritime Customs Service nearly forty years and was then the commissioner of customs in Hoihow, visited Kachek and planned to visit the Miao country: "He is an officer of the Chinese government so had a body-guard of eight or nine soldiers, and when he was all ready to start up to a Miao village the military authorities in Kachek wouldn't let him go because of the soldiers on the other side. He was distinctly peeved, I think. We foreign missionaries go any where up there without a gun and nobody says anything." [15]

Mission Business

Shortly after Margaret arrived in China in 1915, the Presbyterian women missionaries were given the right to vote on mission business and also began to assume more of the responsibilities of running the missions. During the mission meeting held at Kachek during the Chinese New Year holiday in 1923, Margaret was "somewhat overwhelmed with the job that has come to me. Mr. Leverett, the secretary of the Mission, goes home on furlough in July and I have been appointed secretary during his absence....Usually the job goes to one of the younger men....it is quite a job to get the minutes in order for transmission to the Board and the printer." Two weeks later she wrote that the Campbells were leaving for six months on health leave and that the "station treasury has been turned over to me. It took ten men to carry the safe up here." [16]

The magnitude of the treasurer's job was revealed a few weeks later when she told her mother that the quarterly station accounts amounted to $15,192. In another mention of the mission finances, she again revealed the extent of the money involved. On that occasion the Kachek budget totaled $18,000, and she noted that the Reverend Mr. Byers and Dr. Nathaniel Bercovitz had moved $2,000 in silver dollars from the station safe to the doctor's safe in the hospital and in the process discovered that $1,000 in silver weighed sixty-two pounds. She also mentioned that sometimes when she had carried as much as "two or three hundred dollars back from the market my arm has been numb for quite a while afterwards, and when I have had several hundred dollars in my road baskets, bringing money down from Hoihow it has increased the weight of my baskets considerably." The money also concerned Margaret when the missionaries prepared to go to Kiungchow for their annual mission meeting: "Miss Schaeffer is not going to mission meeting but is looking after the property. I'm glad she's here as I'm leaving $3100 in the station safe. However, no one can open it and it would take sixteen men to carry it off."[17]

Although Margaret had previously expressed the dim view she took of the schoolboys' cheating, she generally had a good opinion of the Chinese where financial matters were involved: "The Chinese are very nice to deal with in money matters—I never had trouble but once and that over two false dollars I took back to a store and none of the clerks wanted to admit they had taken them in. And it is always a pleasure to send money to the government school students. Their families prefer to send money by us because they consider it safer."[18]

China Council

Margaret was selected by the other members of the Hainan mission to represent them at the Presbyterian China Council, and in September 1924 she traveled to Shanghai to attend the Council meetings. After the meeting had been in session a few days, she reported that Margaret Frame from North China had arrived: "I'm mighty glad to see her as for the first few days I was the only woman present. I've been elected Minute Clerk so have quite a job on my hands, but I am glad to take that much of the routine off the regular members, who have such heavy committee work."[19]

Only three women attended the China Council meetings and as one of them Margaret was to represent the South China [Canton], Yunnan, and Hainan missions. In a letter addressed to all these women, she stated, "I feel that I absolutely *can not* adequately represent the women of the three Southern Missions" since she had met only a few of the women of the South China mission and "none of the members of the Yunnan mission."[20]

From Shanghai Margaret wrote to her mother, "The China Council continues to be very interesting indeed. I'm enjoying it tremendously but of course am finding out how very, very much there is in connection with our work that I never dreamed of, much less thought seriously about." One of the problems concerned whether or not the missionaries needed to maintain passports while in China and how they would be paid for. Since American passports then cost ten dollars in gold and were only valid for two years, the expense for China would have exceeded two thousand dollars a year. If the Board of Foreign Missions adopted the policy, it would then apply to all countries, further increasing the expense. It was finally decided that "where a passport was necessary during working time in China," the China Council would pay the expense.[21]

Margaret noted that the Council meetings were "strenuous": "Twenty-three days is the shortest session they have ever had." In a letter to the women she was representing, Margaret wrote that she found the experience at the China Council "very broadening" and had gained a better understanding of the ramifications of mission work. She reported that each issue brought before the Council was considered "as to (1) its relations to other missions and stations of our Board, (2) its relation to our Board, (3) its relations to other denominations working in the field, (4) its relations perhaps to non-missionary foreigners in China, (5) its relations to the Chinese Church and, (6) its relations to the Chinese and perhaps our own government. I have realized that this is one great function of the China Council—to keep the forward march of our Church and mission here in China consistent, unified, correlated, sane." She also wrote that the Council had decided to appoint a third secretary: "It is tacitly understood that this third secretary should be a woman."[22] Within a short time Margaret Frame became the third secretary of the China Council.

The Council members had their picture taken twice, because, as Margaret Moninger noted, "the first time was not very flattering to anybody except one or two of the men and the other men, vain creatures, wanted it taken again so it was." She described serving on the China Council as "one of the biggest experiences I have had since I came to China, perhaps in all my life. I've enjoyed it very much indeed. It certainly was fortunate for me that the appointment came this year when I was free to accept it."[23]

Whenever any of the Hainan missionaries traveled to one of China's major cities they were asked to shop for their colleagues. In Shanghai, Margaret bought "seventeen dozen hair nets for different people in Hainan who had ordered them!" In Hong Kong more shopping orders awaited her, and she reported that she "never had such a grand orgy of shopping in my life, as I had in Hong Kong this time, spending other people's money fast and furiously for them. In a day and a half I spent over $200 and the purchases ranged from sewing silk to water faucets, Chinese dishes to colanders, dried apples to clinical thermometers, pith hats to baby chairs,...lace to aluminum cleaner, and so on."[24]

Time for Fun

Margaret always found time for fun in her life, and initiating new missionaries into the exotic life in Hainan was apparently one of the pastimes she found most enjoyable. In early 1924 Caroline McCreery and Margaret went to the market: "We had been trying for some time to see some live pythons, as I wanted to introduce her to them. At last we found some yesterday. They were in their baskets wrapped with gunny sacking and the shop keeper obligingly undid one and poked it until it stuck its head out and spit at us in proper style. It was about twelve feet long and they said the other one they had was over fourteen feet. They had gotten four, killed one the day before to sell the meat, one had gotten away and crawled off somewhere and one is to be killed today. They paid about $9 Mexican for the medium sized one."[25]

Several years later she reported that she and Caroline McCreery were "making some New Missionaries' Alphabet books for the Seatons and Ensigns. I've written some little jingles and she is making the pictures."[26] Margaret's alphabet went through many editions, as it was presented to all missionaries arriving on Hainan for the first time. Some verses were

> *D* for the dirt,
> Any old kind,
> Scattered 'round everywhere—
> Sure you don't mind?
> Smells to high heaven,
> Odors galore—
> From the old dump heap,
> To the dirt floor.
>
> *H* for Hainan,
> Island of palms,

> Sometimes of storms,
> More often of calms.
> Soon you will love it,
> Pearl of the sea,
> Out of all China
> The best place to be.
>
> S for the sacks,
> Now sails for boats,
> Or coolies' trousers,
> And summer coats.
> Once filled with flour,
> Now filled with men—
> Which is the better—
> Now, or as then? [27]

On another occasion, the fun was provided by Margaret's cats. The cook had fixed a pork roast on Saturday night to be eaten on Sunday, but the cats opened the oven door and consumed the roast. After the cook discovered the kitten in the oven in the morning, Margaret commented, "We opened a tin of sliced dried beef and had gravy for dinner!" [28]

Attitudes toward China's Leaders

Almost as soon as Margaret returned from her first furlough, her letters began to reflect her opinions of China's officials. On Christmas Eve 1922 she wrote her mother, expressing her disgust for Chinese government officials: "The man who has been chief magistrate [in the Lengtui district] has killed a lot of people and has especially injured one family, even going so far as to crucify three of the men of that clan. Soldiers have been sent down to get him and word came up a day or so ago that they had captured him and were going to give the widow of one of the crucified men the say about how he should be killed. You can't blame the people of China for rising up against such officials. When that class of men are no longer in power China will be much more peaceful." [29]

But it was during her vacation to Hong Kong and Canton in 1923 that Margaret expressed her strongest feelings about Chinese officials. The medical committee of the Hainan mission insisted that everyone take yearly vacations away from the island, so that year Margaret used her vacation to visit Canton for the first time. Sun Yat-sen, the Christian, Western-trained medical doctor who was the architect of the 1911 revolution, had struggled for more than a decade to establish a workable Western-style government for China. Many American missionaries mistook China's 1911 revolution for the American revolution, and although Margaret sometimes made this mistake, she was no admirer of Sun, whom many missionaries called "the George Washington of China." On this trip, Margaret saw his redoubt near Canton: "As we came up river yesterday we went past a fleet of six gunboats belonging to Sun Yat-sen. They were anchored about ten miles below Canton, at Whampoa. Governor Sun doesn't dare to live in his governor's palace but lives in a cement factory on the river bank where he can take to his boats any time he is scared. As a matter of fact his boats are not very formidable looking." She went on to describe Shameen Island, where the British and French had concessions, and noted, "America holds no territory in China, but our consular buildings are there and we have a gunboat in the harbor. The Stars and Stripes sure do look good. All we see in Hoihow are the British and French flags, as the British Consul there acts for the Americans."[30]

Back in Hainan, the political conditions continued chaotic: "We have rather been expecting a change in government here in Kachek for some time. The soldiers here now belong to the military governor of the island, Deng Vun-in, who is a Sun Yat-sen man. The people generally favor a local man, who is a supporter of Sun's arch enemy. So we rather expect the market to change hands soon. The districts to the south of us have been more or less disturbed for some time, as far as soldiers are concerned." Eventually, the political unrest had an impact on the mission school. In January 1924 the boys and girls in the mission high schools in Kiungchow went on strike. Margaret observed that "other more advanced parts of China had trouble with their schools years ago when things were just getting adjusted and we are so far behind we are just getting it now. The trouble seems to have been instigated by the teacher Mr. Tappan brought down from Nanking and came to a head over some amateur theatricals the boys were giving to raise money for the library. The Chinese students always use the strike method to obtain what they want in native schools but it doesn't work with us—I imagine the schools will simply close down entirely perhaps for a whole term."[31]

In August she wrote, "Judging from the situation in Canton at present

Sun Yat-sen is about at the end of his string, as the people there are repudiating him entirely. He forcibly took the arms and ammunition ordered by Canton city for their merchant police, so the stores in the city have gone on strike and refused to open their doors to do business. The people generally think there will be trouble yet over the matter." Two weeks later she told her mother that "Sun Yat-sen is about to the end of his rope, I believe and most of us hope he is." In October of the same year she wrote from Shanghai that the unrest there and in Peking made it seem unlikely that a consul and a cruiser would visit Hoihow any time soon. The unrest in Canton, she noted, was in the business districts, and mission property had not been harmed. She assessed it as "the old trouble between Dr. Sun and the merchant police," which was "certainly costing the city dear. If only Dr. Sun Yat-sen would fall into the sea and forget to climb out China would be much better off than she is now."[32]

Several months later Margaret mentioned that she thought the unrest at Yale-in-China in Changsha, Hunan, was "very bitterly anti-foreign and anti-Christian." She agreed with "an editorial in *The North China Herald* [that] it was largely due, they thought, to the failure young China had made at government and that they were trying to shift the blame from their own shoulders to the foreigners and the Christians." She compared the unrest to that of the "Boxer times but in a very different sort of way. Physical violence will not be the result, but it is quite likely foreigners will end in some anomalous position."[33]

Death Strikes the Mission Twice

Despite its difficulties, Hainan was one of the safest locations for a mission in China. Armies supporting one or another of the political factions in China did periodically create mayhem on the island, but generally the violence did not touch the missionaries. More important, perhaps, the missionaries felt safe on the island. Indeed, although the missionaries all suffered from malaria, as a group they had suffered few serious illnesses, and only three missionaries had ever died on the island.[34]

This sense of tranquillity was shattered first by the murder by bandits of the Reverend George Byers at Kachek in June 1924 and then by the death in November of the Reverend William Stinson in a sawmill accident, as he was supervising the construction of new buildings for the mission. The murder of the Reverend Mr. Byers shocked the missionaries and precipitated a quintessential extraterritoriality case that lasted more than a year. Since according to treaty agreements, all foreigners resident in China were living under their own countries' laws and not under Chinese law, American diplomatic personnel from Canton, the nearest consular post, handled the Byers case. Whenever a foreigner was killed in China, the foreign government insisted that the Chinese arrest the perpetrators and then demanded an indemnity to compensate for the lost life. The Byers case was no exception, but it proved to be an extremely difficult one to resolve because of the distance between Canton and Kachek, because of the reluctance of diplomatic personnel to pursue it vigorously, and, most of all, because in the chaos prevalent in China in the 1920s no one was exactly sure who held political control at any given time in Hainan, where various strongmen gained and lost territory and created and broke alliances with compatriots on the Chinese mainland with great rapidity.

At the end of the school year, when the Hainan missionaries left for their vacations, it was customary to leave one of the missionaries or one of the families at each station to take care of the compound. Thus in June 1924 all of the Kachek missionaries departed, except for the Byers family, who were left alone at the station. On this occasion Caroline McCreery and Margaret had traveled to Hoihow, and Margaret was planning to depart for Hong Kong. In Kachek, the Reverend Byers conducted the evening religious services on the twenty-fourth at the mission hospital. He was returning to his home, located across the road, when he was attacked by bandits who were apparently intent upon kidnapping him for ransom. As he struggled with his assailants, he was shot through the abdomen. He died in the arms of his wife, who had heard the commotion and responded to her husband's call for help. A military telephone line had recently been installed between Kachek and Hoihow, and Mrs. Byers was able to have Chinese officials call the port with the news. Upon learning that the Reverend Mr. Byers had been shot, several of the men of the mission went to the British consular officials and then to the military governor's office and arranged to leave for Kachek at daylight. The Byers family and the Reverend John Steiner accompanied the body back to Hoihow on the twenty-ninth, and the funeral, which was attended by most of the foreign community in Hoihow, was held that afternoon.

At the time of the murder "the cable between Hoihow and the mainland was not working," but Margaret, as mission secretary, wrote a letter to the Hongkong and Shanghai Bank in Hong Kong, where the missionaries had their accounts, "asking them to cable New York and Shanghai 'Bandits kill Byers Kachek. Family, Bercovitz Moninger McCreery safe.'" Margaret thought the China Council and the Board of Foreign Missions would notify relatives in the United States of the situation. The news of the Reverend Mr. Byers's death was telephoned to the Moninger family by officials at the Board of Foreign Missions, who followed up with a letter, although they admitted they knew no more of the matter than what Margaret had cabled via Hong Kong.[35]

As there were no American diplomatic personnel on Hainan, the British consul took care of matters for the missionaries, but in the aftermath of the Byers murder an American consul was summoned from Canton. He arrived on a gunboat in July. Margaret had a vast network of friends in Iowa, partly because her grandparents and their siblings had been early pioneers in the state and partly because she had joined both the Congregational and the Friends churches when living in two small towns while attending college and teaching. Just how extensive that network was became evident when the gunboat, the *Sacramento,* arrived carrying Vice-Consul C.B. Chamberlain, who was to investigate the Byers case. On the Fourth of July the missionaries invited the sailors ashore for a picnic, and Margaret discovered that the commander of the gunboat was a "Mr. Fletcher, who went to Annapolis from Marshalltown. He remembered Grandpa Moninger or at least the old place well, said he had been out there. He asked first thing if I didn't have a 'cousin'...who was a nurse, and he remembered Aunt Tot well." Margaret also knew the wife of M.M. Hamilton, the American consul, who arrived on Hainan in 1925 to investigate the case, since the woman had been a missionary and had traveled to China on the ship that returned Margaret from her furlough.[36]

After the Byers murder Margaret went to Hong Kong for a brief vacation, and when she returned to the island she lived at the port where all the other missionaries were then residing. From there she wrote, "Robber bands are operating very vigorously still in the region around Kachek but do not attack the market itself." The Byers case dragged on and on, proving extremely difficult to resolve. In December 1924 Margaret wrote, "We are hoping that the officials will get busy and produce the men wanted soon so we can go back to the interior stations."[37]

With all the members of the Hainan mission living at Hoihow and Kiungchow, the 1925 mission meeting was the most unusual ever held, in that everyone was able to attend. Margaret reported that they "had a strenuous week of mission meeting" and continued, "We certainly are up against it—unable to go into the Kachek and Nodoa [stations] until the Consul allows it, and then with not enough missionaries to man more than two stations really full. There has been some talk of closing either Kachek or Nodoa for a year or two....I'm to be in Kiungchow in either case, I believe, to help Miss Chapin this spring and to have the school while she is home. But the final vote hasn't been taken yet." In mid-November the missionaries were still living at the port, and Caroline McCreery and Margaret, who had left Kachek planning only to be gone for a brief vacation, sent for their bedding and their winter clothes, since it appeared they would not be returning to the interior soon. Then in March 1925, when some of the men went to Kachek, Margaret asked "Mr. Thomas...to pack up my things, or rather part of them, and send them out to me. I certainly shall be glad to see them again."[38]

As the Hainan missionaries continued to wait for permission to re-enter their interior stations, the Canton mission requested that Margaret be assigned there. She wrote home that the "Hainan Mission Executive Committee do not approve of my going to Canton. Apparently their line of reasoning is that to allow some of the force to go away from the island would be a tacit admission that we did not expect to go back to the interior and that would weaken our case with the officials and the government....Then I think possibly they were afraid the temporary transfer might become permanent."[39]

The American consul, in consultation with the missionaries, finally made some decisions about the compound at Kachek, even though the matter with the Chinese government continued unresolved: "Mr. Hamilton is still pegging along on the Byers case but doesn't seem to be getting anywhere very fast." By the first of March the only progress that had been made was the decision to wall the Kachek mission compound.[40]

With the Byers matter unresolved, news came of the death of Sun Yat-sen in March 1925. The missionaries were greatly concerned about the impact Sun's death would have on China's political turmoil, and they were careful to observe mourning for him: "I did not have my Bible classes as the native schools are having a three-day period of mourning for Sun Yat-sen....Our school was closed Thursday because of Sun and the pupils had a little meeting out on the lawn late in the afternoon for him." Later Margaret mentioned that Sun had been worshiped, but it is uncertain whether she misunderstood the Chinese customs concerning mourning or if he truly had been worshiped: "Yesterday the students of the government schools had a big meeting in honor of Sun Yat-sen. We heard from very reliable sources that he was to be worshipped in the old style and I presume he was. The part of the procession of the students which we saw was almost a mile long. It remains to be seen what effect his death will have on political conditions in South China generally."[41]

The death of Sun did nothing to ease the political turmoil in China, and those in Hainan were particularly concerned, since the local governor was not a supporter of Sun and thus very likely to be involved in the fighting. Margaret voiced the concern that the governor should settle "the Byers case before he skips to parts unknown to live in luxury on the money he's squeezed out for himself while being an official." She added, "If the Byers case isn't settled before he leaves I'm afraid it never will be! Unless the new official would do it in a hurry just to show his superiority." The American consul had forbidden the missionaries to discuss the progress of the Byers case, but they knew Mrs. Byers had requested an indemnity be sought by the American government, and Margaret was very concerned that raising it would "make it very hard for us to preach the Gospel when money payment has been demanded from people who did not ask us to come in the first place and from those who had nothing to do with the murder of Byers." Margaret thought the idea that an indemnity would prevent further attacks on foreigners was "a weak point in that...the enemies who did the deed aren't the ones who have to pay the money."[42]

Eventually the authorities arrested and executed several men for the Byers murder, although none of the missionaries thought those executed were guilty of the crime. The U.S. government collected an indemnity of ten thousand dollars in gold, which was paid to Mrs. Byers. The consul finally agreed to allow the Reverends David Tappan and David Thomas to return to Kachek to arrange for construction of a concrete fence, lanterns, and sentry boxes at the mission compound.

When the other missionaries were finally given permission to return to the interior, Margaret wrote home, "We are almost holding our breath for fear some hitch will come again. As a matter of fact, bandits are very bad all around Kachek again and the governor doesn't seem to be making any efforts whatever to stop them. Either he is paid to let them alone or else he doesn't care enough about the island to make an effort to clean things up. The letters from Kachek this week said a dozen young boys had been kidnapped from a village school only three or four miles from Kachek, and that a three-year-old child had been taken from another village." After nearly a year at the port, the missionaries returned to Kachek, but the description of their departure that Margaret sent to her family could hardly have reassured them: "The folks started to Kachek last Monday. Some of us went up to the auto station to see them off. Miss Schaeffer, Miss McCreery, two women servants, a kitten, lunches, suitcases, travelling bags and a chauffeur were in one Ford, with a soldier 'boy' on each running board, their fingers on the triggers of their wicked-looking pistols."[43]

But the others were unable to return to Nodoa because of unrest unrelated to the Byers case. Old antagonisms between the aboriginal tribes of the island and the Hakkas erupted into warfare in the area around Nodoa, preventing the missionaries' return. Three of the men started for Nodoa, but "there were such terrible tales of the Hakka-Limko outrages that they had almost decided that it was unwise to go in when a telephone message was sent from the governor here telling them and the two hundred soldiers with them not to go in." The missionaries tried to mediate a peace between the warring factions, with little success.[44]

Such was the situation in Hainan in 1925 when the May Thirtieth Incident occurred in Shanghai. Following a strike by workers protesting the low wages in a Japanese cotton mill, police opened fire on demonstrators who were supporting the strike, killing eleven of them. Unrest quickly spread throughout China and eventually altered the relationships between Chinese and foreigners. Part of the changed relationship took the form of increased anti-Christian activities. Margaret first mentioned these strikes and the impact they had on Hainan in a letter to her family written on 7 June. She indicated that she did not think much of the Chinese students who participated in strikes. Because of "the very disturbed conditions all over China just at present it is hard to tell what may develop. The strikes and riots among the textile workers in Tientsin, Tsingtao and now Shanghai are stirring up the students against what they are pleased to call 'foreign imperialism,' and sympathetic parades are occurring in Peking and Canton. Chinese students seem to have a very peculiar psychology. On the one hand they think they want a republic and on the other hand they haven't the faintest idea of the duties and responsibilities that should go with a republic. Hainan has no mill workers to go on strike, and the schools will soon be disbanding for the summer, but conditions are not very stable. I don't mean that we are in any danger of physical violence here in Hainan, for I do not think we are, but our work may suffer."[45]

It was events on the Chinese mainland, not on Hainan, that caused the American Consul in Canton to order the missionaries to flee the island in June. They went to Haiphong, French Indochina, because that was the destination of the first ship that came into the port. In her last letter written from Kiungchow before the missionaries fled the island, Margaret told her family she was writing on Saturday instead of Sunday, as she usually did, because of the "persistent rumors of a general shipping strike throughout China." She also described the unrest in Hainan: "The students in Kiungchow had a parade last Monday out of sympathy for the students in Shanghai. About two thousand students marched past here with their flags, giving their yell, a call to all students to join them." The mission schools were closed and the local magistrate sent four policemen to guard the mission compound, but it was rain which quelled the disturbance more than anything else. The letter ended, "The consul might order us to Hong Kong, but we do not expect that as the difficulty is with British and Japanese, not with Americans. But don't you worry—we are all right and you'll hear from me whenever steamers run."[46]

Flight to Haiphong

The first word that the Moninger family had of the missionaries' flight came when they received a cable from Margaret saying only "Safe Margaret." From the place of origin, Haiphong, and the date, 29 June, they knew she was in French Indochina on that day, but they could only guess why. Following Margaret's cable, a letter arrived from the Board of Foreign Missions in New York, dated 11 July, stating that the China Council in Shanghai had received a cablegram informing them that the women and children had fled Hainan. The Board assumed they had gone to Hong Kong but noted, "Miss [Mary] Taylor's father has written us that he received a cablegram from his daughter, saying 'Safe,' sent from Haiphong." In the absence of any real information, the Board letter surmised, "It may be, therefore, that our Hainan missionaries, with the exception of those who are coming home on furlough and those who remained on the Island, are in Haiphong until the situation clears in Hainan so that they may return. Haiphong is a port of Indochina, a French dependency, and boats that ply between Haiphong and Hong Kong stop at Hoihow, the port of Hainan. You can readily see that it was just as easy for the missionaries to go to Haiphong as to Hong Kong and they probably thought Haiphong would not be so crowded since all the foreigners from Canton had been requested by their Consuls to go to Hong Kong."[47]

While the Board in New York speculated, Margaret wrote her family an explanation in a 28 June letter from Pakhoi, a port on the south coast of Kwangtung: "Here we are refugees! I told you in my last letter that we were possibly to have troublous times in China, and it seems we are. Last Monday morning a letter came to me as secretary of the mission from the American Consul General in Canton, a confidential warning to Americans. It said that all American women and children were ordered to proceed at once to Hong Kong or other places of safety, all men to come out from the interior, and all 'unnecessary men' to flee. The note at the bottom in handwriting said, 'I do not know how conditions are in Hainan, but this will serve to let you know how things are in Canton.'" Despite heavy rains from an approaching typhoon, Margaret informed the missionaries at Hoihow that afternoon and the next day "sent a special messenger to Kachek to the friends there, sending a copy of the warning and leaving it to their discretion what to do." She went on to describe the continuing unrest, mentioning that Dr. Clarence Salsbury had seen students splattered with red ink "to show their sympathy with the strikers in Shanghai, and to collect money for them."[48]

A British submarine had arrived in Hoihow harbor, and after consultations between the officers and the British consul, the missionaries were instructed to leave. Margaret reported to her family that she had packed hurriedly but said, "We will not be away long, and there are to be soldiers on the compounds, I think." Those fleeing the island included thirteen missionaries and five children and "the Consul's wife, the wife of the Commissioner of Customs, the wife of the Harbormaster, the governess in the Consul's family, and four children." The Kachek missionaries followed the others to Haiphong, while Dr. H.M. McCandliss, the Reverends David Tappan and John Steiner, Dr. Clarence Salsbury, the Customs men, and the British and French consuls remained in Hoihow. The group Margaret left with would have preferred to go to Hong Kong, but the first boat into Hoihow was the *Hanoi,* which was bound for Haiphong. Margaret noted that Hong Kong was "all tied up by the strike" and that the *Hanoi* "wasn't allowed to purchase any stores or unload any cargo except thirty live pigs, [and] stayed just long enough for the captain to go ashore and came right down again, so that is why we could get passage on her."[49]

Indochinese Interlude

The missionaries were not totally tongue-tied in French Indochina. In addition to the Swiss-born Mrs. Madeleine Steiner, both Mrs. Myrle Seaton and Margaret had studied French in college and could communicate at least on a basic level. Margaret's first letter from Haiphong described their arrival and the help given them by a Christian and Missionary Alliance missionary who had been on the *Hanoi*. They had been required to register at the police office after clearing customs. Margaret mentioned that the Hongkong and Shanghai Bank had a branch in Haiphong and "the men there were very nice about cashing checks for us. Fortunately, I have a bank account of over $1000 just now as Miss Chapin turned over various accounts to me before she left, and while it isn't my money it can be used in such an emergency as this, for you see we were ordered to leave by Consular authority....Miss Taylor and I went to the telegraph office and sent our cables home. I'll be so anxious to know whether my word reached you or not. The place 'Haiphong' should appear on the cable itself. It was sent 'deferred cable' which is...a night letter....I paid $5.14 for it and it read 'Moninger Marshalltown Iowa Safe Margaret,' which counted for five words as Marshalltown, Iowa counts as one word, but I had to pay for...the code word meaning 'deferred.'" She also sent her family "the notices about us in last night's papers," asking them to save them for her.[50]

Ever the humorist, Margaret organized a typewritten newsletter for her colleagues, called *The Refugee Rampage*. Mrs. Myrle Seaton preserved a copy of it, which noted that it was "published semi-occasionally," its "circulation strictly limited," and its "price not yet determined—bill will follow." It included news that the missionary children had discovered the zoo in the local park and that Mrs. Tappan's inability to speak French had resulted in her son David having his head shaved instead of his hair cut by a local barber.[51]

In July Margaret noted that it was "the 'Glorious Fourth'—and rather a rainy one." To her sister Helen, whose birthday was 4 July, she wrote that the missionary men had been invited to celebrate the Fourth of July with the men of the Standard Oil Company, who were the only Americans living in Haiphong, but "us women had no part nor lot in the matter, per strict official and international etiquette in a French port." In the same letter she reported that the city had "the red, white and blue of the French tri-color...everywhere" in preparation for Bastille Day, which was celebrated with a big parade.[52]

She described Haiphong: "It's very much quieter here than in Hong Kong. There are no street cars, but automobiles, rickshas, oxcarts to clean streets, pony dog carts, old-fashioned low carriages with a high seat for the driver in front and two seats facing each other below, bicycles, and regular hayracks with sleek-looking mules hauling loads of rice straw. Coolies push and pull wheeled trucks with all sorts of things. There are French, Chinese, Annamese and Japanese shops. The French here treat the Annamese very sternly, and the Annamese are a very different temperament from the Chinese to begin with. They anticipate no trouble in the present disturbances—the Annamites are not friendly to the Chinese anyway." Later she wrote that most of the French military in Haiphong were Moroccan troops, many of whom had been on the *Hanoi* when the missionaries took her to Haiphong. Margaret noted that there seemed to be "no color line...observed. But the treatment of the natives was far worse than anything we had ever seen....one afternoon when a sudden terrific downpour of rain came as I was at the post office, I stood at the top of the steps under the projecting eaves, with several Frenchmen, waiting for the rain to stop. A rickshaw coolie, sopping wet, left his 'shaw at the curb and came up the steps for shelter. There was room enough, but one of the Frenchmen deliberately kicked the Annamite down the steps. In Hong Kong such an incident would have been very unlikely to happen, but if it had the offender would have been hauled into the Mixed Court and sentenced to a fine, at least."[53]

The Standard Oil employees took the missionaries on a picnic to a beach, and later the missionaries visited "Baie d'Along, where there are rocky caves and natural arches and all sorts of curious formations in the bay." Margaret thought the place was "more beautiful even than the Inland Sea in Japan and that's saying a good deal." To relieve the boredom of living in the hotel in Haiphong, Margaret began giving Hainanese lessons to the Reverend and Mrs. S.J.R. Ensign, who had recently arrived in China. Nine of the missionaries "engaged a French teacher to give us two hours a week for each of two different classes."[54]

On 19 July Margaret wrote home that it was her fourth Sunday since leaving Hainan and "still no home mail!...This French post office here is notoriously inefficient for everything except French mail." Some of the married women in Haiphong had received mail from their husbands still in Hainan. From the news they had received, Margaret reported, "Everything seems to be calm in Hoihow." The island's schools were closed for the summer, and the "merchants in Hoihow who are not in favor of the strike referred to the students as having 'five-minute patriotism' and it seems as if they do. For instance, they declare a boycott on English, Japanese and American goods, but continue to wear foreign style clothes, use Singer sewing machines, kerosene sold by British or American firms, etc., and so far we haven't heard that they have demolished their autos, though they did not allow them to run on the days of the parades." 55

In Haiphong, an "out-of-the-way corner of the world," the missionaries got little news of events in China. They did learn that a "soviet government has been set up in Canton, and if it is able to remain in control it would be in control of Hainan, too, geographically. But the present governor of Hainan is a Northern man, nominally loyal to the Peking government, if there is any government in power in Peking, so that probably means war in Hainan." Missionaries passing through Haiphong brought news from Hong Kong and Canton. One British missionary told the Hainan refugees that "the students in Canton are getting out a sermon against 'Imperialism,' and...that every missionary is to be obliged to sign a statement as to whether he or she believes in the Chinese or in the foreign imperialists. All of which, if true, is not especially encouraging to our work in China for a while. We are not supposed to take sides in political matters and we do not want to do it and in this particular case we sympathize with Chinese ideals but not with the means they are using to obtain their ideals." 56

While in Haiphong Margaret had a chance to learn more about the Miao of the mainland: "Some Frenchman loaned Mrs. Steiner a copy of *A History of the Miaos* in French and I'm very much enjoying reading parts of it. Mrs. Seaton helps me sometimes when I'm stuck. I'm glad to get some notes on the subject." (Back in Hainan several years later, Margaret met the author of the *Histoire des Miao,* "Père [F.M.] Savina, the French father who is such an authority on native tribes. He declares our 'Miao' are not Miao but 'Mau,' another tribe group. I shouldn't wonder if he is correct, we have never understood why there was so little in common between the Hainanese Miao and the Miao among which missionaries in other places were working.") 57

In early August the missionaries' mail arrived, and it provided one of the humorous incidents of the refugees' experience. Margaret was anxious that they get "enough mail to impress the post office, and I really believe we did. The Japanese steamer came in last Sunday morning and Monday afternoon they gave us our first batch of letters about 3:00. At 5:00 I went up to the office to mail a letter and incidentally asked for our papers. *Two* Frenchmen appeared gesticulating wildly as they told me our papers were 'plenty, plenty,' so many the office could not deliver them, and I should have the hotel send up two coolies. The hotel clerk smiled indulgently at my request for two coolies and sent up one, but he returned escorting a whole pushcart full of mail, and yesterday again we had almost as much."[58]

About the time the mail arrived in Haiphong, the missionaries decided that conditions in Hainan were calm enough for them to return. Three days before she left Haiphong, Margaret received a letter from her family informing her that they had received her June telegram. Margaret's last letter from Haiphong instructed her family, "Don't worry about us. If things get *too* bad the China Council will tell us to leave, but the Canton situation looks more hopeful now. I do not suppose we [will] do much school work this fall, though." Steamer tickets for the missionaries were purchased, and they sailed back to their island home on 3 August. Others on the steamer included "seven or eight Russians...deck passengers for Pakhoi. They'd come down from Yunnanfu to Haiphong and the French authorities put them out on the first steamer. One of them was very well-dressed and well-educated. He wanted a cabin and as there was none wanted to stay over till the next boat but the police would not allow it. They said they were 'white' Russians and did not want to go ashore at Pakhoi lest they be treated as 'reds.' "[59]

Margaret looked on the interlude in Haiphong as "very pleasant, and not very expensive. I would have gone on a short vacation anyway and this is vacation time." It also caused her to reassess her material possessions, as she noted, "I'm destroying a lot of unnecessary truck I have kept on hand and [am] getting my belongings into such shape [that] the ones I really want can go in my two trunks if we have to leave again."[60]

The enforced vacation in Haiphong had given the Hainan missionaries a chance to see the French colony in operation. A few of them, like Margaret, had been in Manila on their way to Hainan, and some had been in Shanghai and Peking, but most had been only in Hainan and Hong Kong, the transit point for coming and going from the island. Although a few foreign businessmen and customs employees lived in Hainan, the missionaries had little social contact with them. The Presbyterian mission was the only Protestant one on Hainan, and most of the missionaries' acquaintants elsewhere in China were members of other Protestant mission agencies and stations whom they met coming and going from the United States or while vacationing in Hong Kong or in China's coastal cities. The Haiphong interlude had allowed them to become acquainted with foreign businessmen, as well as to meet some of the missionaries stationed in the French colony.

Return to Hainan

Back in Hainan the missionaries had no illusions that conditions there had changed appreciably, as unrest continued on the island. In her first letter written after her return, Margaret observed that most of the students were home for the summer but some had "been delegated to remain here to receive and send cablegrams to other parts of China and to search the stores and shops to enforce the boycott. I understand they are not allowed by General Dong to destroy any goods actually on hand, and they are allowing merchants to sell old stock on hand, but they are forbidding the importation of any new goods from Japan or England. Some people look at us rather askance as we go down the street but most of the merchants are glad to see us back. It created something of a panic in Hoihow and Kiungchow when we left and General Dong gives every assurance that he will control the situation. As a matter of fact, I imagine the worst has probably passed although war threatens Canton again. The Reds are in control there now and we'd all be glad to see them driven out, so we are hoping the fighting will soon come off."[61]

Margaret was concerned about the missionaries' food supply with the boycott in place, so she and Caroline McCreery "scouted around the stores...and managed to get a sack of flour,...eighteen big tins of Carnation milk and a box of Borden's sweet milk, [and] a few cans of fruit and vegetables....The milk we got was sent up from Singapore and Bangkok, the compradore said."[62]

Margaret continued to worry that Britain was going to go to war over the situation in Canton and that Hainan would be dragged into it. "General Dong, his military chief of staff and his civil chief of staff with soldiers, left the island the first of the week ostensibly for Pakhoi to settle a scrap between two of his lieutenants there, but he (General Dong) had a permit to enter Hong Kong. Then the next night about 8:30 there was a soldier fracas in which 'little Dong,' the man left in charge in Hainan to a certain extent, and a number of others were killed. It looks like a frame-up....Of course Dong is an anti-Sun man." But a week later she thought that things had calmed down and were "going along quite as usual."[63]

Then in mid-November the British consul ordered the missionary women and children out of the interior stations. They again resided at the port. Margaret reported, "Governor Dong, who is also General Dong, is fighting over on the mainland against the reds and he is losing. If he loses two or three more places then he will retreat to Hainan and there will be trouble here, supposedly. The reds would come here to fight him and his own men would probably turn over. Then the other side of the tale is that should the soldiers here rebel or leave, the robbers would take a hand. The Hainanese generally are not fond of Dong, as he has taxed them pretty heavily, but they would find the reds infinitely worse, I think." She did not think the missionaries would be involved but noted, "We are right in line with the powder factory on one side and the main city gate on another, [and]...bullets have no eyes." She did not personally feel in any danger but wrote, "The poor Chinese are frightened to death. Many are trying to get away to Singapore, Siam, Annam or Hong Kong. The latter place is not very keen on receiving Chinese since their difficulties last spring and summer. The Chinese make remarks about foreign powers in China, but they have to flee to places under foreign government when things get too hot in their own country."[64]

Margaret revealed just how much tension accompanied the situation in Hoihow when she wrote her mother, "The expected soldier turnover has not yet taken place, as we are going along as usual. But I am certainly sorry for the Chinese, they are so afraid. Last Friday some gamblers lost their game so got wrathy and tore up the gambling den. Everybody in that part of Kiungchow city thought sure looting was beginning and the people began running hither and yon. At least the gambling tale seems to be the true [one], others say some small boys flying a kite ran along the street and other people saw them running and began to run, too. You can see how tense the atmosphere is." As head of the mission girls' school, Margaret refused to allow any of the schoolgirls to go home "unless adult members of the family come for them." She ended her letter by saying, "The last Hong Kong papers say General Dong has won back some of the places he lost on the mainland, so it is hard to tell what the next developments will be."[65]

Chinese Refugees at the Mission Compound

If Margaret knew the missionaries could not guarantee Chinese protection from the hostilities, many Chinese felt otherwise. Hundreds fled to the mission compound as the political unrest continued and General Dong seemed to be losing on the peninsula. Margaret wrote to her brother, "I do feel so sorry for the Chinese....If there is a turnover it will work something like this: The soldiers here will rebel, loot the city and leave before the opposing army can come to stop them. The bandits who are waiting to pounce on the city will come and loot again before the new soldiers from the mainland come, and when the new soldiers come they will loot if there's anything left to loot. That sounds awful, but it is almost the way it works." She went on to relate that one night an elderly man had died and when his family lit firecrackers at the moment of death to accompany his spirit onward, as was the Chinese custom, the people in that part of the city panicked, thinking the fighting had begun. Margaret assured her family that the mission compounds had never been looted. With the unrest the missionaries were "besieged with people who want to come here to stay, and to bring their boxes of valuables here. We can't guarantee protection or freedom from looting in any case, certainly not if we take in goods, so we refuse to do that but say when trouble begins that women and children may come as refugees. It's not an easy thing to be in a sense responsible for the physical protection of one hundred and thirty girls and young boys in a time like this....So we just go on about our work as best we can when the pupils are so frightened. They can't go home as conditions in the villages are so bad because of bandits."[66]

As the threat of Dong's arrival on the island intensified, Margaret reported that the local people were selling all their fowl and livestock in Hong Kong before the city was blockaded. The missionaries found it hard to decide just what they could do. "The British consul [in Hoihow] and the American consul in Canton insist that it is 'extremely inadvisable' for women to remain in the interior and that the men do so 'at their own risk.'" Yet the missionaries also believed that the British consul "hasn't much interest in, or sympathy for, mission work, and being a Britisher he is worse off under present conditions than we Americans are." One of the primary concerns for the missionaries was how they would handle their money if Hong Kong were completely closed to them, as the mission funds and all personal monies were in British banks in Hong Kong. Margaret noted, "There are branches of two Chinese banks in Hoihow but we would hardly care to do much business with them in such unsettled times." She concluded, "I'm hoping things will adjust themselves more peaceably than we fear. The poor Chinese are simply panic-stricken. They are so fearfully afraid *of their own people*. It isn't a foreign power coming after them, it is merely Chinese from another place, and they'll suffer worse than they would from outsiders."⁶⁷ Later Margaret wrote that Governor Dong had returned to Hainan and "Wu Pei-fu [one of the northern leaders] has promised him help if he can hold the island three months."⁶⁸

Margaret occasionally remarked on the treaty relations the Westerners had with the Chinese. In December 1925 she expressed her opinion that she hoped the Gospel had its own appeal for the Chinese and that missionaries did not need to rely on the treaties, yet she also took advantage of the provisions of those treaties when the missionaries' property and personal possessions were threatened by military factions: "I have sent daddy a copy of the November *Chinese Recorder* this morning, as I thought you might both be interested in some of the statements about treaties, etc. It doesn't follow that I agree absolutely with all that is said, but certainly I would not want to think we were dependent entirely on government backing for permission to preach the Gospel and protection while doing so! Treaty revision is far more vital to business men than to missionaries, i.e., we missionaries would be less affected by it than business men would. Until China puts her own house in order no one can say much either way."⁶⁹

Some things continued on as usual, political turmoil notwithstanding. Margaret reported that "there was a big dragon idol festival on in Hoihow and even the day pupils from our school ran away to attend it." When Double Ten Day arrived in 1925, she wrote that "our pupils had a patriotic meeting in the afternoon on the lawn which went off very nicely and nothing at all disrespectful to foreign countries was mentioned."⁷⁰

Gradually the missionaries decided to return to the interior stations. Just after New Year's Day 1926 Margaret noted, "The political situation remains quiet at present. Dong's men are all back from the mainland. The general opinion seems to be that fighting is sure to come eventually but probably not before Chinese New Year. The anti-Christian literature is beginning to flood the country. Mr. Tappan received a set of five posters by mail yesterday, anti-Christian and anti-British." Missionaries in charge of schools faced a major problem in trying to decide whether or not to open them for the coming term. Margaret, who was still head of the girls' school in Kiungchow, and the Reverend David Tappan, who headed the boys' school, were in favor of opening the schools, but those engaged in other types of work did not share their view. Margaret knew that the decision might not be the missionaries' to make. "The government of course may make such drastic regulations about religious teaching we will have to close, or compromise, which we would not do, unless by having all our pupils take their Bible work outside of government school hours, which could be done."⁷¹

But the schools did open, despite "rumors that the troops have come over from the mainland and are landing in the south of the island, planning to come up...to the city. In that case I should judge we would have time to finish school before the excitement could reach here. I certainly hope so. The district magistrate has stamped our six higher primary diplomas without a word so I feel pretty good about that." Other rumors reported that the missionaries' servants would be forced to leave and that the schools would have to close, but despite everything the schools continued until their usual closing time just before Chinese New Year.⁷²

The unrest in China caused many missionaries to reassess their dealings with the Chinese and to turn over to them some of the control and money associated with the running of the missions. In 1926 the Hainan missionaries decided on a plan, which was being used by Presbyterian missions elsewhere in China, to turn all the evangelistic work and the elementary schools over to the presbytery to administer. Margaret thought, if the plan were accepted, it would "take away the idea that Christianity is just a foreign thing foisted on China from outside." She wrote, "I personally favor the idea very much. It will help the Chinese pastors and elders to see the difficulties of carrying on the work with the funds at our disposal."⁷³

Margaret undoubtedly had an easier time than some of the other missionaries in adjusting to giving the Chinese more control over affairs of the mission. Several years before the issue had become a political one, Margaret had written to her family about hearing an excellent sermon by Elder Ngou on the topic "Go and make disciples of all nations." She said, "Try as hard as we will, we foreigners never can express ourselves as fluently as the natives do. We may have better messages to give (which I doubt, in the case of men like [Mr.] Ngou and one or two of our other assistants) but we cannot make ourselves understood as well." When the new plans for the Hainan mission were adopted, six Chinese and five foreigners were selected to run the mission. Margaret informed her family, "This past week I've had one of the big experiences of my life in China. I was very much surprised to be one of those chosen to serve on the committee." She also thought that the new arrangement gave the Chinese insights into "the problems and difficulties we are up against in the matter of funds, etc."⁷⁴

Anti-Christian Activities

A great deal of uncertainty about the conduct of the schools still remained, even after the Chinese became more involved with the business of the mission. School was scheduled to resume after the Chinese New Year holiday, but Margaret admitted, "We still do not know whether we will have any pupils or not—there doesn't seem to be any open opposition but the method probably will be to scare the pupils and prevent them from returning by threats, etc." School did begin, though, and as usual the students straggled in over several weeks' time until more than one hundred were enrolled at the girls' school. Margaret thought the number was a good one "considering the anti-foreign and anti-Christian propaganda that continues to go the rounds. It's likely to be a more or less turbulent term, with so many student meetings being held in the city and so on. I do not personally approve of the girls going to all such meetings but see their point of view. They are brave to come to a foreign school anyway and if I do not allow them to take any part in outside affairs the school might even be closed."[75]

During the term the question of registering the schools with the Peking Bureau of Education plagued the missionaries, as they found the regulation that stated that "the purpose of the school shall not be the propagation of religion" to be a difficult one. Margaret acknowledged that "the next step may be that the government will close all schools not registered. They would have a right to do so but it would be manifestly unfair for Christian schools still have a great place in China." Yet she also recognized that since Hainan was still "under the rebel Kwangtung government instead of the real Peking government...we haven't any way of knowing what may come. If I can get through this term without a fracas I'll breathe a big sigh of relief."[76]

Margaret had been writing a news-filled, four-page letter to her family every Sunday since 1915 detailing her life in China, but on a rare occasion in 1926 she penned the lines, "There doesn't seem to be very much to write about this week, for a change! We've had quite an uneventful week considering the excitement we had been having." But then she revealed how much she had become accustomed to the political and economic turmoil of China: "The most excitement seems to have been over the questions of kerosene and quartering soldiers in the church. We've been paying the $3.00 tax on kerosene, as I wrote you. Now a new tax has gone into effect, or perhaps more properly speaking a new monopoly, whereby dealers were to be forced to sell their kerosene to the holder of the government monopoly at the old price. The compradore sold to us before the tax took effect and then the strike pickets caught the Ensigns' coolie carrying their kerosene, arrested him, and confiscated the oil. It's all been settled, but we are going to bring the rest of our kerosene up at daylight in covered baskets. It's ours and legally so, but the strike pickets apparently do not recognize the fact." The missionaries had further difficulties when the Reverend Mr. Tappan was informed that soldiers were going to be quartered in the church and vacant school buildings. The missionaries were required by American diplomatic personnel to have official dealings with the Chinese government through the British Consul on the island, and finally, with his help, succeeded in getting a letter from a Chinese government office forbidding the use of mission property for the quartering of troops. Margaret noted, "It's about time for a gunboat to come down on the periodic trips advised by the Commanding Officer when he was here before. The presence of a gunboat in the harbor might make some difference. It's hard to know what to do, we don't believe in forcing things by brute force, and yet the conditions in China are such that nothing else seems to have any effect."[77]

If Margaret considered those events to constitute a dull week, in her next letter she described "rather an exciting week in some ways." The Chinese army officers returned to seek permission to quarter their troops in the church, and again the missionaries refused. "The Commissioner of Foreign Affairs reiterates that he has given orders no soldiers are to come here, so we are hopeful." One of the difficulties was that the military had no funds to pay their troops and had decided "to allow gambling and opium smoking again" to compensate for the lack of pay. During the same week there was a mass meeting involving students and workmen. Some of the mission schoolgirls attended, and while they were at the meeting, Margaret, who had remained at the school, watched "three soldiers decorate the school buildings here...with anti-Christian posters...but made no attempt to prevent them. When they left they said the posters had been put up by the orders of those in authority and were to be left up, but we took them down ourselves. It was some job. I would like their recipe for paste! We had to scrape them off with pieces of broken glass, even though the paint was not yet dry." Anti-Christian sentiment had spread throughout the island, and "Christians in several villages have been told by the village people they would not be allowed to worship in the villages."[78]

Amid the turmoil the position of the missionaries was further complicated by the withdrawal of the British consul. He was reassigned to central China, and the British government had no plans to replace him. As the boycott of Hong Kong continued, Margaret thought that British steamers would stop calling at Hoihow, but she mentioned that, as there was still a French consul on the island, French steamers bound to and from Indochina would likely continue to call. (The French consul would act informally for the Americans.) She also noted that Chinese companies were adding steamers to service the port. To her family Margaret wrote, "Don't worry about me any more than you just have to, we know unpleasant times are likely to come but we are not expecting anything worse than inconvenience and the possible closing of our schools and hospitals. If we have to leave the island I'll cable you if it is at all possible, and we know everything works out in the end according to God's plans."[79] After the British consul withdrew, the American consul at Canton ordered women and children to leave the interior stations, but Katherine Schaeffer remained at Kachek until she was warned that bandits were after her. Then she departed to prevent an extraterritoriality incident.[80]

At Kiungchow the missionaries attempted to carry on as normally as possible. As Margaret remarked, "We've had our usual school schedule with the usual(!) one day out for patriotic meetings." She thought the mission school students were "much less keen than they were about going to these meetings, but I absolutely do not see where the students in the government schools get any time to study at all. We lose one day a week, and we don't pretend to go to all the meetings."[81]

Inevitably, the missionaries heard rumors about anti-Christian activities that were being planned, such as the one that was to observe the anniversary of the Shanghai and Canton affairs. Despite the uncertainty, Margaret's school continued as usual, "except for the organization in our schools here of a society to inquire into the teachings of Sun Yat-sen." As examinations approached, Margaret hoped they would not be interrupted, remarking, "Truly it is no easy job to be principal of a school in China these days."[82]

In the midst of the turmoil of anti-Christian activities and boycotts, disease struck in the form of cholera and dengue fever. Since Margaret was responsible for the girls in her school, she sent everyone who even seemed sick to the hospital and began a "swat the fly" campaign. She also tried to ensure that all water was boiled and all food thoroughly cooked.

"The devil pidgin flags indicating epidemics are flying both in Hoihow and Kiungchow—black triangles with white snaky looking figures on them and red streamers with bells attached. We have this much comfort, if the epidemic continues there will be little if any demonstration over May 30th and the Shanghai affair anniversary."[83]

Even though the interior mission stations had been evacuated, the missionaries were concerned about their property there. In May 1926 the Reverends H.H. Bousman and David Thomas went to Kachek to survey the situation. They discovered that the compound had been looted. Margaret wrote her family that she had lost "the head of my sewing machine...[but] they didn't disturb my books." Because the missionaries were protected by treaty rights, the men informed the local officials of the losses. "The district magistrate came over and saw the remains, he would only look at three rooms. He is responsible for protection of foreign property in his district so this mess probably means he'll be degraded in rank, at least. We hope so because if this affair goes unadjusted consequences are not hard to foresee for property in other places....Conditions of course are worse here in South China than in North China because of the Bolshevist slant we have down here." It was a worried Margaret who ended the month by writing, "There are to be only about a thousand soldiers left in Hainan, we hear, and that is not enough to keep the country in order."[84]

Despite the unrest the school year ended with examinations and the departure of the students for home. Because the Chinese were determined that all schools be registered with the government and not teach religion, Margaret, as head of an unregistered school, faced a dilemma about the diplomas for the girls who were finishing their course. Near the end of May she explained the problem to her family: "We are not a registered school, so the Board of Education can't stamp them, but the district magistrate always has done it. Just now I hardly like to call the magistrate's attention to ourselves to the extent of asking him to do it, as he's Japanese-trained, and none too friendly, I've been told, though we've had no dealings with him. But I hate to give the girls diplomas which are not stamped." Margaret did not succeed in getting the diplomas stamped by graduation, but after several weeks she figured out what to do. Her solution was typically Chinese: she used an intermediary and did not directly ask the government official to do what he was unable to do for political reasons. She wrote, "I finally succeeded in getting my three junior middle school diplomas stamped, through the kindness of a man for whom I wrote some treasurer's orders. The magistrate told this man when he asked that he couldn't do it publicly but would do it privately and we should buy the revenue stamps ourselves. That way I suppose there will be no record of it in the magistrate's office, since no fees were paid him, and I've asked one of our teachers to buy the revenue stamps at the regular office where they are for sale and no questions asked as to what they are to be used for. So now the girls will have the necessary stamps on their diplomas, should they decide to go to a government school later, even though our school is not yet registered." [85]

Boycotts

Throughout the political unrest Margaret relied on her letters from home to keep up her spirits, even though with cholera in the port, few ships stopped. After more than three weeks during which no mail arrived on or left the island, the trusty *Hanoi* provided the much-awaited letters from home: "There were over two hundred bags of mail for Hoihow on the *Hanoi*, and yesterday about a hundred bags came on the British boat so we are caught up with ourselves again." [86]

Even though school was not in session, the missionaries were most interested in the activities of their students who participated in the boycotts. A Students' Union was organized in Kiungchow that had delegates from all the higher primary and middle schools of the island. At one of its meetings "some anti-Christian sentiment [was] manifest at first but it seems to have been entirely quashed. Every one of three resolutions introduced which had anti-Christian statements in them was refused or changed. We had two girl delegates, one a Christian and one not a church member though I think a believer, and there was one delegate from the boys' school." Margaret knew that "the students could have made the situation practically impossible for us, as they have done in some other parts of China," but she could see "no reason why we should not open as usual in the fall, though our pupils are offered class promotion if they enter government schools and our upper grade enrollment may be smaller than usual." [87]

As the strikes continued, Margaret wrote that American goods purchased in Hong Kong were allowed to enter the port only if they had been shipped to Haiphong first. And as the turmoil persisted, Chinese government officials became the object of demonstrations. When the government tried "to levy a tax on every shop and house...the people were very much incensed at the idea...[and had a] parade in protest. Each person carried a small triangular paper banner with characters expressing their unwillingness, and each group had a larger white cloth banner on a bamboo pole with appropriate sentiments written thereon." The parade went past the mission compound in Kiungchow "to the old German consulate, where the governor and head civil officials had their quarters, and practically filled a town square. They yelled and beat their drums while their representatives interviewed the governor, and in the end he agreed not to collect the tax and the people dispersed. But now when there are robberies in Hoihow, as is happening more and more frequently, the police make no effort to interfere because they say the people would not pay the house tax. See how it works. The money is lost by the people either way—great government, isn't it?"[88]

Margaret went on that the Chinese government officials had moved into the city from the old consulate, fearing that the place was too accessible to robbers, and just after they moved the building was struck by lightning. "I expect the Chinese wish the officials had been in the place when the lightning struck! But the men in power down here belong to the moderate wing of the party and are not the rabid extreme communist wing, so we might fare far worse." She also expressed her concern for the Chinese government officers who were Western-trained, such as the local commissioner of foreign affairs, who knew "the government isn't fair to the common people, but...hadn't any military power" to rely on to make changes.[89]

Just how much the violence had become a part of her everyday life was evidenced when Margaret reported in mid-August 1926 that "bandits continue quite lively. A village just near this end of Hoihow was entered the other night and ten or more men were kidnapped and held for ransom. Miss Schaeffer said she heard guns popping last night. I was too sound asleep to notice, I guess." Robbers were interrupting the island's food supply, as it was impossible for farmers to get their produce to market. Margaret felt that the island would suffer economically for years if order were not restored quickly, and she wrote pessimistically, "There are only eight or nine hundred regular Cantonese soldiers in Hainan, nowhere near enough to police the place properly, and the anti-Canton party has soldiers that are difficult to distinguish from robbers. Then any village that wants revenge on a nearby village goes and takes it, because there is no real authority that will punish them." As the chaos continued, those living at Kiungchow learned that their compound at Kachek had been looted again and that people at the "Bolshevist school next door...are intimidating the servants and workmen."[90]

Sojourn in Hong Kong and on the Chinese Mainland

Margaret was a member of the Presbyterian China Council, and in May 1926 she learned her schedule for the meetings to be held in the fall. Board officials from New York were scheduled to hold a regional conference with representatives of the South China, Yunnan, and Hainan missions in Canton on 6-12 November, followed by a meeting for special delegates in Shanghai on 19-30 November. Then the regular meeting of the China Council was to take place.[91] As Margaret was preparing to leave Hainan for these meetings, she thought about security for her personal possessions and decided to "carry some [of my private letters] with me on my travels." She had "others in my trunk where they can be rescued if we leave Hainan precipitately again! Not that we anticipate any such event in the immediate future, but the last news in the papers is rather bad. What with the fall of Wuchang, Hankow and Hanyang and the killing of British officers up the Yangtze and British marines dispersing pickets in Canton things may be lively. Poor old China—we wonder and wonder what the outcome will be."[92]

Heading northward, Margaret stopped in Hong Kong, where she enjoyed the luxury of attending a church service without having to worry about being one of those in charge. "It will seem good to go to a real church service in English again, and a service where I have no responsibility for anyone but myself. It is a trifle hard to be in a truly worshipful spirit and keep an eye on seventy or eighty youngsters at the same time, and greet the latecomers as they come in. So I hope to enjoy services every chance I get while I am here."[93]

Hong Kong was also a place to get away from other problems. Often the Americans had encounters with the British in the colony, which were not always congenial, but many of the missionaries used the opportunities they had in Hong Kong to catch up on life outside of China. On this occasion Margaret went to see the latest movie, *Forty Winks,* in the company of another missionary and her "two men friends...from the Canadian Pacific offices." But the outing was not entirely pleasant, as Margaret reported. They "saw some American navy boys off the destroyers, just dead drunk. That always hurts me, and it was worse to be with two

Englishmen, because they always contend that the men who can get liquor whenever they want it never get dead drunk, as prohibition is bad! I surely am ashamed of Americans out here in the Orient when they get drunk because they do such a horribly thorough job of it....I feel sorry for the pastors of the Union Churches here in Hong Kong and Kowloon, as there are so many people in the colony who ought to be in church but never come near. There are so many temptations out here to help the young men especially go wrong, and the young men won't take advantage of the few influences that would help them go right."[94]

On the way to Shanghai Margaret engaged in a bit of business for one of the silversmiths in Hainan. Although she did not identify the craftsman, she sold wares for him worth about $150. In November Margaret wrote that in Shanghai "there are wars and rumors of wars around here all the time but...[the] city itself would not be very liable to attack. The arsenals outside the city would be taken but the armies are not near enough yet to cause any immediate flurry." While at the Council meetings she had an opportunity to get to know missionaries stationed throughout the country. After meeting some who had had to flee Szechwan, her opinion was that "altogether, we have fared much better in Hainan than some, in fact many other places, and of course fared worse than some places, too. In China a good deal depends on the individual governor or military official who may be in charge in your particular district."[95]

Margaret was skilled at spoken Hainanese, but that dialect was of little help to her in Shanghai. Yet she had lived in China for more than a decade and was familiar with Chinese customs, so she did not hesitate to travel around the city alone. After visiting the Mary Farnham School, she wrote to her family that "the city was partially under martial law so taxicabs could not run in the Chinese city and I went out by ricksha, about a forty-five minute ride. I did enjoy seeing the school so much, and am getting various ideas which can be adapted to our work in Hainan. This is the first time I've ever been able to visit mission schools in session and I'm enjoying it very much indeed. Miss [Annie R.] Morton insisted that I stay for tiffin with her and then I went back by tram car, all alone, which makes me feel quite proud of myself as it involved two or three different cars. I can follow directions if some one starts me out."[96]

It was on this trip that Margaret visited Nanking for the first time. Bang Hin-zong, the girl Margaret had sent to school in Hainan as a memorial to her grandmother, had journeyed north in 1924 to attend Ginling College in Nanking and, apparently inadvertently, had became involved in the country's political turmoil.⁹⁷ Margaret learned of the girl's plight in the Hong Kong newspapers and wrote home that "Hin-zong...was held in custody for several days in Nanking as a spy for the southern government, and...Dr. Tu (our Hainan doctor who was in the Kachek hospital a few years ago and is now the physician for the Baptist College in Shanghai) who was escorting her up from Shanghai was in prison, chained, for a week and nearly shot. You see the southern government hasn't yet taken Shanghai and Nanking, and because Hin-zong had a picture of the Kuomintang groups in our schools and some books they were sure she was a spy." Margaret went on to write that Hin-zong had been fortunate because the official who investigated her case had been kind to her and had allowed her to stay with his family, and Minnie Vautrin, who was head of Ginling College, had helped Hin-zong by assigning the college's Chinese secretary to deal with the official and to secure the release of the girl and the doctor. Dr. Tu had visited Margaret in Shanghai and told her the entire story. While in Nanking, Margaret visited a Presbyterian girls' school, the Bible Woman's Training School, and the theological seminary, where she met several other students from Hainan. She also visited Ginling and a missionary language school, where she found some new methods for learning Chinese "tremendously interesting."⁹⁸

Margaret used her free time in Shanghai for a trip to nearby Soochow, where she visited a Presbyterian school and then took "a wild and woolly fifty-minute ride through the crowded narrow streets and over the high arched bridges of the canals to the beautiful Laura Haygood Memorial School of the Southern Methodist Church." Then she visited a Southern Presbyterian school, where the assistant principal was a Hainanese woman, Sarah Liang, who had been educated in the United States.⁹⁹

While in Shanghai Margaret stayed at the Missionary Home, which was the permanent home for a few people but primarily served as accommodations for transients from the interior stations or those in the city for conferences. Margaret informed her family that at the home "prayers are held in the parlor every morning after breakfast and every night after dinner. You can go or stay as you like, most people stay unless in a big hurry, though they do run sometimes and speak of the back stairs from the dining room as the 'prayer escape.'" She also related that a major distraction had occurred one afternoon during the China Council meeting, which was held on the fifth floor of the Missions Building in a room overlooking the river. "One day when the tide was high and the northeast wind blowing a gale we watched the *President McKinley* trying to go around the bend of the river against wind and tide. She's a great big boat and simply couldn't make it under her own steam. Once the tide swung her clear around against a river wharf, crushing some small boats and killing several boat people. Ten thousand taels damage done to the wharf, I heard. The fifth attempt finally got the steamer around the bend, five tugs pulling her from the bow and other tugs fastened alongside. I'm afraid my mind wasn't entirely on Council business that afternoon, but neither was other people's. I had one advantage, my seat faced the windows so I didn't have to turn around every time I wanted to look out."[100]

Leaving Shanghai proved to be difficult, but finally the captain of the freighter *City of Tokio* agreed to take Margaret and the Reverend Wilbur Campbell as a favor so that they could be in Hainan for Christmas. The ship proved to be an interesting one, and Margaret reported, "The engineer told us about the cargo. Besides the four hundred live pigs on the foredeck, they were carrying tea, soy beans, tallow and sixteen hundred tons of eggs. Half of the eggs were frozen, shelled and in tins, the other half were chilled eggs, in cases, to be kept at 33 degrees. The refrigerating plant was interesting, the big engines in one room, where the temperature was 130 degrees, and the tanks of CO_2...were in the next room, covered with frost an inch deep, the temperature only ten degrees. The engineer said when the steamer got to the Red Sea it was so hot the men often like to get in the storage tank room to cool off." Arriving in Hoihow, Margaret found that there were still difficulties in getting freight cleared for landing, so she smuggled her purchases ashore as hand baggage, which was not checked by the student strikers. "The steamer men and the Customs men simply do not see it, they understand the situation and are glad to help us out." Her contraband included "twenty boxes of milk, sugar, flour, and canned goods for various people in the mission, three boxes of apples, two baskets of potatoes, our own baggage, and three heavy cases containing Mr. Stinson's tombstone."[101]

More Anti-Christian Activities

Christmas 1926 could hardly have been the type of holiday Margaret anticipated when she became a missionary. She spent the day in Kiungchow with the other single women, since "there was so much anti-Christian disturbance in the air...[and] oodles of anti-Christian posters were pasted up all over Hoihow—not anti-foreign, especially, other than the usual

'Down with Imperialism.' " The schoolgirls had awakened the missionaries about 3:30 A.M. by singing carols, and the church service was held at eight o'clock, when "there would be less likelihood of disturbance, but no [protesters] appeared." About noon a "big anti-Christian parade went by our compounds...[with] one continuous yell of 'Down with Christianity' for at least twenty minutes, while some thousand pupils and workmen marched by with banners and paper flags, scattering anti-Christian tracts broadcast. Some soldiers brought up the rear, and there was no violence and no attempt to enter the compound. We stayed out of sight and allowed no pupils to hang around the gates. The Commissioner of Foreign Affairs had assured us no violence would occur, but a mob spirit is never very certain and we are always careful to give no occasion for trouble when parades are on. We all breathed easier when it was over. There was no trouble in Hoihow, either, just some more posters pasted on our compound wall while the service was being held."[102]

By February 1927 political conditions in Hainan, associated with the Northern Expedition on the mainland and the growing anti-Christian attitudes throughout China, were such that the missionaries were again advised to come out from Kachek and Nodoa. Several of them decided to go to Hong Kong, while others, who were remaining at the port, sent trunks to Hong Kong for safekeeping. It was again the *Hanoi* that carried the missionaries and their belongings, although Margaret remarked, "The captain...is terribly crusty...and...nearly had spasms while the baggage was being taken on. I'll admit there *was* a lot."[103]

It was not only the Presbyterians who were threatened by the political unrest as the French Catholic missionaries in Hoihow also found the situation difficult. In one of her rare references to the Catholic mission, Margaret mentioned that the Catholic missionaries were sending "the Chinese sisters and ten or a dozen of the oldest orphans off on the boat, too. They did not want a repetition of the Foochow affair, which started at the Catholic foundling home there. Some one saw twenty-seven bodies laid out in the morgue, during a cholera epidemic, and said their eyes had all been removed....People on the streets here are talking about the orphanage here, saying so many girls are taken there every year and never heard of afterwards. As a matter of fact,...the babies taken there are those abandoned by their parents because they are sick so it is no wonder they die. And, too, when the ones who live are grown they are taken to Haiphong or Hanoi or Fort Bayard, where French is spoken, and married to young Catholic men. When we were in Haiphong we met a girl clerk in a store who had been raised in the Hoihow orphanage. We can help the sisters out a little bit by counteracting some of the stories. The Chinese say they know where the girls in the American school are, they are teachers and principals in other schools. Of course, the comparison is unfair because we do not take babies in our schools." [104]

The situation at the Catholic orphanage became extremely tense. Margaret wrote, "There was a lot of excitement at the French orphanage over on the south side of Hoihow, apparently an attempt to imitate the Foochow affair. A story was started that someone was seen coming from there with two brainless, eyeless babies in a basket. About a hundred women armed with sticks and stones went to the orphanage and demanded to see the babies. Père Savina and Père Juliet managed to quiet that crowd but about 11:00 a mob of men, women, and children went there and did considerable damage to the wall and the garden before the French Consul could get soldiers and police down to scatter them. Fortunately no one was hurt." [105]

Following the incident at the French orphanage, the Commissioner of Foreign Affairs and the military authorities issued proclamations "saying all foreign lives and property were to be respected." Margaret noted that "the riot didn't concern us Protestants at all and we are assured time and again that we will have no trouble." The Presbyterians had decided not to try to open their schools because of the political unrest, and Margaret, at least, sensed that the situation was more serious than previous troubles they had experienced. She wrote, "Hainan is not a very good place to get away from in a hurry. Of course if serious trouble breaks out up above a British gunboat will come for the acting consul and his wife and the Britishers in the Customs and I presume we would be ordered to go along. However, we are hardly anticipating anything so drastic." She noted that "the newspaper items aren't any too reassuring and we heard that news was so serious that Hong Kong papers were censored and Hong Kong itself might be put under martial law, presumably to prevent any trouble from Chinese [there]. Pickets seem to be beginning work again." [106]

While all of this was happening, some Chinese women were modernizing themselves. In Kiungchow one afternoon Margaret discovered that "the girls are having a regular spasm of bobbing their hair. One girl whom I've been helping some wrote me yesterday that she had cut her hair for three reasons—it was a saving of time, it was a saving of money (hair-oil, combs, etc.) and it was more hygienic! I don't object if they cut their hair, but have always said their fathers and mothers should have a say about it."[107]

Preparing to Flee

As the unrest intensified, Margaret noted that conditions for both Chinese and foreigners in Hainan were not good and that many people were trying to leave the island. By February 1927 the mission had only three people at Nodoa, the Kachek station had been totally evacuated, and only nine people were left in Hoihow and Kiungchow. Margaret, apparently weary from the tension, momentarily forgot that she was a guest in China when she reported, "Hoihow is crowded with people leaving for the South Seas. Some five thousand tickets have been sold and about two thousand people have left on the Siam steamer which came in a few days ago. I'll be glad when they get away, the streets are just crowded with them and they gamble, drink and go to the dogs generally while they are waiting."[108]

The Chinese government had ordered the mission school to register or close, so the missionaries paid off their teachers and rented them the buildings to run their own schools "with government curriculum but with Christian teachers." Margaret recognized how difficult it was for them as "the anti-Christian and anti-foreign element scold them and say they are running dogs of the foreigners just the same. As the teachers themselves say frankly they are not against us but it is very hard to make it appear that they aren't. I tell you it isn't easy for them these days, patriotism has to be the great thing and religion or education or family or anything else does not demand any consideration. Parents are beginning to get disgusted though and I do hope the saner elements will soon get control. Students in government schools have gone around smashing idols and urging people not to believe in any god at all and that's about the surest road to destruction I know of for individuals, social groups or government. I'd far rather see a person ignorantly but sincerely worshipping a false god than brazenly casting aside all spiritual values, you can win the former to a true faith in a true God, but it's mighty hard to reach the latter especially if he once professed faith in some religion and fell back....There are plenty of government proclamations out about protecting foreign lives and property and we really have very little annoyance except now and then some yelling."[109]

As the tensions continued, Margaret began packing up the furniture of the missionaries and sending it out of Hainan. Surveying her own possessions, she gave her portable phonograph to the bride and groom when she was invited to a Christian wedding. "As it was a gift to me I didn't want to sell it, it was hardly expedient to take it back to America as baggage, and I'd rather see people like these have it than have it seized if our property should be looted and go nobody knows where, as my sewing machine did." The groom was a widower who had taught at the mission school, and the bride was a graduate of the girls' school in Kachek. Margaret described the wedding to her mother: "The bride had a lovely pale blue brocaded silk suit with apricot tints in the brocading, and her white silk cap-shaped veil was caught with a wreath of white chrysanthemums, but we nearly fell over when we saw the groom, he had on a high silk hat, frock coat and grey striped trousers, evidently a rented costume, I should judge. He must have seen foreign church weddings in Peking or Hangchow, to get himself up in quite so much style."[110]

In early March 1927 Margaret noted that the Hainan mission was "asking the China Council to hold our furloughed missionaries in the States temporarily. If we on the field have to go to Hong Kong why call more people back to stay there too? Anyhow, as long as Kachek is unoccupied we are not short of workers." The tenuous situation continued. On "the second anniversary of Sun Yat-sen's death...there were big patriotic parades in Hoihow and Kiungchow and we foreigners kept off the streets as a matter of expediency....A three-funnel Japanese cruiser sailed in here the other day, to the great delight of the Japanese friends. It was only a passing visit but the Chinese were greatly excited when they saw it coming in. We were only relieved that it wasn't a British or American gunboat coming to order us off."[111]

China's political turmoil was soon to be a faraway problem to Margaret. Her regular furlough was scheduled to begin on 1 July 1927.[112] Since the missionaries were unable to continue their work, the China Council decided to send home early those who were due for furloughs within six months. To her mother, Margaret wrote, "From the way it looks now you may see me very soon after you see this letter. Authorization has come from Shanghai for all whose furloughs are due before August 31 to leave immediately." Margaret had many things to do before she could leave, and she worked hard at finishing up the mission accounts: "The station turnover for the year was something over $71,000 so there has been a good deal of book work to do."[113]

Margaret left the island hurriedly. Repeating the cable she had sent two years earlier from Haiphong, she sent only the word "Safe" to her family from Hong Kong on 13 April. The Moningers soon received a letter from the Board of Foreign Missions informing them that "a cable received on Saturday April 23 states: 'Leaving on the 23rd, Seattle, Washington, Miss M.M. Moninger.' The boat is the *President Taft* due on May 9. This, we are sure, will be most welcome news. We shall hope for a good voyage and safe arrival on the scheduled date." [114]

En route home Margaret cabled her family from Kobe, "Seattle Taft May Ninth, Margaret." Later from the boat she wrote her sister Dorothy, asking, "Did my cable from Kobe ever get to the folks? Somehow I can't quite trust the Japanese though I don't know why I should feel that way." She also mentioned that "the steamers are crowded full. I was lucky to get passage so soon. There are about a hundred missionaries on board travelling 'first class steerage,' sleeping in bunks down in the steerage but having first class dining saloon and deck privileges. They are paying $200 gold where the regular rate is $345 from Shanghai. I have a bed in a good cabin." Margaret knew of the seriousness of the political climate in China and wrote, "We are all very anxious for news of the situation in China. There is a radio news sheet put out every morning but it gives no Chinese news. We hear the captain forbids it on account of the Chinese crew on board, lest trouble should be started. Perhaps it is wise, but we surely are anxious for news ourselves." [115]

From Seattle she cabled her parents in Iowa, "Arrived safely so glad for letters start east tomorrow...Love Margaret." [116] And so Margaret arrived home safe from the turmoil that was convulsing China, but she would have only a visit. At its conclusion she went back again to Hainan.

CHAPTER FOUR

Come Rejoicing
1928–1935

MARGARET ORIGINALLY PLANNED to use her second furlough to work on a doctorate at Grinnell College.¹ After arriving home, however, she decided to accept a position teaching Latin and mathematics at the high school in Washington, Iowa, in part because of the financial difficulties the Board of Foreign Missions was facing.² While employed as a teacher, Margaret was placed on the rolls of furloughed missionaries by the Board, yet she found that the Board continued to rely on her for various tasks.

In February 1928, for example, Board members found themselves preparing for the annual General Assembly of the Presbyterian Church without an up-to-date account of the Hainan mission's work. In a somewhat frantic letter to Margaret, Frances Graham asked for "six or seven double-spaced pages within the next week." Margaret responded that a December letter she had received from the Reverend Paul Melrose indicated that the official mission report was being prepared and that her information was not complete, she had no typewriter, she feared she was usurping Mr. Melrose's prerogatives, and she was entertaining a visiting Methodist missionary from Argentina but that she would try to send something by the end of the week. The following week Margaret dispatched a twelve-page handwritten report to the Board in New York, apologizing for not having been able to type it. She was told that her handwritten report was "much more legible than some typed reports."³

Leaving Hainan in the turmoil that swept China in 1927, Margaret, whom one of her colleagues called the closest the mission ever had to an official historian, carried home a box of the early records of the mission, lest they be lost if left behind. Several letters about them to the Board of Foreign Missions resulted in the records being sent to the Board for placement in their archives.[4]

Margaret's second furlough was marked by tragedy when her mother died in March 1928 following surgery, leaving Margaret without her strongest supporter. The changed circumstances in her family led her to extend her furlough for a second year, so that she might remain close to home, even though, she wrote, "neither my father nor I contemplate my permanent withdrawal from the field." Margaret also acknowledged that the "chaotic conditions in China, the closing of the schools in Kiungchow, and the number of people now on the field [made it seem] as if there was very little, if any, need for me there just now."[5]

By 1929 Margaret and the Board agreed that she should return to Hainan. Arriving on the island in August, she was first assigned to the girls' school at Nodoa, but in the following year she moved back to Kachek to head the girls' school there. Previously, Margaret and her father had corresponded only when a fifth Sunday occurred in a month, but now she adopted a new system, writing "to her father every Sunday and to her sisters and brother in rotation to the oldest on the first Sunday of the month, to the next one the next Sunday and so on."[6] Most of the letters that survive were addressed to her father or to her youngest sister, Louise, who was living at home. But without her mother to save them, fewer of Margaret's letters were kept, so the details of her life in China in the years 1929-42 are not as extensive as those from earlier years. Yet the few letters that do survive indicate that it was in her third term of service in Hainan that her career as a missionary was fulfilled. She was fluent in the language and accustomed to life in Hainan, and she now worked as an itinerating missionary traveling to places in the Kachek region while the women she had educated earlier ran the mission school. During these years Margaret assumed positions of leadership in the Hainan mission, representing her colleagues at the meetings of the China Council in Shanghai and at the general assembly of the Church of Christ in China. At this time, if her life were described in terms of a hymn it would be *Bringing in the Sheaves,* for the farmer's daughter from Iowa was truly reaping the benefits of the career she had chosen for herself. Margaret was essentially a happy person, content with the life she led and glad to be in China, thus in her third term of service she would truly "Come Rejoicing."

Dr. Esther Morse Joins the Mission

In 1930 Margaret was joined in Kachek by Esther Morse, M.D., the only woman medical doctor ever to serve the Hainan mission and the only woman at the mission who was better educated than Margaret. Dr. Morse was to live with Margaret for a number of years, and from the doctor's diary and letters home a view of Margaret emerges that is quite different from the one presented in Margaret's own letters. Despite the tensions of living in the same house, the two women developed a deep respect for each other. Dr. Morse hated the gossip of the isolated mission compounds, so rather than voicing her own complaints to the other missionaries, she wrote them to her father, brother, and sister. Because of their living arrangements, Dr. Morse often complained about Margaret in her letters. Margaret's few written references to Dr. Morse, in contrast, are all positive ones.

Margaret and Dr. Morse first met in Hong Kong when the doctor was on her way to Hainan and Margaret was en route to a China Council meeting in Shanghai. Dr. Morse's first impression was that "Miss Moninger is a woman of about 35 or so, blue eyes, dark wavy hair, tendency to plumpness but with well-turned ankles and feet, jolly and likeable." In a letter written a few days later she added a few years to Margaret's age: "Miss Moninger is about 40, I judge....She is very pleasant and capable....She is a very fine person to be with." When Margaret returned from Shanghai, the doctor noted, "Dr. Bercovitz brought Miss Moninger down to Kachek on Saturday and she is making things 'step' around here now. She's from the middle west and has more energy than anyone else here almost." A few months later Dr. Morse wrote, "Miss Moninger is a very strong-minded woman under a soft and rather appealing exterior. Her judgment is good, too, I would say, regarding the problems we face here."[7]

This assessment by a new colleague of Margaret indicates how much the mission had become a part of her life. When she returned from her furlough, she traveled to Nodoa by car, and in her first letter to her family she remarked, "This was the first long trip I've ever made in Hainan by car. Our chariot was an ancient Ford chassis with a wooden top. The driver, another Chinese man and I occupied the front seat....In the back of the car the board seats run lengthwise. One was folded up against the side of my baggage and some other freight stacked in. Six or seven Chinese occupied the other side. There were six or seven inner tubes tied on one side, all patched up and mostly needing more. A five-gallon tin of water, one of gas and one of oil were tied on the running board along with freight. Each car carries one or two mechanics and a coolie along also as part of their equipment." The driver was willing to continue after dark, so Margaret arrived in Nodoa about 9:30 P.M., "surprising the Melroses very much as the letter I sent telling them I was coming didn't arrive till this morning."[8]

At Nodoa Margaret assumed the duties of station treasurer and continued her practice of serving as a banker, issuing money orders for Chinese people who requested them, on one occasion writing five hundred dollars' worth at one time. Since counterfeiting was always a problem, Margaret had to ring "every one of those dollars...to see if it were good, but Dr. Tong, who brought the men, rang some of them for me." Money orders were not the only banking service the missionaries provided. Margaret informed her sister that "before [Mother] Melrose left she had accepted a thousand dollars for safekeeping for the local magistrate. The money was supposed to be a reward for the capture of the leading communist in this region. The money was to be here 'only a little while' but it was here six months before we succeeded in turning it over to the magistrates' representatives. I doubt very much if it is ever used for its original purpose but that doesn't concern us." Margaret remarked to her father that she was "glad I enjoy [treasury] work, some people find [it] an awful bore and have lots of trouble with it but I like it. And somebody has to do it. I have had my turn at all kinds of it here now, treasurer of each station, treasurer of Administrative Board, and mission agent." She had learned some Chinese skills to help her with these tasks, writing once that she used an abacus for addition and subtraction but had not learned to do multiplication and division on it.[9]

Even though she was highly skilled at languages, Margaret did not speak the dialects used around Nodoa at the time of her arrival, but three months later she reported, "I listened to the elders examining the girls and women for church membership and was surprised to see how much I understood of what they said as of course they were speaking Hakka." A month later she was wanting "to get at my Hakka and Limko study." Margaret became the supervisor of language study for the new missionaries who arrived in Hainan in 1930. Living in Kachek in late 1930, she was supervising the work of the Reverend and Mrs. Arthur French and Dr. Morse. Dr. Morse noted that Margaret "has too much energy to suit me and as our Language Study supervisor keeps on our trail and insists we do certain things and study in certain ways and at certain times, which is arduous for me. I hope, when I'm in my own room, to study more as I choose. She doesn't want us to even think of language study at night and then fills the rest of our day so full there is no other time and then 'jumps' us if we do try to study at night. So lately I've just folded my hands and said 'All right, Language—soak in if you can' and I'm not studying a bit except when the Chinese teacher is here. I hope, as I say, to do differently when I have the privacy of my own room."[10]

When Margaret had to go to Shanghai to a meeting of the China Council, Dr. Morse wrote home, "While I'm alone...I'm not leading as ordered a life as I probably would if [Margaret] were here....She thinks I shouldn't spend much time at the hospital, even this year, so I go to the hospital every day for an hour or two. My teacher says of the situation, when the mother-in-law is away the daughter-in-law doesn't work as hard!"[11] Eventually the two women worked out most of their differences, and Margaret's frequent trips to do itinerating work and to attend meetings at the other stations and on the Chinese mainland gave them time apart.

Chinese nationalism, which had caused much unrest in the years before 1927, had diminished in importance in Hainan. The Chinese schoolboys had been upset in 1920 because they had to postpone their Independence Day celebration from Sunday to Monday to accommodate the missionaries' beliefs about the Sabbath, but in 1929 their younger counterparts in Nodoa postponed their celebration from Thursday to Friday so that it would coincide with the local market day! Margaret observed, "We have had vacation all this week except Monday and Saturday because of Chinese Independence Day. Thursday was the day but because the market day was Friday they had their celebration then. Everything went off very nicely. The lanterns were the prettiest I have ever seen although of course the procession was not nearly so long as it usually is in either Kiungchow or Hoihow....*Nobody but the school children seem to pay any attention to Independence Day* [emphasis mine]. We are to have a special patriotic service at church this morning, arranged by the Church of Christ in China, and a patriotic service at Christian Endeavor."[12]

Margaret's third term of service was a relatively quiet one, compared with the years 1915-27, but as 1929 ended she wrote again of violence and the uncertainty it caused for the mission schools. "We don't know yet whether we can open school for another term or not...[after Chinese New Year]. The war situation doesn't bother us much locally except that lawless elements are always more bold when there is no central authority. Some soldiers executed rather a spicy manoeuver last Saturday and took possession of Hoihow and Kiungchow for the new government. Our local military man went out to Hoihow and enrolled himself and his men under the new party and came back with his same rank—so easy as that it is to change sides out here." In January 1930 the missionaries at Nodoa temporarily evacuated the station when some five hundred Cantonese soldiers took the town.[13]

Later, in the spring, Margaret wrote of a "little trouble around Hoihow and Vunsio," which included "burning of ferry boats, cutting of telegraph poles, and the like, all of which seems to be part of the May 1 red demonstrations planned everywhere." How little Margaret understood of the ramifications of Chinese politics was evident in a letter she wrote in August 1931 to the Board of Foreign Missions detailing events in a nearby district. Margaret wrote that one of the districts near Kachek had "gone communist" and the land was being divided among party members. "Rightful owners who do not enroll in the party have no share at all and are forced to flee. They do it so meekly, it seems to me, but I don't know what else they can do as authorities do not interfere." The soldiers and the Communists, she wrote, had fought a battle in which "the soldiers lost about a dozen men killed and as many wounded, the communists many more so we hear. I tried to find out which side won. 'The communists lost more men.' 'But who won?' 'Why the side that lost fewest.' Another man said, 'No, the ones who ran last.' I asked, 'Which side ran?' And nobody knew, although the trouble occurred two or three days ago in a precinct of this district and not more than twenty miles away! Results should have been reported to officials and military headquarters here. So it goes and I see no hope of change for the better unless a real responsible government is set up or the substantial farmers and merchants take things into their own hands and get busy."[14]

Nearly a year passed before Margaret again mentioned any trouble. In July 1932 she and Dr. Morse were the only foreigners at the mission compound, as the others were away at a meeting. "All the soldiers left and the market was much afraid of an attack by Reds. So it seemed wiser for Dr. Morse and me to go out to the market chapel to sleep nights and we have been doing so. I understand soldiers are expected today but it remains to be seen whether they really come or not. Some did come in Thursday evening and we stayed out here that night and then the next day they were withdrawn as suddenly as they had come." Dr. Morse also wrote home about sleeping in the street chapel, but she indicated that Margaret did not like doing it and was, in fact, wracked by doubts about the wisdom of it. The doctor said, "On the advice of the Chinese on the compound Miss M. and I went to the market chapel for the night. Wednesday was a quiet day and no soldiers came in so we slept in the chapel again. Thursday about 5:00 P.M. soldiers returned, only to be removed again on Friday afternoon so we went out again last night....Miss M. has been in a curious state of mind about going to the market chapel to sleep, these few days and nights. She knows that the responsible Chinese feel we should go, that it is in accord with the wishes of the men of the mission (who are not here now, it is true, but they'd want us to go, if they *were* here) and it is in line with consular advice. But there are several old Chinese Christians who say 'Why do you run away? Can't you trust the Lord to care for you? What is there to be afraid of? etc. etc.' and it gets Miss M.'s goat, completely. Whatever the market people think they are most kindly and courteous to us." [15]

Dr. Morse wrote several weeks later that Margaret "wants to cooperate with the Chinese and when the most responsible Chinese on the compound told us it was safer to go, we decided to go, of course. But old Elder Li accused us of being afraid and of 'running.'...Miss M. takes Elder Li's comments very much to heart and grieves because she *is* running away. She says she prays about it but what good does it do when you know you *are* running away. And every person whom we meet while we are en route to the market says, 'Are you going to market?' the regular accustomed greeting, but she construes a meaning of reproach into that simple greeting. And frets about it. I don't care to go either, but Elder Li or anyone else needn't think they can buffalo me if I have made up my mind that I'm doing what is the right as far as I can divine it. Miss M. admits that we ought to obey the responsible Chinese but says we are cowards and quitters just the same. So her state of mind isn't happy when we *must* go to the market. I can't see why one must put up with such worry and stewing. It really seems a lack of faith, for one thing and a lack of self-control, in another way." [16]

At the same time Margaret wrote about sleeping in the street chapel, she reported that on the way back from a village wedding she "saw a lot of soldiers coming back from an expedition against the Reds. They had nine captives and three big Red battle flags they had gotten. I wasn't where I could see the symbols on the flags, but the pastor says the hammer and sickle are what they always do have, and that is the regular Soviet Russian flag. I certainly would have liked to verify that fact with my own eyes." She also reported seeing twenty prisoners being transported to Kiungchow for trial, and she was "of the opinion that some will probably be executed, but the authorities are proclaiming amnesties in many places."[17]

In July 1932 Margaret reported that airplanes had dropped bombs that sank a gunboat in Hoihow harbor. She and Dr. Morse were in Kachek when the event occurred, but they heard rumors that "the gunboat had been sunk which really was true, and also that the highest building in Hoihow, a five story 'hotel' used for military headquarters, had been hit and that part of it had collapsed, which was not true." Again because the women were alone at the mission compound and no soldiers were in Kachek, "the acting head of the local militia sent word to us that there were some rumors of communist threats for that night and that we were to go out to the chapel to sleep...so we did." The Reverend David Thomas returned and stayed one night at the compound while the women slept in the street chapel, and then all of them left for Hoihow, which was somewhat safer.[18] Margaret's next comment about the political situation came in December 1933, when she thought that civil war was about to break out. She feared that Hainan would be dragged into the fray when Canton became involved.[19]

Margaret as an Itinerating Missionary

Margaret spent much of the time during her third term in Hainan as an itinerating missionary, which freed her from work at the school and gave her the opportunity to travel to places around Kachek she had never visited before. In addition, she was able to observe aspects of Chinese life she had not previously seen, with the result that her letters contain much rich detail of the lifestyles of the local people.

Margaret developed a more anthropological interest in the local customs, and she was less likely than before to condemn them as superstitious. She and Dr. Morse went to a big idol festival in the market to see the images on display. "They put up a pavilion about twenty feet square and thirty feet high, roofed with matting and enclosed on three sides with matting. The images were made of papier-mâché, with paper clothes. There were four fairly good-sized ones on the front of the stage, that was about eight by sixteen feet in size, and two great big hideous ones that grinned from each end of the platform. All along the walls, in three tiers, were about a hundred and thirty small images in groups representing various historical and legendary figures. The whole thing cost about $500 silver and was burned the last night of the festival in honor of the spirits who have no one to worship them, that is people who died and have no sons or other descendants to carry on ancestor worship. Kachek market is supposed to have a festival every seven years in honor of the boatmen who died as their junks were caught in storms while bringing goods in from Canton and other places." [20]

While on an itinerating trip to a city near Kachek, Margaret and several of the other missionaries witnessed a dragon dance that was being held despite the fact that the district magistrate did not favor the celebration because there were rumors of Communists in the area and very few soldiers were around. "The streets were jammed full of people and they were just beginning the dragon procession....They had two 'dragons.' They are made of bamboo frames, the body of circles some eighteen inches in diameter, the circles held together by bamboo and covered with cloth painted to represent the dragon [with] twenty-eight men holding up one of them, the men walking about eight or ten feet apart." Idols, symbolic figures, and children "dressed in robes of ancient style" completed the procession.[21]

Kite flying was a Chinese pastime that always interested the foreigners, and Margaret noted that regional differences existed among the kites on the island. "Kachek market isn't very much on flying big kites, as Hoihow is. A Hoihow firm with a branch in Kachek recently brought a big 'centipede kite' down here. The head or face was like a big tiger's head and the body part was over a hundred paper circles, perhaps three feet in diameter, strung four feet apart on a fairly heavy rope." After several days of attempts to get the kite airborne, it finally "went up a ways but fell in the river just back of the compound and that's the end of it."[22]

That the Hainan missionaries had made some cultural accommodations to China was evident in March 1935, when Margaret related that she had accompanied Pastor Ngou, and the Reverends Thomas and French "to a village to have a Christian ceremony of breaking ground for a new house....It was interesting to me to hear Pastor Ngou talking about how Christians did not fear the powerful demon the Chinese always think will be disturbed when ground is broken....I have never been at this village before although I know the family. The husband is the man who was to act as go-between to collect the ransom money for Mr. Byers when the plan was of course to kidnap but not to kill him. The village people have said he can never come back home. The man and his son are in Singapore, the old mother and the wife in the village."[23]

There were aspects of Chinese life that the missionaries could not or would not adapt to, as was evidenced when Margaret described a school field meet, noting, "There's one trait in the Chinese I dislike. When a boy sees he can't get a place in a race that counts—first, second or third—he just quits running and walks off the track. Of course to us Americans that's a 'yellow streak' and we try to get the boys to the place where they'll finish the race even if they don't get a prize."[24]

On itinerating trips Margaret observed other aspects of Chinese life, as when she commented on the food that the Chinese ate, which she shared. On one occasion she encountered a man who was "skinning a big rat. As the Chinese do not ordinarily eat rats, in this section of the country, I asked why. He said he was fixing it for his grandchildren to roast over the fire and eat so they wouldn't have boils! And then the small boys skewered it with pieces of bamboo and did roast it and I saw the youngest grandson, four or five years old, devouring his share with great delight a little later." Small boys also captured Margaret's interest on another itinerating trip, when they gathered to watch her write. She reported, "One feels sure he could write English if he only had a pencil like the one I am using, and another, in great superiority, is assuring him that even a pencil won't make him able to write English if he doesn't know how anyway."[25]

It was also during this time that Margaret made her only trip to the south end of Hainan, where Carl C. Jeremiassen, who had originally interested the Presbyterians in establishing a mission in Hainan, had worked in the late 1890s. Accompanied by Arthur French and Alice Skinner, Margaret visited the only Muslim village on the island.[26]

Having grown up on a midwestern farm, Margaret was keenly interested in the crops the Chinese grew, and many of her letters contained references to the weather and its effect on the farmers of the island. Rice was Hainan's major crop, of course, and the weather could create serious problems if drought or rain came at the wrong times. In January 1934 Margaret informed her father that the fields were so dry that the rice could not be planted but that in many places six or eight families were joining together to make big bamboo wheels to irrigate their fields. Later she noted, "Rice is rather a temperamental crop. It took me a long time to come to that conclusion but I really believe it is true. If conditions aren't just about right for it all the time it doesn't make a crop at all."²⁷

Although Margaret, the foreigner, was often a source of curiosity on her trips, she frequently was able to gain at least as much information about the people she saw as they did about her. Once while itinerating near Kachek, she spent the night in a village "which seems to be dying out." There were vacant, crumbling houses, and many of the men had been "killed by the Reds or...gone to the South Seas, and I haven't been in a village for a long time where there were so few children." She also reported that on the trip "we came past the salt pans and salt kilns and I was interested to see the way they 'cook' the salt. I haven't all the processes in mind except that they dry the salt-water soaked sand in built up 'wells' and then scrape off the crusted top and pour water through it, drain off the salty water and boil it. The boiling pans are made of kerosene tins nowadays, about thirty tins to make one some fifteen feet in diameter and six to eight inches deep. One cooking takes about twelve to fourteen hours and yields 300 to 400 catties of salt. The duty on salt is quite high—$2.10 a 100 catties. A soldier from the salt gabelle goes to each kiln as the salt is to be taken out and sold, weighs and stamps with a big wooden stamp each small round basket ready to be carried away, and the market authorities are careful to buy only stamped baskets." Margaret hoped to write an article on salt for the *Lingnan Science Journal,* as the editors "seem quite willing to print everything I send them." The article appeared in 1934.²⁸

One innovative Chinese farmer had asked Margaret to obtain some oat seeds from her father, which she did, but the oats did not grow properly in Hainan. Later, while out itinerating, she spent a night at the man's house and described his farming techniques to her father: "He has quite a 'garden' as he calls it, which he has worked for over twenty years. Originally he planted it to cardamon seed but the price of that fell. Then he grubbed it out and planted rubber trees. He went to Singapore and saw how rubber really should be gotten from the trees, and came back and took out all his trees. He says that the ground there in his garden was not suited to rubber trees and the yield was far less than it should be for the expense of the garden. Now he has pineapples, coffee, carambolas, the trees whose nuts yield oil for the best quality hair oil, sweet potatoes, several varieties of peppers, etc. and especially guavas."²⁹

Automobiles had arrived in Hainan by the 1930s and had radically altered the missionaries' style of itinerating, but sometimes the cars proved a difficult means of transportation. In 1934 Margaret and several other missionaries went by car to a nearby town. Rain delayed them, but they finally set off with chains on the car. Then they "had difficulty getting on the ferry to cross the Kachek river, and almost thought the car was so dead we could not go. Then we got off the ferry and had to cross a bayou so deep they covered the radiator with matting before they let us start across and two men stood on either side of the wheeltrack so Mr. Thomas would know where to drive. It took us nearly three hours to go thirty-two miles, part of the road was pretty bad." She also related that the "lovely ten-span concrete bridge" that had been built the previous summer was now "just terrible to see....Three sets of pillars have settled and the bridge is buckled in two places....They say the contractor is sitting in prison in Kiungchow and deserves to, very evidently he didn't put his pillars down to bedrock. Mr. Thomas and Mr. French both think the sections could be raised and put back in place...if sufficient leverage could be gotten." On the return trip "we ran off into a ditch and had to have men help lift the car back onto the road and push it through the deep water and over a bridge, and it took a while for the engine to dry out so it would start. We got to the Kachek river about 8:00 but had to leave the car and the coolie there as the river is so high cars aren't being ferried across."[30]

Chinese people owned most of the island's cars, which were used both for passengers and for freight. On one occasion, Margaret reported traveling from Kiungchow to Kachek in a Chevrolet touring car loaded with two thousand pounds of rice: "I crawled over the bags, (of course the doors are blocked shut) and dropped into the seat beside the driver. There are two widows' arches just near the compound. Cars usually go under one unless they are loaded too wide, and then they go around. And the two arches are so near together it makes rather a sharp curve in the road if they go around the first one. But our chauffeur had to, and his car was so close to the second arch he ripped a hole in a rice bag and spilled out a good deal before he could stop. So we were delayed half an hour while they picked up rice and mended the bag."[31]

Miao Country Again

February 1934 found Margaret planning a month-long trip to the Miao country. "A hospital assistant is going with us with medicines this trip and I am awfully glad for then I won't have the responsibility for selling medicine and treating sick people. And if any of our party should be laid up there's somebody to look after them."³² In the Miao country the temperature dropped to 50 degrees Fahrenheit, and it was damp and rainy, so the group was glad they had extra clothing. "Mr. French said yesterday morning he cheated the weather the night before because he slept with all his clothes on, and I said I did one better than that, I even kept my little felt hat on nearly all night! I am sleeping on a board bed and have two wool blankets and a steamer rug for bedding so really haven't any reason for being cold and am not after I once get the bed warmed up, but these houses are drafty."³³

She continued her description by stating that the missionaries had left by car in the rain and took the riverboat. Then they were to walk three miles "to a Christian village. We had sent word to them to have carriers meet us as we had quite a load of baggage and no carriers with us. So we were poling along up the branch of the river...when a man with a gun appeared on the bank and told us to stop. A militia officer came along to see who and what we were and told us we couldn't go on up that river unless we registered our names and even then he couldn't guarantee protection as a band of communists were making trouble and soldiers were after them." The group returned the way they had come and used another landing, from which they had to walk twenty miles to their destination. "We didn't have carriers. So...the boatmen carried our stuff to the nearest Miao village, [which] was a heathen village and wouldn't give us carriers, and anyway the men were nearly all away hunting." Carriers were summoned from the nearest Christian village, and "we were able to get off Sunday morning at 6:30 and we surely did do more than a Sabbath day's journey!" The group walked three hours to the first Christian village, where they had a service. Then they climbed a mountain, which took nearly two hours. Descending the mountain, they conducted another service at a village in the valley and then walked almost two hours more to yet another village for an evening service.³⁴

The missionaries had made the trip to conduct a Bible school for Miao Christians. Margaret reported that everything was "going along very nicely," as twenty-two men attended the classes. "This is the first time we've tried this sort of a project up here and we are I think all pleased with the way it has worked out so far. My own thought is we should do the same thing next year, perhaps in another village and perhaps at a different time of year, as the Miao are beginning to open water rice fields like the Chinese now and this year we struck their rice planting season. And perhaps women will come another year."35

Margaret had not reached a town that had a post office where she could mail her letter to her family, so she continued writing it. The local people had received word that a district magistrate was planning to visit, so they "hustle[d] carriers off to meet him, men out to widen the road and build bridges, [and] a platform...in the village, and everybody [had] bonfires cleaning up. At eleven Thursday night a courier came saying his honor wasn't coming and the head men were to go down nearly to the river to a meeting there instead! But we had the advantage of his road coming out yesterday and today."36

The political unrest that had wracked Hainan in the 1920s had an ecological impact on the island. While in the Miao country Margaret noted that the area "was having a regular plague of wild boars" because no one had ventured out of the villages to hunt for several years because of the Communist threat. To protect the crops, "every night the young men take their dogs and go out to [thatch] shacks to sleep....[Before retiring] they call and yell...to scare the boars, and last night I heard them yelling again in the middle of the night, as the boars came to root up the crops. They have killed over a hundred in the last few months, one weighing about two hundred pounds."37

School Problems

Margaret again served as principal of the girls' school in Nodoa in 1930, and as the spring term approached, she reported, "The Chinese all say it is just like it used to be several years ago before the persecution began," as many new students flocked to the mission schools. Many of the newcomers had been attending coeducational schools but were now "too big to be with the boys any longer." Others came from the Nodoa market school, which had "more or less gone to pot." Always interested in her students, Margaret was anxious to maintain contact with the women who had graduated from the mission school, and in 1933 she planned a reception for them. Margaret sent out ninety invitations, but as "all our school record books were destroyed when the compound was looted [in 1927] we haven't anything to go on but memory."38

As the anti-Christian movement in China intensified, the government continued to insist that all schools be registered and not teach religion.

For the mission schools, this posed a real dilemma. The Hainan mission had struggled with the issue throughout most of the 1920s but had avoided a confrontation over it in 1927 by closing the schools. Finally, in 1930 the government in Nodoa issued a proclamation, but it only applied to the boys' school. "The word 'girl' or 'woman' wasn't used at all and only the term *long koang* which is the name of the boys' school, so our Chinese assure me we are perfectly within bounds in keeping on. If they want us to stop too they can send out another proclamation. We are sorry to have to close the boys' school but believe pretty much everybody concerned knows we closed rather than give up our privilege of Bible teaching. That fact was definitely stated in the proclamation." Even though the girls' school was not ordered to close, Margaret thought she would close for the term at the end of May, "before the big Chinese Dragon-boat festival....Of course we may receive a definite order to close sooner, just like the boys' school did, in which case we obey. The Nodoa church session is beginning special Bible classes for the boys tomorrow and quite a number of Christian boys and boys from Christian homes will probably be here. The officials didn't quite dare to tell us directly we had to close but sent an order to the local 'sheriff's' office to tell them to arrest our teachers if they continued to come here to teach and to urge parents to take the children out of school." [39]

The registration issue caused Margaret to rethink the kind of education the Hainan missionaries engaged in. The mission school board wanted to create a coeducational middle school at the Pitkin School in Kiungchow but had heard "that the school inspector in Kiungchow said he wouldn't recommend registration for us as co-ed." Margaret thought "the church and mission should specialize in primary schools, and possibly the one middle school for girls, and not try to compete with the government middle schools. The Chinese government works on the English educational system—going from the top down, beginning with the university—as opposed to the American system of beginning with 'the little red brick schoolhouse' or the primary. Consequently, although they expect eventually to have a complete system at present they are just beginning to get middle schools. The Kachek middle school is the thirteenth provincial middle school and I don't suppose there are more than twenty-five in all Kwangtung Province yet, they are numbered in order of establishment. Of course there are privately established middle schools too but both together make a very small total number for such a huge province." [40]

The Kachek school had fewer problems than the ones in Kiungchow and solved its difficulties with the Chinese authorities in 1933, after which officials monitored its examinations. "The district magistrate sent the head of the Kachek police force to be the official observer of all exams for the graduating class. He mostly sat around and smoked cigarettes but he was very pleasant and made no trouble at all. He is not a Hainanese and some one said he had attended church schools."[41]

Finally, in 1935 the question of registration was resolved for the Kiungchow school when the government granted it official status. Margaret knew that the registration wouldn't "solve all our school problems, of course, but it does mean that probably from now on we will have enough pupils so that finances will not be so difficult. Students graduating from non-registered schools have difficulty entering registered schools and so as long as we were not registered pupils hesitated to enter our school."[42]

After being officially registered, Chinese participation in school governance was essential, but it is evident that some of the Chinese who took positions of responsibility were not the sort the missionaries might have hoped to have associated with their endeavors. Margaret once wrote, "We heard a few days ago that the president of our school board fell down a flight of steps in Hoihow and fractured his skull and broke an arm. He drinks more than most Chinese do and was pretty well tanked up when it happened, we understand. I personally haven't much use for him but he did help the school a great deal with all the red tape at the time we were registering. He has a son who is in our second year class here, a little rascal he was last year but he has been doing very much better this year."[43]

The Church of Christ in China

The effects of growing Chinese nationalism and the Depression in the United States in the 1930s resulted in the involvement of more Chinese in the operation of the mission schools and churches. As appropriations from the Board of Foreign Missions in New York decreased, Margaret noted the impact on the work in Hainan. She wrote to her sister Louise in March 1933, "We have had word of another 10 per cent cut and that we are only to get 75 per cent of exchange gains after April 1. Also, the Board is urging postponement of furloughs but I do not know yet whether that will affect us next year or not. I've been looking forward to furlough in 1934 but can stay over if necessary so far as my health is concerned." The following month she reported that her furlough had been postponed until 1935.⁴⁴

In 1933 Margaret was one of the missionary delegates to the General Assembly of the Church of Christ in China held in Amoy, Fukien. The Reverend David Tappan, the regular delegate, was unable to attend because his wife was ill. Dr. Morse noted that Margaret "was tickled pink at the chance [to go and] will do our fall buying in Hong Kong, such as butter, coffee, sugar, and so on." Writing to her own family about the meeting in Amoy, Margaret informed them, "There were four foreigners...and eleven Chinese on the boat who were General Assembly delegates. Nifty-looking boy scouts and a Chinese gentleman came out to meet the Chinese and some foreigners came for us." Since the hosts had been expecting Mr. Tappan to room with other men, Margaret was found accommodations at "a great big rambling house where the American Dutch Reformed single ladies live. They have six or seven living here all the time and have four delegates—two ladies from Foochow, Mrs. [Frank R.] Millican from Shanghai, and myself." The oldest resident of the home was an eighty-year-old woman, Katherine M. Talmage, who had been born in China and had served as a missionary for more than sixty years. Another of the elderly missionaries had visited Grinnell, Iowa, before Margaret had gone to college and had known a friend of Margaret's Grandma Kellogg. The Assembly meetings were conducted in Mandarin, so Margaret did not understand very much, but she was able to follow the discussions from the printed statements she was given. She commented, "Our two Chinese pastors understand [Mandarin] so that is the essential thing."⁴⁵

Margaret's Religious Life

One of the little known aspects of Margaret's life was her personal religious beliefs and, more specifically, what she told the people of Hainan about the Christianity she had come to teach them. One of her rare references to exactly what she talked about on her itinerating trips appears in an April 1933 letter written to her sister Louise. Visiting an outlying chapel, Margaret said she "called on some of the Christian women in the market. A big crowd of women and children and even men came in in the evening and then after some informal talk on the Parables of the Sower and the Ten Virgins the men went out and we had some very good opportunities to talk with the women." The next month, while on another itinerating trip, she reported that in one village "fifty or sixty people came to hear us sing and 'talk doctrine' and for the most part they listen[ed] very well. People everywhere are ready to listen these days, since the disturbances of the past few years are over and promises made by enemies of Christianity have proven false." Although she was specifically interested in talking to women, she noted that in the area she was visiting "there are some thirty or more men baptized [but] there are only one or two women who are members of the church. For the most part they are not against the Gospel but don't know a great deal and still don't realize they are just as important as individuals in the Heavenly Kingdom as their husbands are!"[46]

In her memoir of her years in China, written in retirement, Margaret remembered village women visiting her house: "I was sitting in the little front room with them, answering their questions, telling a bit of the Gospel story from a picture on the large Sunday school roll we always kept hanging in full view, and listening to their excited comments over things in general." Margaret's servant entered to obtain a hammer and nails, since the pig had broken out of its pen, and the women wanted to know why she did not consult a fortune-teller to learn if it were a lucky day before allowing the man to repair the pen: "I calmly assured them all days were equally lucky for us, given us by the Heavenly Father who cared for us, but that we considered one day in seven especially sacred because it was set apart to worship the true God, and that we did no unnecessary work on that day. And the pig would certainly come to grief if we did not keep it in the pen. They left very soon, still shaking their heads, and prophesying dire calamities for the pig and all of us."[47]

Despite the fact that Margaret wrote little about her personal beliefs, she was a dedicated church attender. One Sunday in 1932 Margaret was aboard a ship in Hoihow harbor that was taking on cargo for Hong Kong when she wrote to her sister, "It seems so strange not to be at church. It has been literally years since I have not been at some service on Sunday but there is none on these small boats except as we perhaps have a 'sing' in the evening if we wish."[48]

Some of the aspects of Christianity that Margaret conveyed to the Chinese were evident to other members of the mission. Dr. Morse wrote, "In her room where she greets the Chinese Miss M. has several pictures and rolls with illustrative texts. The postman asked for one one day. The one he wanted was a pictorial illustration of the broad way to destruction and of the narrow way to life. So at Christmas time Miss M. wrapped up one of those rolls for him and a Scripture text calendar for each of the two men in the Post Office. When we went to the Post Office next we saw all three of these up on the walls, a witness to all who enter. Scripture calendars were given to practically everyone on the compound and to others roundabout. Miss M. and Mr. Tappan made these their Christmas gifts to the Chinese." Dr. Morse also sent to her family "a set of cards that Miss M. is using to teach her little market youngsters. They are a series taken, as you see, from events in the life of Christ. Those that she gives to the children have little holes along the right margin and each successive card is put with the others to make a little booklet and when there is a certain number the child receives a prize. Numbers 7 and 8 are lessons illustrating 'Giving' and the 'Evils of Gambling' and are Chinese in appearance, rather than Biblical."[49]

Margaret once commented on the problems that Chinese families encountered when some members were Christian and some were not: "The principal's father died and the funeral was Monday. The principal and his wife are Christians and the mother wants to be but the father would have nothing to do with the doctrine. The daughter-in-law said to him at the last, (the son was here in Kachek) 'You know we can't do the old rites for you.' The father said, 'I know and that's all right, but if the second son wants to, let him.' The second son isn't a Christian at all. The pastor here decided though that we should go and have a little service 'for the comfort of the living,' as he said." Even though the Christians did not perform the traditional ceremonies, Margaret said that "according to custom we each put in twenty cents, a cloth banner was bought and a suitable message put on it, and food purchased with the rest." The missionaries and Chinese Christians went in the morning and "ate the funeral meal, had a little service, followed the coffin to the grave side and had prayer, and then came back, leaving the other son to do as he desired. It is awfully hard for the families like that where some are and others are not Christians."[50]

Margaret was concerned not only about the religion of the Chinese but also about that of the members of the Kachek station. She felt they needed to get together for a prayer meeting, preferably daily, but certainly at least weekly. This proved to be a difficult issue for the missionaries, who could never agree on a time. To her family, Dr. Morse detailed the problem and Margaret's view of it: "An old subject came up this week again and irritated some of us. It was the matter of station prayers. There are some who feel each station ought to meet for fifteen to thirty minutes each day for prayers." Dr. Morse went on to write that other stations had tried having prayers together, but it was "an admitted failure in the Kiungchow and Hoihow stations, it is going on in Nodoa but not everyone attends, even there." The doctor had "in theory...no objections whatever, I'll admit we need praying for and praying with...[but] I'd like to tell [Margaret] *why* she takes the tack she does. I don't believe she is innately more religious than other people in the Mission, only she is unwed and her physical desires are being sublimated in religion. But she'd perish of shame, such being her temperament, if anyone told her why she does as she does."[51]

The issue of station prayers came up again a few months later, and the doctor related that Margaret, "the senior member, has been a more or less constant thorn in the flesh of some of us for a long while. The ideas are 'station prayers,' and 'English service on Sundays.' Station prayers, ideally, are the thing to have, a period of daily united prayer." Again the issue of when to have them could not be decided and probably masked the larger issue that the missionaries did not truly want to have the prayer meetings. According to Dr. Morse, "Miss M....thinks we are committing at least one, if not several deadly sins, in that we meet as a station to play Rook once a week, but can't find time for station prayers." The issue was finally resolved by deciding to have "station prayers *once a week* on Wednesday at 4:30 P.M. Regular prayer-meeting comes at 5:00 that same evening so that would tend to break up the meeting before it could get much of a start at either gossip or fussing." Margaret was away from the station when the matter was decided, and the doctor thought the missionaries had "spiked her guns, temporarily, at least, even though station prayers are only once a week. She insists on some sort of station get-together on Sundays and would prefer a sermon every week. But lately we've just been singing and that's all."[52]

Dr. Morse went on to write that the two ordained men at the station, Arthur French and David Thomas, did not "like the idea of reading sermons when Miss M. spends hours preparing one, and yet neither have the time to prepare the sermons she would demand. And I don't blame them for being irritated. Her expression when she's preaching irritates me, too, it's like the cat that's been in the cream and is congratulating itself that none shows on its whiskers." The issue was finally resolved by having song services on the first, third, and fifth Sundays in the month; a service by the women, in rotation, on the second Sunday; and English sermons by the men on the fourth Sunday. By this schedule, Dr. Morse noted, Margaret's turn "will come once every five months and I reckon we can all live through that." But the doctor concluded, "Aren't we awful to try to circumvent a fellow-missionary that way? She does pin-prick so." Dr. Morse also observed that "Miss M. always outlines her talks and gives them without reading them, she says it keeps her in better shape to give talks when she is home on furlough."[53]

Family Problems at Home

None of the archival collections of Margaret's papers contain any letters written in 1931, and very few dated 1932 survive. A letter from Dr. Morse to her father written in early 1932, however, suggests that Margaret was having difficulties with her sisters and perhaps her brother about her continuing on in Hainan. Dr. Morse wrote, "Her father is the only one who seems to really care about her work out here, and he has not asked her to come....She is already sending home all of her salary that she can spare and if she went home now, would have to spend her small savings on fare, for the Board would not pay her way, and if in America, without a job, she would be in less of a position to help than she is right now. She has been much upset all week, but I think she has decided not to do anything until she hears from home again."[54] It is clear from letters Margaret wrote later that her sister Louise was ill on several occasions and had difficulty continuing for more than one year at her teaching jobs. Her sister Helen, whose fiancé had died in World War I, also continued to suffer as a result of that loss. Since their mother had died in 1928, it is also possible that the Moninger siblings were feeling their loss deeply and hoped that their extremely capable eldest sister might return home to take their mother's place.

Although Margaret regularly destroyed the letters she received from her family, her father obviously once asked her about the details of her work, perhaps as a means of expressing his support for her continued presence in Hainan. Margaret responded to his request by writing, "It seems to me I do a little of this and a little of that and not much of any one thing. The mission...assigned me to women's evangelistic work. Then I am mission secretary, which means I keep the mission minutes at mission meeting time, carry on necessary correspondence with the Board in

New York and with the China Council, and with any one else that occasion demands, including the American Consul in Canton. I am also a member of the mission executive committee, which means that I meet with the committee two or three times a year to decide on various items of mission business and policy. I am the Kachek member of the mission language committee so hire language teachers for the student missionaries in Kachek and supervise their work....And I am editor of the newsletter, which means that three times a year I go after the members of the mission for their articles, edit the material, and put it through the press. So much for mission assignments." Margaret then said that for the Kachek station she was "station secretary, which means that I keep the records of the station meetings, make out statistical blanks, make out reports of work, and carry on the station correspondence with the Board and China Council." For the Chinese church she served as "treasurer...so have accounts to keep and session meetings to attend. I am organist for church and Sunday school, teach the women's class in Sunday school and have a children's meeting in the market chapel twice a week on Sunday afternoons and on Wednesday or Thursday morning each week whichever is not market day. The average attendance is about fifty." Additionally, at the McCormick School she taught "three English classes this last semester, each meeting three times a week, and the voluntary Bible class for the girls, who came twice a week." She concluded her list of official duties by writing, "I am in charge of the Bibles, hymnbooks, tracts and other Christian literature we keep on hand to sell or distribute free, and have to order supplies, keep accounts of them, etc. I am also a member of three school boards of directors—the Pitkin Girls' School and the Lingnan Branch School for boys in Kiungchow and the McCormick School here. Do you see why I said my work was a little of everything and not much of anything?"[55]

She also reported, "I entertain all the Chinese women callers who come and try to tell them as much of the Gospel story as I can, and visit the women in the hospital wards every day for a few minutes, and call on women in the market a little—not as much as I should. The country is so unsettled we can't get out to the villages as I long to do, going out and staying a week or ten days in a place and having classes with the women. Then every once in a while Dr. Morse and I invite various Chinese friends here to a meal, and try to help out the social life a bit." Within her household she alternated with Dr. Morse as housekeeper, and she also canned fruit, as the doctor did not particularly like that activity. At the time Margaret wrote this account, she clearly had been busy: "On the storeroom shelves now are canned tomatoes, yellow tomato preserves, roselle jam, pineapple jam, pineapple canned in rings or in pieces, canned lychees, yellow-skin [kumquat?] jam, cucumber pickles, whole green tomato pickles, sliced green tomato pickles, and mango chutney, and there will be guavas and guava jam to make later in the summer."[56]

Life at the Mission Compound

Margaret's letters revealed other aspects of life on the mission compound. The compound at Kachek contained the school buildings, the church, the missionaries' homes, and the buildings where the Chinese servants lived. Many people were always on the compound, so it was impossible for the missionaries to know exactly who was there at any given time. This produced a difficult situation in 1934 when one of the servants hid some runaway women. Margaret told her family, "A strange thing happened the other night." The gatehouse servant had called for Dr. Morse about 10:30 P.M. The women, thinking someone was sick, asked the servant to bring the person to the house. The servant responded that the "law office people" wanted the doctor. Those who arrived at the house were "the chief of police and a policeman and a man from the law office and the proprietor of a tobacco shop in the market, whose small wife [concubine] and another young woman had run away. They insisted the women were on the compound at the Frenches! I said we didn't take in runaway women, but went over to the Frenches with them and sure enough the two women were in the room with the Frenches' woman servant. Of course, the women had to leave which they did quite peaceably but we are pretty much disgusted with the amah. Of all things we don't want, a reputation for trafficking in women is the special one." Margaret said that "the men who came were perfectly polite and proper about it—regular police authority and all. I hear the women are in prison now, along with the man who was trying to get the small wife to elope with him."[57]

Sharing her house with the mission doctor meant that Margaret knew of many of the cases at the hospital, but she often learned more details of them from the Chinese women on the compound. One such case concerned a man who was "brought into the hospital quite badly burned. The people who brought him told the doctor he'd been burning brush getting ready to make charcoal and when the wind shifted suddenly he couldn't move quickly enough to avoid the flames. But at Ladies' Aid last week the women said he was really a Taoist priest and had been attempting to carry an idol through the fire and had fallen and been burned." Margaret thought the man was "ashamed to admit his idol hadn't protected him" or fearful that the hospital would not treat him if he told the truth. Dr. Morse had treated his badly burned legs and tried to get him to straighten them "lest he be permanently crippled," but one day he departed, saying he could no longer endure the pain. Despite the details of this case, Dr. Morse had a very different opinion of Margaret's interest in the hospital work, writing that she "has an insatiable curiosity about sickness and sick people—almost a morbid interest and asks all sorts of uncomfortable questions. I have talked more freely than I should have, I admit, but I'm trying to curb my speech about hospital affairs, outside the hospital and it is hard when most of my interests lie there." [58]

Loneliness was a major problem for all of the missionaries, and Margaret was no exception. Once she told her sister Louise that she wanted "Grace Livingstone Lutz's two books, *Recreation* and *The Search*," but asked that Louise not laugh at her choices. "When I am tired it is easier to read an old familiar book." Although Margaret rarely mentioned to her family which books she was reading, perhaps because they had sent her many of them, Dr. Morse, who also loved to read, often mentioned Margaret's books and reading preferences. At the beginning of 1931 Dr. Morse wrote, "Miss Moninger received several books for Christmas and in the interval since our guests departed I have read one of them, *Cimmaron* by Edna Ferber. The others are *The Little French Girl* by Ann Douglass Sedgwick, *The Kramer Girls* by Ruth Suchow and *The Waters under the Earth* by Martha Ostenso." A few weeks later the doctor observed, "A while ago some friend of Miss M.'s sent her *The Art of Thinking* by Dimnet. Last night when I opened *The Story of Philosophy* she said, 'Now you can't make fun of my *Art of Thinking* any more, you've got a deeper book than that now!'" [59]

In 1935, when Margaret was preparing for her third furlough, she sent a list of the books she had read during 1933 and 1934 to the Furlough Study Committee of the Board of Foreign Missions. She listed twenty-five works, ranging from Lytton Strachey's *Queen Victoria,* Van Wyck Brooks's *Life of Emerson,* and Julius Meier-Graefe's *Vincent Van Gogh* to R.F. Johnston's *Confucianism and Modern China* and Nora Wahn's *House of Exile.* Her readings on religious topics included Rabbi Abba Hillel Silver's *Religion in a Changing World* and Justin W. Nixon's *An Emerging*

Christian Faith, as well as *Re-thinking Missions,* the recently published critique of a century of mission work. Although Margaret read many novels during the years she was in Hainan, she had a curious attitude about secular magazines. Dr. Morse reported, "Miss M. gets the *Christian Herald.* She thinks I'm foolish to like the *Saturday Evening Post.* Her dad has lately taken to reading the *Post* and she feels he has quite fallen from grace!" On another occasion the doctor wrote, "Miss M. gave me a book of hers to read some time ago, *John Brown's Body* by Stephen Vincent Benét. It is all verse, mostly blank verse, which she detests."⁶⁰

After arriving in China, Dr. Morse suffered severe eye problems and was unable to read for some months, so Margaret frequently read aloud to her. One of the books the two read this way was George Sokolsky's *The Tinderbox of Asia,* which the doctor thought was "the clearest exposition of the Manchurian situation I've yet heard." A few years later Dr. Morse commented that she could not persuade the Reverend Melrose, Mother Melrose, or Margaret to read Edgar Snow's *Red Star over China.* "They are prejudiced against communists and have bourgeois prejudices of sundry sorts also. I suppose some of them would have resented the slurs against the missionaries, too, though that's of minor significance compared to their other attitude, probably."⁶¹

In reply to a query from her family, Dr. Morse wrote, "You ask how Miss M. and I get along. Oh, some days are okay and some are not so good." The doctor mostly complained that Margaret was too concerned about "missionary and religious propaganda." She admitted that "I *may need* it, but I can think of easier ways of spending spare time. And I like to get things done on time and in order, etc., etc. but if ever anything would cure me of those habits, it would be living with Miss M. She is so previous about things that she makes extra work for herself, and if other folks don't see doing things as she thinks they ought to be done she talks about them and nags enough to drive one to drink, if one took her seriously." Margaret's preoccupation with mail schedules also irritated the doctor, who wrote that her colleague "knows every mail steamer from America, when it is due in Hong Kong and when that mail should get a steamer to Hoihow and then how long it should take before it reaches Kachek, she knows all this, and also *talks* about it."⁶²

Although Dr. Morse frequently complained to her family about Margaret, she once told them, "I write to you just as I feel, without choosing words or items or details...but I think I ought to spend more time on the good points of my housemate, rather than enlarge on the points that are a source of aggravation to me. Life with her is not all cheerless or unpleasant, and I think I have learned how to adjust better these last few months, than before. In general, we are congenial, and have never had a knock-down-and-drag-out yet." When the doctor was having a particularly difficult time living with her housemate, she wrote to her family, "Mr. Thomas unwittingly gave me the cue the other day. He said that when Miss M. and Miss Schaeffer were living together, Miss Schaeffer stood just so much and then she'd move out. I've heard Miss Schaeffer extolled to the skies, to hear about her one would think she was ready for canonization as a saint, and if *she* had to move out, well, I think I can 'let go' in my own interests, too." [63]

Crossword puzzles had become popular in the United States, and some were sent by friends to the missionaries. Dr. Morse reported, "Miss M. is having quite a time with the cock-eyed puzzle. She said she only got four words the first time over and she said, 'it's the new slang that makes the difference, I don't know it and I can't understand it.' But she will try again and again before she gives up—that's Miss M." [64]

Mission meetings were always a time of tension, as the missionaries from the three stations got together to discuss the work of the mission and to make their plans for the future. In the isolation of the mission compounds, differences in individual personalities often caused friction, and these manifested themselves at the mission meetings. As mission meeting approached in 1933, Dr. Morse wrote to her family that David Thomas was quite upset because Margaret was hinting that she wanted to move to Nodoa. Dr. Morse and the Reverend Mr. Thomas thought Margaret "wish[ed] to leave [Kachek because]...she doesn't get on very well with some of the Chinese down here. Well, there *are* differences between Nodoa and Kachek Chinese. These folks down here must be worked *with* and not lorded *over,* and in Nodoa the Chinese haven't gotten over [Mother] Melrose's high-handed way of ordering them here and yon and maybe Miss M. is still in favor of the old methods, I know she is in some things." After mission meeting, Margaret was still at Kachek. The issue had never been brought up because the Reverend David Tappan "nipped it in the bud." [65]

The dynamics of the mission, with its handful of foreigners isolated from their own culture, meant that the missionaries depended upon one another for emotional support as well as for companionship and collegiality. The Board of Foreign Missions selected for service only individuals whose letters of recommendation mentioned leadership qualities, which undoubtedly added to the tensions of the far-flung mission compounds. Nevertheless, deep personal relationships formed among the missionaries, and when Katherine Schaeffer, the senior missionary at the Kachek station during Margaret's first term, died in Hong Kong in 1931, she willed all her possessions in Hainan to Margaret.[66]

Concerning Margaret's relations with another colleague, Dr. Morse noted, "Miss M. and Miss [Grace] Macdonald are not too fond of each other at best, and the enforced proximity isn't adding to their good nature. The latter has a sharp tongue anyway and it is a lash at times. Little flicks of the lash on her part brings response in like kind and degree from Miss M."[67]

Sometimes the simple desire to have time to oneself was thwarted by other members of the mission. In March 1932 the missionaries went to Nodoa for a conference. Margaret, desiring some time away from the other missionaries, wanted to travel in one of the native cars. Dr. Morse reported, "Several of the mission wanted us to go in the foreign cars, rather than go in in native cars, but Miss M. had her mind made up that there was not room enough and nothing would do but she must go in a native bus. She was making rather a fuss about it all, so the men of the mission decided to say nothing more and let her have her own way." When they were ready to leave Nodoa, it was raining, and there were no native cars, "so there was nothing for the recalcitrant member to do but to go in the foreigners' car."[68]

In 1934 Margaret Frame, from the China Council office in Shanghai, visited Kachek. Dr. Morse observed that "Miss Frame and Miss Moninger are pretty good friends. As nearly as I can figure it they are both cut from the same piece of cloth or very nearly so. I hope I can be courteous to her, especially as she is to be our house guest. That sounds as if Miss M. likely finds me continually discourteous to her, it really isn't that bad. As a whole we get along pretty well, and I expect she irritates me less than any other unmarried woman in the Mission with the exception of Miss Skinner or Miss McCreery. At any rate she doesn't inhale her soup, and that habit of one person in the mission has driven me to the verge of well, if not murder, bodily injury, at the very least. And as to whether I irritate Miss M. I've no doubt but I do, and in some minor respects, I am sure she will be as glad to go home next year to be rid of me as she will be to see her family."[69]

Despite their differences and arguments, the missionaries were virtually the only Westerners around, and entertaining each other was also a means of escaping the loneliness of the mission compound. The Hainan missionaries rarely let a week pass without sharing a meal with their fellow workers on the compound. Every event was cause for a party. Margaret entertained the Thomas family at a Chinese dinner before their sons, David and Dan, returned to Shanghai for school. Margaret later described the event: "After dinner the boys and the Chinese servants sent up the 'heaven lamp' they'd been working on all day as this is the time of year for such lanterns. They had taken native blue tissue paper and made a great big paper sack, and inverted it over a round bamboo rim. They made a wire support or net work in the circle and piled on it sheets of paper soaked in peanut oil, and tied strings of firecrackers to the rim, with punk lighted and attached. They heated the air in the bag over a fire of coconut leaves till the bag was all inflated, then lighted the paper in the middle and the whole thing went up like a balloon, the firecrackers popping after it was up quite high. Such lanterns are pretty up in the sky, we saw ten or fifteen around last night and heard the crackers popping." [70]

Entertaining Guests

The missionaries always observed American holidays, and Dr. Morse once noted, "Yesterday was Valentine's day....Miss Moninger and I made some [valentines] for the Thomas children....We didn't have very much to make them with but Miss Moninger makes up verses as easy as she can think so she wrote the verses on a couple of them." [71]

Hainan had no hotels to accommodate foreign visitors, so the missionaries customarily housed any foreigners who appeared and requested lodging. At Thanksgiving in 1931 Dr. Morse and Margaret were the only missionaries at the Kachek station. They were planning to observe the day together when they received unexpected guests. The doctor wrote home that "Miss M. and I were the only ones on the compound and we had planned to have a big dinner ourselves. Then on Wednesday afternoon two Customs men from Hoihow, Mr. Appleton and Mr. Vantvort, English and Dutch respectively, came and asked if we would put them up for a day or so, as they had been informed that smugglers were due on the coast about fifteen miles below here....We had our Thanksgiving dinner...on Wednesday evening, with all the fixings." [72] None of Margaret's letters of this time survive, and the doctor did not mention in which of the mission houses the men stayed, but clearly Dr. Morse was not bothered that the two single women missionaries provided accommodations for visiting men.

Christmas presents from home were always most welcome. In 1933 Dr. Morse told her family, "Miss M.'s father sent her some black walnuts, butternuts and hickory nuts from home this Christmas. Yesterday she made some taffy and put in some black walnut meats. She was laughing about it, she used molasses from Jamaica, sugar from Hong Kong, butter from Australia and nuts from America. Rather geographical taffy." Margaret's enjoyment of Christmas was observed by the doctor, who in 1935 wrote home that she had had trouble waking up on Christmas morning, as the schoolchildren had sung Christmas carols at 2:00 A.M. and "I didn't have Miss Moninger to get me out early, she is like a child on Christmas morning herself."[73] Margaret was home on furlough that year.

Chess became a favorite pastime for Dr. Morse and Margaret, with the doctor noting in early November 1931 that Margaret was "a very keen antagonist in any game." Several weeks later the doctor wrote, "This week I won a game of chess, the first I had won from Miss M. She plays to win every time and I usually play to see how long I can keep her from winning! She was so surprised when I finally did win a game, so was I!"[74]

On one occasion Margaret reported that the local soldiers asked to use the church "to show moving pictures to a group of soldiers and selected guests, and they invited us too. It took them a long time to get their picture machine adjusted and their little engine going but when they did get at it they had nine rolls of film showing Sin Hau-koang, the head military man in Hainan, cleaning out the communists, and it was really good. The pictures must have been made in the Loi country, it was just such trails as we travel in the Miao and Loi trips we take."[75]

Serious Illness

Margaret sometimes wrote home that she had had an attack of malaria and had gone to bed for a few days, but she also suffered two more serious illnesses that she either never mentioned in her letters home or described in letters that were not kept. From Dr. Morse's letters one learns that "Miss M. had been ill. She had a continuous fever for six days, when it came down and has been approximately normal since. But during those six days I was trying to make a diagnosis and finally decided it was like nothing else on earth but typhoid fever. Dr. [Herman] Burkwall agreed with me that that was probably the case, though why she should have typhoid with inoculations every two years is beyond me." It was after this illness that Margaret had to reassess her role at the mission, because while she was ill "one of the Chinese girls played the organ for church and now that Miss M. is up again, the girl wants to keep on playing the organ....In theory Miss M. agrees, but she had done it for so long that she rather hates to give it up now."[76]

Two years after the attack of typhoid, Dr. Morse wrote that Margaret had "a small fleshy tumor on her side, had it for years and never had any difficulties with it but a few days ago she noticed all at once it was swollen and of a different color so, as she is very scared of cancer anyway, I took it off for her. I sent the specimen to PUMC [Peking Union Medical College] for microscopic diagnosis, but I didn't tell her I had done so. She'd worry until the report came back and then some. As it is she thinks it is of no consequence, and I sincerely hope she is right. I'm not betting."[77] Dr. Morse's suspicions apparently proved groundless, as she never again mentioned the tumor. Neither did Margaret, who lived another fifteen years and four months.

Margaret's Hainanese-English Dictionary

During these years Margaret developed the hobby of working on a Hainanese-English dictionary. It undoubtedly grew out of the phrase book that she had written when she began studying Chinese. In its final form it comprised two large handwritten volumes, some accomplishment for the author who had once claimed to her family, "This Chinese language is a mess."[78] In her dictionary Margaret included many Chinese proverbs, for which she provided English proverbs that were the closest equivalents. She reported, "I've been working on my Hainanese-English and English-Hainanese dictionary as I could get a bit of spare time and that is always interesting to me. It's a good hobby to have on hand." References to it appeared in many of her letters.[79] "I'm putting in my time these days working on my English-Chinese vocabulary to my dictionary," she wrote, "I have the Chinese-English part in fairly good shape although I am continually adding words and phrases to it. It is quite a job to put the English-Chinese part in alphabetic order. There are over 8,000 Hainanese expressions in it....I've finished the As, Bs, Cs, Ds and Es, and have over 1600 English words. It's really fun—the kind of work I very much enjoy doing, but of course it gets tiresome to stick at too steadily. And then I have other things to do, too."[80]

Although Margaret was skilled in the spoken language and was rated the best of the missionaries at the written language by many of her colleagues, she realized that she needed the help of a Chinese person if the dictionary were to be accurate. Thus she sought the help of Arthur French's language teacher while the Reverend Mr. French was away.[81] The teacher had been "educated in our Kachek and Kiungchow schools and has a B.A. degree from a Shanghai college."[82] Margaret described "Mr. Iap (Mr. Leaf) [as] the first teacher I've ever had to help me with this sort of work who really gets the idea and gives me the colloquialisms I want." She also noted that the teacher was "very much interested in the whole thing."[83]

Margaret worked on the dictionary whenever she could, but she realized she would not have it finished before her next furlough, especially since she was to spend the last three months before leaving for home teaching at the school in Kiungchow, replacing Mae Chapin, who had resigned from the mission.[84] Still, she continued to work as much as possible on the dictionary and just before leaving for Kiungchow wrote, "I have finished work on my dictionary through the Ks and there it will have to stop until after furlough as nearly as I can figure. The Chinese isn't anywhere near all written in yet so I will leave the book with the teacher to do, and I surely hope that when I get back from America he will be available to help me finish the rest of the book as he is exceedingly good for this sort of thing."[85]

Although Margaret was skilled at written Chinese, sometimes the spoken language still caused her trouble. The doctor said that when the wife of one of the elders gave birth to a girl, her sixth child, "Miss M. asked the fifth youngster, also a girl, what the baby's name would be and she said 'A-voe.' Miss M. asked, 'A-voe?' which when the tone is broken, means 'the tail.' A-seng quite scornfully repeated 'A-voe' which means 'a rose.' When Miss M. told Mrs. Li she laughed and said no name had been selected yet, so that was A-seng's own choice."[86]

Margaret spent the last months before her furlough in Kiungchow, and just before leaving for home, she spent a day seeing the sights of the city: "We visited the grave of a famous ancient worthy [likely that of Su Dung-po, the famous Sung dynasty poet exiled to Hainan], went out to the leper colony (first time I had ever been there), out to the beach for a swim, saw the progress on the new jetty, and came home."[87]

Leaving Kiungchow for home in 1935, Margaret had an eventful farewell. The car she was using had several flat tires, and she finally boarded a bus carrying some of the school students who were on their way to see her off. When she boarded the steamer, both its cabins were occupied, "but the English Methodist clergyman in the one cabin has kindly moved out so I share a cabin with his wife and the men are taking camp cots on the upper deck....They have 130 water buffalo and several hundred pigs on as cargo and a lot of Chinese deck passengers."[88] She journeyed across the Pacific on the SS *President McKinley* and arrived home on 31 July. When Margaret returned to Hainan the following year, she would begin her final sojourn on the island.

CHAPTER FIVE

Warfare

1936–1942

MARGARET SPENT MOST of her third furlough traveling to churches to give talks about her mission work. Shortly after she returned to Hainan, World War II began in China. The Japanese bombed Hainan in 1937, occupied it in 1939, and placed the missionaries under house arrest in July 1941. But these events were in the future when Margaret returned to the island in 1936 and took up her post as head of the Pitkin School in Kiungchow. With the others at the school, she would flee to the relative safety of the inland town of Nodoa in 1937. During these years she continued to write home about her work, and although the mail was frequently interrupted by the activities of the Japanese, many of her letters of this period survive. Throughout the turmoil she continued working on her dictionary, and then, while under house arrest, she wrote her memoir of her childhood, "Cedarcroft," which she continued after returning home. She also wrote "Somewhere in Occupied Territory" about living in Nodoa under Japanese occupation, and she revised this manuscript after her return to the United States, when she also wrote "Twenty-three Thousand Miles of Miracles" about her repatriation experience and "Hainan Was My Home," a summary of her life in China.

Before the 1937 mission meeting, Margaret wrote to her family that at the gathering the decision would be made whether she would remain as a teacher at Kiungchow or return to evangelistic work in Kachek. She wrote that she did not dislike Kiungchow but preferred Kachek. "I've enjoyed the school work immensely and we have an awfully nice group of teachers and students. The worst difficulty to me is that nobody in

Kachek could take the evangelistic work for women. We are so shorthanded we haven't enough people for the places we are needed."[1] Margaret continued to work at the school in Kiungchow after mission meeting and was still teaching there the following year when the school personnel were evacuated to Nodoa.

As graduation approached in the spring of 1937, she wrote, "We will hate to see this class leave the school but the next class is a splendid one, too. The present third class isn't so good in general though there is some very good material in it. As you know sometimes you get a class which isn't so good." Inevitably, the problems of all teachers affected the schools in Hainan; Margaret noted in June, "I had to make out a second set of arithmetic questions as some student got hold of the first set down in the school office." As the school year ended, Margaret's pupils stopped by to tell her goodby, some asking her to teach them math the following year, which she "considered quite a compliment." As always there was the difficulty of finding funds to help the most capable students continue their education. The young man who was "second in the class for the whole three years wants to be a teacher and has every mark of making a fine one. He's worked part of his way through our school and won scholarships, but if he goes to the government normal school here in Kiungchow there's no chance to work." He needed only about twenty U.S. dollars, but Margaret said she was unable to help him since she was then putting another student through his last year of school. The mission school graduates all took the government exams, and Margaret noted: "I was pretty much disappointed over the record our pupils made...but I've heard...that we had the best record of any school in Hainan. That's not saying much but it is a consolation. They count failure in one subject only as virtually passing since one subject is easy to make up, and on that basis we did have seventy-five per cent pass."[2]

After a vacation in Hong Kong, Margaret returned to Kiungchow, where she was to live with Alice Skinner: "I don't mind living alone and I am not afraid to be in the house alone, but it is always [more pleasant]...to have company, especially when the company are as nice as Dr. Morse and Miss Skinner! I always enjoyed living with either of them."[3]

Margaret had frequently served as mission treasurer, and, as a foreigner, she was sometimes sought out by Chinese to help them with their currency problems. While visiting Hong Kong that summer, she reported she had some Hong Kong money with her, which she had obtained in Hainan: "On Monday A.M. the premium was $4.00 per $100. A friend of mine in Kiungchow wanted me to change $500 Chinese currency to Hong Kong money for her so I went back to Hoihow that afternoon and the rate was $4.80, and by Friday it was $7.25! The Chinese are afraid their currency will fall in value if war actually occurs between China and Japan and they jump to get Hong Kong currency, which is as stable as the Bank of England."[4]

Other Chinese seemed to think that the foreigners could solve money problems for them more easily than they could themselves. Margaret once wrote, "I had to go to the bank [in Hoihow] to cash a check sent out from Nodoa for school fees, and to get some money out of a postal savings account for one of the girl teachers. The post office department suddenly announced without any previous warning that only 5 per cent of deposits could be withdrawn at a time, and at weekly intervals. This teacher has over $400 in the postal savings and needed $100 right away. I know the postmaster slightly and so went to see what I could do for her and did get $100, but she has to take her book down once a week for the four weeks to have it properly stamped. The Bank of China did the same thing though I believe they only allow one to draw 5 per cent per month and the week before [I] went to them and rescued $95 one of the school girls had deposited when her brother sent it to her to pay school fees for herself and her little nephew and she thought it safer to open a current account in the bank than to keep so much money in her own hands."[5]

The increasing warfare in North China began to concern the missionaries in Hainan and then to encroach upon their lives.[6] Margaret, like other missionaries who had lived many years in China, refused to believe that tiny Japan could wreak any real harm on China and thought that, at most, the warfare would be confined to a small part of the country. Those in Hainan got their news of the war by radio, and after Shanghai, Swatow, and Amoy were attacked, Margaret reported that the Hainanese said, "Japan has to depend on her warships and air craft to do anything in China and if she gets the heaps of ruins which are all that will be left of coast ports before they are surrendered she will not get much, and meantime the interior will sow and reap as usual and if it takes three years or even five China will win in the end, which she will. But it is terrible to think of the destruction of life and property involved." Previously, whenever hostilities had occurred on the mainland, the American consul in Canton had ordered the Hainan missionaries to leave the island, but this time Margaret reported that the government was taking a new attitude: Americans remained at their own risk. Margaret thought the new policy was "a much more sensible attitude because in countries as big as China often trouble is confined to one comparatively small area."[7]

The Japanese Come to Hainan

In September 1937 the fighting arrived in Hainan, preceded by rumors. Because of the rumors, Margaret wrote, "the people are panic stricken." Arriving at Kiungchow one afternoon for station prayers, the missionaries from Hoihow reported that a Japanese cruiser was in sight of the harbor. The group's prayers were interrupted as "the Chinese fort guns opened fire," forcing the cruiser to depart. Margaret reported, "The people were just scared silly, [and] there has been a regular exodus of people fleeing to the inland villages." Among those departing were "all our primary school pupils and teachers...all the middle school girls and some of the boys." Margaret held classes for those left at the school, "but it was the hardest teaching I ever did as the youngsters were so scared. They had been badly frightened Wednesday night when the city police had come out and told us to dim our electric lights if possible as they were so bright." She reassured her family, "Schools have not closed, pupils have merely left! All our middle school teachers are here on the job! Don't be worried about me. This is a very different situation from previous times of trouble in China. There is no anti-American feeling whatever, we would be welcomed to any village where we would seek refuge." Yet she admitted that while "Kiungchow is out of range of warship gunfire...Hoihow is not." For once Margaret was glad that Hainan had such a poor harbor: "No landing parties of any size can come ashore because they dare not leave the warships very far and the harbor at Hoihow isn't a near one, a fact which is fortunate now though we grumble a lot about it when we travel." She acknowledged that aircraft were still a threat but added, "We can get outside the range of any bombs which would be thrown at our buildings very easily as on two sides of us are open gravelands where any number of people can scatter and hide temporarily. I'm taking no extraordinary risks, so...as our Chinese say —'put your heart away,' and don't be anxious. The [Japanese] are not after Americans either particularly, you know."[8]

Margaret went on to note the rumors and the ability of some people to believe nearly anything were major problems. "The people were dead sure there was to be an airplane raid on Kiungchow at 4:00 Friday afternoon, we asked them how they were so sure of the date and hour. Many say Japanese spies are everywhere, i.e. Chinese in Japanese employ, who are to give out rumors and scare the people. Others say the rumors just give petty thieves a chance to rob houses that have been deserted or to hold up the people who are fleeing. Certainly car drivers are holding people up, prices of car tickets have jumped 400 to 500 per cent and there aren't cars enough to carry people who want to get away to the interior." A week later a Japanese sea plane "dropped pamphlets in Chinese laying all the blame for the war on China, [while]...a three-funneled [Japanese] cruiser in the harbor shelled the fort again and the sea plane dropped two bombs. One dropped in a rice field and the other in the fort but neither exploded. The shell did no serious damage to the fort, but the other one injured some people in a nearby village." Just before this episode Margaret had sent letters to the parents of her pupils, "saying classes were going on as usual and nothing had happened and urging them to send the children back." The government schools were expelling students who did not return, but Margaret did not think that was fair. Rather, the missionaries began thinking about moving the school inland to Nodoa or, if that were too far away, as Margaret believed, then to some other location.⁹

The School Moves to Nodoa

The danger to the students if the missionaries continued to try to conduct classes in Kiungchow was so great that the school officials made a hasty decision to move inland. A week after Margaret had written that she thought Nodoa was too far away, she wrote from that town: "We have moved our school in to Nodoa temporarily, since bombs were getting rather plentiful in Hoihow." After an observation plane appeared over Kiungchow and Hoihow, the missionaries told the students that they "were planning to move to Nodoa and they were all agreeable." On Tuesday bombs were again dropped, this time on the military headquarters in Kiungchow. The military headquarters was "only two blocks from our school, and about four blocks from the house where Miss Skinner and I live. We stood on our upstairs veranda and watched the plane" as it dropped its bombs. Following this incident the decision to move was made, and everyone packed up quickly. Transportation was hard to obtain, but they finally got the Hoihow hospital ambulance, which carried "seven girls, seven boys, Mr. Iap (the dean), the chauffeur," and Margaret. She thought it would "seem ridiculous to have moved if there is no other bombing but we will work here probably until the end of the semester anyway. Public opinion is getting so hot against the indiscriminate bombing of non-combatants, when war hasn't even been declared."[10]

The missionaries were fortunate to have a station at Nodoa to which they could move. Only one boy and one girl from the senior class failed to join the school in the interior. Margaret knew that the students "must really want to study and really have confidence in the school to be willing to come so far as many of them have come....Of course it isn't as convenient as in our place but everybody is being good sports and working hard."[11]

Very soon after moving, the school settled into a familiar routine, and "the school office [sent] notices of fees due to parents after the first six weeks exams [were] over." Margaret did most of the bookkeeping work, which turned out to be quite complicated. "Some Kiungchow pupils who were only day pupils out there have to be boarding pupils in here and some Nodoa pupils who were boarding pupils out there are only day pupils in here, and some sleep in the dormitories here but eat at home." In the chaotic conditions, it wasn't long until thieves struck, but this time there was a different result than usual, as Margaret reported. "There was a great excitement here about 1:30 A.M. Wednesday. We heard a great commotion and got up to see what was the matter. A thief had gotten into the dormitory where the seventh grade boys sleep. He had been caught or at least one was caught (I believe there were supposed to be two) and was being tied to a post when we arrived and shortly the local police came and took him away. They said he was known to be a thief from previous acquaintance. He hadn't gotten any loot. But it made enough excitement to last the youngsters awhile. The night watchman hit one boy who he thought was a thief just as the boy was going to hit the watchman for a thief, etc."[12]

As a registered institution, the Pitkin School had government officials overseeing the work it did, and Margaret expected the "middle school inspector from Canton...to be pleased to see us going along on regular schedule because so many schools aren't. We have all our regular work but are shy on laboratory equipment and library. We brought some books in with us but of course could not bring very many."[13]

Even in such unsettled conditions, everyone tried to carry on, and before long an invitation came to visit one of the local tin mines. Even though the visit was scheduled for a Sunday, they went, since "under the circumstances we can't very well dictate when we will go." Seventy students participated in the event, and Margaret wrote, "We visited four of the six [mines]. They mine tin and they are also setting out rubber trees. The tin isn't a very heavy deposit and as it is all used the rubber trees will be ready to tap. They don't have machinery at the mines, but use human labor entirely....It really was a nice outing for us all."[14]

But of course, the continuing warfare was uppermost in Margaret's mind. She thought it was unlikely that Nodoa would be attacked, since it wasn't "a county seat and there are no soldiers here at all except local militia and we aren't near the seacoast." She also mentioned that "the Hoihow bombing...wasn't serious, [and] a French gunboat was in Hoihow and we hear through the Chinese that England, France, and U.S.A. have agreed to patrol south China waters,...seeing that Hong Kong, the Philippines and French IndoChina are near."[15]

War in Hainan

Japan continued to menace the island, as Margaret, still hopeful that China would emerge victorious, reported: "Japanese gunboats continue to go through the straits, but Hoihow has had no raids of late. Japan is apparently realizing she can't eat up China in one mouthful as she planned to do, and I hope she's realizing how the civilized world feels about some of her doings." The Japanese attacks interrupted mail service, and this concerned Margaret greatly. By 31 October she had received only the Hong Kong newspapers to 19 October, and thus she did not know what was going on. Mail from home was always of concern to Margaret, and when a fire broke out in the mail hatches of one steamer, she was quick to mention it. "There were over a hundred bags of mail. The report is that ten sacks were destroyed and about sixty damaged. We do not know how much we may have lost, the Hong Kong post office will probably know whether the destroyed sacks were for Hoihow or Haiphong." Since very few people got mail addressed in English, the post office managed to identify one of Margaret's letters after the fire even though "one end of the letter was charred and burned and the address only had enough on to show Miss M.M. Mo. Apparently, the Hong Kong post office knew which bags were for Hoihow and the Hoihow post office guessed at the rest. It was my April salary statement and was so burned as to be unrecognizable but we had already asked the treasurer to send us duplicates."[16]

The war continued, but even after Shanghai fell to the Japanese Margaret wrote, "I think China will win yet." In her optimism she observed in December 1937, "We hope very much to move our school back to Kiungchow next semester, if there is no more trouble in Hainan than there is now." But the missionaries decided to continue the school in Nodoa, as it seemed safer than the area around the port. The decision to remain in the interior proved to be the right one, since Hoihow and Kiungchow were bombed in early April 1938, even though damages were slight. Several months later Margaret commented, "The war situation seems about the same. Japan has certainly bitten off more than she can chew, much as she hates to admit it. She captures places but can't hold them, and does not get anything out of what she does capture. I surely wish the end of it could come soon."[17]

Inevitably, the warfare on the mainland brought back to Hainan some of the students who had left the island to continue their education, and the warfare in Canton brought advice from the American consul there that the women and children in Hainan might want to consider leaving the island. As in the past, Margaret refused to believe that the Japanese would risk engaging Britain in war by attacking Hong Kong or risk antagonizing France with a move against Indochina. Margaret and the other Hainan missionaries considered themselves safe on the island. She thought that "if China just hangs on a while longer the enemy will have to retreat." Complaining that she had seen neither her father's nor her sister's handwriting for a time, Margaret speculated, "There is a possibility though that one batch of our home mail may have gone to Canton just before that city fell to the [Japanese]."[18]

The 1938 Double Ten Day celebration saw manifestations of Chinese nationalism, as the country continued to confront the war with Japan. Margaret observed that at both "the lantern parade and the theater afterwards...patriotic emblems and war materials were much in evidence. There were submarines and tanks and anti-aircraft guns and battle axes and swords and maps of China and all sorts of things."[19]

Dr. Morse joined the Nodoa station in early 1938, and she again lived with Margaret. As before, the doctor frequently wrote her family about Margaret, providing another dimension on the situation in Hainan. Margaret had been the first of the missionaries taught to speak the Kachek dialect, and she always considered Kachek her favorite location on the island, even though in 1938 she was living at Nodoa. Dr. Morse wrote to her family that she was "amused and amazed at Miss M. not so long since. We were talking about sundry limitations to work...and she remarked that everything in here—people, habitations, food, ideas, all—was *su,* in other words, cheap and coarse. To Kachekites, anything called *su* can have scarcely any other criticism that is so damaging. And to think Miss Moninger said it! In fact, she said *su ti,* cheap to the death or to the limit, the strongest anathema she could give!"[20]

Margaret herself had an experience in Nodoa that she said made her feel old. As government-registered schools, the mission schools had self-government societies as part of their required extracurricular activities. Margaret wrote that even though the school had relocated to Nodoa, these activities continued. "The self-government society is under the direction of the party headquarters and they send representatives to the [student] elections." On this occasion the military also sent a representative, and "after the meeting when we were having tea, the military representative said he knew me, that when he was a student in the normal school in Kiungchow I was teaching in our girls's school there. So I'm beginning to feel quite old!"[21]

As Chinese New Year approached in 1938 Margaret was hoping that the school would return to Kiungchow. The return was also sought by about sixty of the students, who "presented the teachers with a petition asking for the return to the city. The teachers passed [the petition] on to the school board without comment, and the very next day [Japanese] planes bombed both Hoihow and Kiungchow. Damage was comparatively slight, a few people were killed, some wounded, and some buildings wrecked, but if there is going to be more of it we will just stay put in here." Many Chinese traveled home for the New Year's celebrations, but "cars are being held up between here and Hoihow so our pupils, most of them anyway, will not even go home for vacation."[22]

Near the end of the New Year period, Margaret did go out to Kiungchow, but "it was quite a trip....robbers are apt to be bad so all cars leaving Nodoa carry soldier guards, two to each car, with their fingers on the triggers of their Mausers. And all the cars going out leave at the same time and keep together for the fifty-five miles to Simtoa market." At that location the cars from Hoihow met those from Nodoa, and the guards switched cars for the return journey. Margaret reported that on her trip there were "eight cars loaded till you could hardly see the cars." Margaret went in a "Ford touring car [loaded with a]bout 2000 pounds of black beans, in gunny sacks,...roped on the running boards, fenders, and back." The car held eight people, and "all baggage and some miscellaneous freight were tied on and packed in....I tell you car men at home don't know how to load cars!" Margaret reported that she knew "how to scramble up on to the load, swing my feet in first and slide down into my corner, or to reverse the process and crawl out head first, pivot on the sacks and slide down. Sacks of rice or beans are easy—live pigs in crates or bundles of rattan or packing cases aren't quite so advantageous!"[23]

When the missionaries held their annual mission meeting in April 1938, Margaret was assigned to teach at the Pitkin School wherever it was located. She, of course, hoped that the school would be able to return to Kiungchow for the coming year, but conditions on Hainan were to keep Margaret and the school in Nodoa for the coming year and on into 1940.[24]

Normal Life under Abnormal Conditions

Despite the continuing war news and the ever-present possibility that the hostilities would reach Hainan, the missionaries continued some aspects of their lives unchanged. During these years Margaret continued to work on her Hainanese-English dictionary, which she had had to put aside shortly before going home on furlough in 1935. In early 1937 she wrote home, "I didn't even get all I wanted to do on my dictionary done. Tomorrow is a school holiday though so perhaps I can catch up." Always interested in improving her spoken abilities in various Chinese dialects, she noted several months later, "[I] have studied a couple hours every day with the teacher, part time working on Mandarin and part time on my dictionary. And of course I have to write up in the dictionary what we get done." She did not mention the dictionary very often but obviously continued to work on it. She reported in the summer of 1938, "This week my dictionary has progressed pretty well." A year later she was still "working on my dictionary with Mr. Iap, about two hours at a stretch on Monday, Wednesday and Friday afternoons and then at odd moments I copy in what we have worked out....Maybe I'll get it done this summer."[25]

Although she was able to report finishing a revision of the work, she knew it was the sort of project she could always go back to, commenting, "It's a good kind of hobby to have as it never gets finished! I can always begin another revision if I run out of something to do!" With the arrival of the Japanese in Hainan, the mission school in Nodoa ceased to have classes, but Margaret observed that "my dictionary is always ready to be worked at." As time began to weigh heavily on her hands, she wrote, "I keep working away at my dictionary and enjoy it very much. It's a good long job that will keep me busy for a long time yet."²⁶ She clearly recognized how important the work had become to her: "My beloved dictionary is a most satisfactory hobby for a time like this....I have sorted out...22,000 expressions in Chinese, many of which have more than one English meaning, and now I am arranging each letter group alphabetically within itself and copying in the final book....[It] is a fine review of my Chinese. If when I am home some time and can do some university work again in phonetics and allied subjects, grammatical and idiomatic structure of languages, for instances, it ought to do for a thesis or a good part of a thesis, seems to me."²⁷

Margaret, who always loved to entertain, refused to allow the unstable situation to interrupt this activity. In December 1938 Dr. Morse remarked that Margaret "had a dinner for the school teachers and their wives. With me present there should have been fourteen at the table. But one of the faculty wives didn't come so there were thirteen. Neither Miss M. nor I were sensitive about the number thirteen and the Chinese don't have such a superstition so all were happy and the meal went off very satisfactorily." Shortly after that occasion, the doctor left Nodoa to return to Hoihow. Margaret wrote, "I shall miss her terribly. She's so jolly to live with and she's been so nice to take care of the students."²⁸ That same month, Margaret Melrose, one of the pioneers of the Hainan mission who had been living in retirement with her son, Paul, and his family at Nodoa, left for home. With the departure of Mother Melrose, Margaret became the senior member of the mission at Nodoa.²⁹

Christmas greeting cards posed a problem for the missionaries in Hainan, particularly after the cards became more popular in the United States. Margaret wrote that "the Christmas and New Year greeting cards that are so lovely at home have appeared in China too. Here they only greet the New Year but our Christians write Christmas greetings on them too. I have a lovely set on my desk shelves, given me by Chinese friends." She also purchased some of the "devil pidgin lucky paper" used by heathen families at Chinese New Year to use as "Christmas cards next year!"³⁰ Whether or not she actually sent the lucky paper is not known.

The new year brought still more concern about the warfare on the mainland, but no one could foresee that 1939 was going to bring the Japanese in force to Hainan and greatly restrict not only the missionaries' work but also their personal movements. At the beginning of the year Margaret's primary concern was still that she receive her mail from home promptly. To her family she reported, "Our mail has been delayed but I think we will get it all eventually. At long last the Hong Kong post office is to handle Canton pouch mail for Swatow and points north, and Hainan and points south, thus circumventing censorship in Canton and avoiding delays." In the same letter Margaret reported that the 1939 mission meeting was to be in Nodoa at Chinese New Year: "I'll be hostess to Miss Skinner, Miss Macdonald, Miss McCreery, Miss Taylor and Dr. Morse, and have two other people eating here, and be mission secretary for the first part of the meeting at least and probably have the job another year as it is sort of a thankless task nobody hankers after and the New York Board doesn't like frequent changes in it."[31]

With the increasing threat of war, the extended family nature of the Hainan mission became more important to Margaret. It was customary for the missionaries who were in the United States on home leave to visit the families of other Hainan missionaries. The Thomas family had met Margaret's brother, John, and she related to him that the Reverend David Thomas, who handled the school accounts in Kachek and so corresponded with Margaret, "often asks what I hear from you. When I was writing him last night I put in that part of your letter telling of your drive from Marshalltown to Seattle as I knew both he and Mrs. Thomas would enjoy hearing about it....They are mighty nice people and we have always been very good friends." She also observed, "It makes any of us much less lonely out here when some one else on the field knows some of our family or friends at home and we can have an outlet when we want to talk over news that comes."[32]

Despite the tension of the mission's situation, Margaret still had time for fun. She once wrote home that Mary Taylor had received a pair of silk hose from her family, one sent in each of two letters, and that there had been no duty to pay. Margaret thought it was lucky neither letter was lost. The Moningers tried the same thing. The first arrived in December 1938, and the always humorous Margaret inquired if *hoe* were the singular of *hose*. She reported the arrival of the second *hoe* in January 1939.[33]

But the following month brought greater concerns to the missionaries. Early in February Margaret visited Kiungchow, and when she wanted to return to Nodoa she "had a streak of good luck. The organizer of the Red Cross work in Hainan had two military ambulances. When he left for Hong Kong last month he put them in Dr. Bercovitz' care." One of the ambulances had been delivered to Kachek, and the other was intended for Nodoa. "There was no license on the car, so Dr. Bercovitz wanted a foreigner to escort it in, so his chauffeur would have some one to help out if the military or police or car company officials along the way made any trouble....I was glad for the job." She also escorted "twenty-four tins of kerosene," which she said had been smuggled onto the island and which "the Customs had confiscated and sold to Miss Macdonald at $7.10 a tin when she agreed to buy seventy-five tins. Then we paid no local tax on it since we bought direct from the Customs, and that's a source of grievance to the tax gatherers. We had our official permit to ship the kerosene to the interior but it was wiser for one of us to be along."[34]

The Japanese Capture Hainan

Margaret was in the interior when the Japanese took Hoihow later in the month. Writing to her family, she speculated, "Probably you know more about it than we do, as communications are cut off." The Nodoa school had started classes on Wednesday, and the Japanese took Hoihow on Friday, so the schoolteachers had a meeting on Saturday morning with the hundred students who had already registered to make arrangements for refunds for those who wished to leave. About fifty, mostly those from distant locations, decided to remain at the school. Then "about 9:30 A.M. the airplane alarms were given (police running through the streets beating big brass gongs). A dozen planes flew past but so far away they could scarcely be seen. About 11:00, three planes flew very near and very low but did no bombing here." People from the community again poured into the mission compound to try to escape the hostilities, although Margaret warned, "We can't guarantee protection of course from air attacks but our American flags are flying and if soldiers should come we have our signed consular notices fastened firmly on the three gates to the compound." The missionaries had been planning to host the annual mission conference, so they had a larger supply of food than usual, yet with the coming of so many refugees they feared they would run short. Dr. Herman Burkwall and the Reverend Henry Bucher "each made two trips with the ambulance to Namfong market, nine miles away, and brought back loads of paddy or unhulled rice which they put in the granary here. We ourselves have bought two live pigs to feed, and have some chickens and ducks, and of course now our gardens are furnishing vegetables."³⁵

Knowing it was useless to try to mail anything, Margaret continued to write the same letter for over a month. She wrote that on one occasion she and Mrs. Bucher and Mrs. Burkwall went out looking for food in the market, only to discover that "the shops have their doors closed tight, or open a wee crack and have moved most of their stocks to the villages. If planes should bomb Nodoa market to bits, I don't believe more than fifty people would be there to be bombed!" Margaret continued her letter, reporting that one day "a single scout plane, carrying no bombs, circled over the compound twice, flying very low and apparently inspecting our U.S. flags. We have to mend our flags frequently and are just wondering how long they will last. We really should have two more and will make them if we can get the cloth. Sui-moe says she has the right colors in her store and will try to bring them back from whatever hiding place they are in." The only news the missionaries had came from a radio, which they could use "when the electric light plant is running." English news was broadcast from Chengtu, Szechwan, and sometimes they could hear a report from Manila or Hong Kong.³⁶

Margaret wrote some shorter letters while she continued to work on the long one. She wrote to her family on 20 February that the missionaries continued to display their "symbols of our patriotism...from our houses and the church and hospital. Aerial visitors a few days ago were near enough to observe them carefully and apparently were satisfied as there were no reports. There are lots of women and kiddies on the compound. Yesterday was a very quiet Chinese New Year compared to the noise of firecrackers we usually hear."³⁷

Just how effectively the missionaries at Nodoa were cut off from the outside world was evident on 2 April, when Margaret wrote to her father, "Haven't seen any planes here for over a week now and hope we don't see any. Dr. Burkwall's radio has been out of kilter almost all week so we don't know any outside news. No Hong Kong papers since February 7." The psychological impact of the war was also clear: "An airplane came along, we hadn't seen one for three weeks about. It was a lone seaplane with no bombs visible and just circled around a few times and departed, but people were scared as usual. The more so as rumors have been extra numerous this week and telephone messages say a few tens of Japanese have actually landed on the coast of Damtsiu some thirty miles from here. We don't anticipate any immediate arrival of soldiers here, and hope there will be no bombing. In any case our compound will not be much involved, likely." [38]

The Japanese did indeed land near Nodoa, and the town immediately felt the impact of the invading army. As the Chinese retreated, "the district magistrate burned the yamen, the [government] school buildings and the People's Hospital before he fled, in accordance with the 'scorched earth' policy. But the word came yesterday that the Japanese, who had put up tents, had all gone back on the cruisers. Whether the cruisers have left or not we don't know." Very few people were left in Nodoa market. "We know the invaders are at the district city. A big bridge between here and there has been destroyed. There are persistent rumors that they are rebuilding it." In the turmoil, Margaret reported that "two of our former schoolboys came to get their baggage. I think both are guerrillas now. They did not say so, in so many words, but they had their native style bamboo hats marked with their district city militia insignia." [39]

In Occupied Nodoa

When the Japanese army finally took Nodoa, the action happened quickly. Margaret wrote, "The entrance came so suddenly that it was practically painless. It was about 4:15 or 4:30 Thursday morning when I heard a couple of shots, which didn't surprise me much. Then I heard a machine gun volley, and was dressing in a large hurry before the second volley came." She went at once to the gate that she was assigned to guard, and "soon I heard knocking on the gate and opened it. A Japanese officer and his bodyguard of six or eight men with bayonets were there. The officer asked if I were American, asked a few other questions, and went on. Soon a second officer (I believe he is the second in command) and a number of men came along but there was nothing then either but a few questions. Later in the morning their medical officer and a few others came in and asked various questions about the hospital, the climate, and various diseases here." [40]

In order to find out exactly what their situation was vis-à-vis the Japanese, the missionaries approached those who were in control of the town. Margaret and Dr. Burkwall went "to call on the Japanese officials...to ask about several things. The English-speaking officer with whom we talk is always very pleasant and we are so glad we do not need an interpreter. I think he is the officer who censors our English mail also, all our outgoing letters are sent to the post office unsealed." As usual, Margaret was concerned about her mail, which she noted was coming in again, but it took a bit longer since it had to pass the censor.[41]

In April 1939 Margaret received word that her Christmas packages from home had finally arrived in Hoihow. With no way to get the packages into the interior and "knowing...that Dad...usually put in candy, I wrote Dr. Morse and told her to rescue the candy before it melted in the heat and damaged other things. She said she rescued gum drops and hard candy from Dad's package and was sure they would keep in tin until I could get them." Chocolate bars in another package had melted onto a piece of fabric, but the amah washed it.[42]

Food was a continuing problem in Nodoa. About three hundred people lived on the compound, only fifty of whom were refugees. The rest were mission employees and schoolchildren.[43] Margaret wrote to Dr. Morse "referring to [the] compound as Andersonville." But to her father in Iowa, Margaret was more optimistic: "We were going along as usual last Monday morning when our gateman came hurrying up the walk with cards in his hand and we were surprised to know that the Japanese consul-general from Hoihow and his aide had come to call. He speaks excellent English and we had a pleasant visit. He had brought in our American mail....Mail service is irregular here still but the Japanese consul said that Hoihow was to be opened up for steamers June 20 so probably things will move faster now. The carrier here leaves about once a week....We have had several sessions with the military about getting vegetables and wood. Things are not entirely settled yet."[44]

The missionaries in Hoihow and Kiungchow were very concerned about the situation at the interior stations, since they knew that events there could greatly alter the treatment all the missionaries were receiving from the Japanese. The missionaries knew that the Japanese had to assume that the "neutral" Americans were partial to the Chinese among whom they had worked for so many years. Yet it was important for the missionaries, as American citizens, to maintain some semblance of neutrality, since their lives were in the hands of the Japanese. Dr. Morse was worried that "Dr. Burkwall shows his sympathy for the guerrillas to such an extent that the Japanese are making a lot of trouble for him, possibly ultimately for the mission, too. He is impetuous and stubborn and fiery and young so that I don't question that he has been in difficulties with the invaders." As Dr. Morse detailed the situation, the missionaries at the port wanted to send the Reverend Paul Melrose to Nodoa as soon as he returned to the island, as "Dr. Burkwall and Miss Moninger don't like each other much so...any advice she might give he would disregard just because it was she who gave it. So the whole situation in there has been quite tense and the local Chinese are very frightened lest Dr. Burkwall bring down wrath on them as well as himself....[The Melroses] want Miss M. to stay in Nodoa for a year, [but] it won't be possible to have a high school for at least that long, maybe longer, because we don't want to be used as propagandists by the [Japanese]."[45]

The question of neutrality was one on which the missionaries did not agree. Margaret wrote, "To one group, neutrality consists of making friends with the powers that be in every possible way, thus presumably facilitating opportunities for work. So long as the powers that be are of the same nationality as the common people among whom one works that view has its logic. When the powers that be are invaders with no moral or legal right behind them, ruthlessly destroying innocent civilians, it is another story entirely. Granted that we are citizens of a neutral country and are dependent on the invader for many things, nevertheless does neutrality mean we are obliged to welcome them with open arms, as long lost friends, and saviours of a decadent and corrupted government? To the second group, neutrality means aiding the non-combatant people of their adopted country in every way compatible with the position of a neutral—in food, in shelter, in medical treatment and supplies, in sympathetic encouragement, and in giving medical aid to the wounded, whether civilian or military of either side, if such be needed; and in scrupulous adherence to the rules laid down by the powers that be insofar as these can be conscientiously obeyed. This second group has the harder task to stay within bounds, desiring so intensely to help their friends, and believing in China's ultimate recovery."[46]

The Reverend Paul Melrose recorded an incident in which the missionaries clearly violated their neutrality. On the day the Japanese captured Nodoa, about forty Chinese policemen threw their guns over the mission compound wall. The missionaries informed the Japanese of the presence of the guns and requested that they come and get them, but they did not. Eventually the missionaries put the guns in the storeroom of the house where the Reverend Mr. Melrose was living. As he later reported, one of Margaret's students at the Pitkin School had given her his pistol and ammunition for safekeeping when the students left the compound and later returned secretly to recover the weapon. "She gave it to him and then the idea struck her. Those forty police guns would look mighty incriminating if the Japanese ever searched our place. Why not get rid of them? She talked it over with the doctor and me and we agreed to her plan. She then told a couple of her Pitkin school boys that the storeroom door would be unlocked from 6:00 to 9:00 A.M. the next day and they would know what to do about it. Sure enough when we locked the storeroom door at 9:00 A.M. the guns were gone."[47]

Amid the difficult situation in Nodoa, there was still time to laugh at disasters narrowly averted. In trying to find enough food for everyone on the compound, Margaret once got "a chicken big enough for us all and had that roasted. Very nearly came to grief on it, too, the cook had carved it and had it in a pan on the kitchen table covered with a towel, and was going to heat it up in the oven at the last minute. He was up in the pantry working, and...went down the steps to the kitchen...just in time to see a cat enjoying our chicken and the cat ran off with a second joint, too, so the chicken pretty nearly didn't adorn our dinner table!"[48]

Margaret was developing expertise in areas she had not dreamed would become the domain of a teacher at a missionary school. She informed her family, "I'm getting quite expert in knowing what type of gun is booming or pop-pop-popping or just plain popping. Suspect more practice in that line is ahead in the near future, though I don't know." Margaret also had a solution to the morale problem of those at Nodoa: "We have to have a little relaxation, so once a week we get out a mock newspaper, known as the *Sing-Sing Sentinel*. I must confess I perpetrated the first spasm. Then the next week Mr. Melrose did Spasm Two, and then the Burkwalls together did Spasm Three. It is so much fun we have kept it up in rotation, and get a big kick out of it. Just nonsense, of course, mostly comments on current local events and of course absolutely unintelligible to any one else, but we'll enjoy looking back at them later, maybe."[49]

But the missionaries continued to be concerned about the limitations placed on them. So in September Paul Melrose and Margaret "called at the office that looks after our affairs Friday afternoon and were told just what we had been told before, that we could go out when there was a supply ship available. The joke is, partly at least, that the auto road from here to the west coast isn't always open for traffic....Mrs. Burkwall says she doesn't want to discourage me, but she thinks I'll be here for Christmas!" Mrs. Burkwall and Margaret continued to go to the market about twice a week seeking food for those living in the compound. "This last week we bought dried mushrooms, rice flour macaroni, and a sack of Japanese flour there. We have to pay in Japanese 'soldier money' there so have to go to the tobacco shop to get our Chinese money changed....We can buy some fruit and vegetables and sometimes fresh meat now. And we still have plenty of rice on the compound for the hospital patients and people who live here the year round, but we are not selling now to refugees. Quite a number of them are gone, and we are trying to have others go who have places to go near here." [50]

Margaret reported that on her birthday in 1939, she was working on her dictionary when "we discovered that soldiers drilling just outside the compound had a machine gun pointed through the gate, and Mr. Melrose and I went down to the headquarters next door to us (not *the* headquarters but a branch office) to ask them please not to do that again as even in drill it frightens people on the compound. Incidentally we inquired about my trip to Hoihow, and heard some assuring words although we are fairly sure the way isn't open at present." [51]

More Chinese Refugees

In November Margaret was still at Nodoa when a change in the occupation troops in the town caused refugees to again flee to what they considered the safety of the mission compound. The regular Japanese troops were evacuated, and the new troops included "two hundred Protective Corps men...[and] Chinese from occupied areas officered by northern Chinese and a few Japanese. The market people are desperately afraid the Chinese soldiers will attack the market and burn it." As a result of the fear, people again "poured in over our walls, and Wednesday the military and the local market officials told them to come in, all restrictions were off. And they came in in a steady stream." Mrs. Burkwall and Margaret stood "at the front gate trying to monitor those who entered. We said only women and children, boys under fourteen and men over sixty could be in at night, and every evening at five the doctor and Mr. Melrose rout out the other men and I lock the gate. There must be a thousand people in here, every space outside our residence compound crowded full, and all verandas and cubby holes packed. People camp out in the daytime and at night we open the church for sleeping quarters, so no one need lack shelter." [52]

Margaret described the refugees as pitiful and ragged: "The more substantial people long ago left the island or else moved into the mountainous interior." Everyone was expected to provide food, fuel, and bedding, and Margaret wrote that the compound was a "menagerie." She also reported, "The number of big earthen jars on hand is immense—I kept asking people at the gate as they brought them in whether they were going to burn them, eat them, or crawl inside them to sleep!" apparently not realizing the most obvious use for the jars was to contain night soil, to be used later as fertilizer. Margaret concluded her description by stating, "The compound buzzes like a county fair. People sell vegetables, peanuts, etc. and the market baker is in here and selling his cakes and cookies."[53]

At night there was sporadic firing, but "both sides respect our neutrality." When the new commander, a Formosan Japanese, and his aide, an English-speaking Formosan Chinese, paid the missionaries a courtesy call, they "presented us with a case of forty-eight small tins of sweetened condensed milk—a very acceptable gift." The missionaries' gift in return was a pair of live rabbits, which their cook took to the military headquarters. "The commander seemed very, very much pleased. This officer seemed pleasant and anxious to cooperate. Others have not been so friendly."[54]

The fighting feared by the people who had flocked into the mission compound was not long in coming. Within weeks Margaret wrote that Nodoa was a battleground. "All the houses along one end of the upper market street were burned, [as were] some thatch huts down below us. The wind was enough in our direction that we got out our fire-pumps [left for safekeeping by one of the mining companies]....But our buildings all have tile roofs and it's not...likely a serious fire could break out. [However,] the thatch shelters and the firewood the refugees have brought in would [burn.] The market was not taken." As a result of the fighting, Margaret was learning even more about guns. She reported "guns popping every once in a while...[although] both sides carefully respect our neutrality...once in a while a bullet or shell *zings* across over our heads. It's a high whining sound, something like a high pitched meow from a very angry cat."[55]

As the fighting continued, a siege mentality clearly developed in the mission compound. Margaret reported, "A plane was circling and circling over us one morning...and dropped dispatches for the commander, the car roads are not open in any direction unless...towards the interior mountains....The compound is full of refugees. We haven't actually counted the ones who came in with this last scare but there must be a thousand people here....We hope no epidemics get started....There was some firing last night but not much. The Chinese bugler loves to tantalize the soldiers cooped up in [their barracks]. He toots and the machine guns pop and rifles bang. A little later he toots from an entirely different position and off go the guns again, wasting ammunition but not daring not to do it."[56]

Characteristically, Margaret was concerned about the mail, which did not come for more than a month. "The carrier we expected...a week ago Saturday...didn't come and didn't come and when the next carrier arrived Tuesday he said the man had been killed when the car in which he was [riding] back from Hoihow, was attacked about fifteen miles out of Hoihow....The mail bag is reported missing but we know from Hoihow letters the other carrier brought that no steamer had come down from Hong Kong."[57]

Unfortunately, the situation got worse. On 17 December 1939 Margaret reported that the compound had had a bad week, with fighting every night from Sunday to Thursday, when "we were up from about 1:30 until daylight. Some buildings very near our hospital wall were burning and our fire brigade had their hand pumps ready. Non-combatants came over our walls in greater numbers than usual. The doctor had some wounded civilians to look after. He has to do his work without chloroform—is all out." The missionaries were determined to maintain their neutrality, so when the doctor took a wounded man into the hospital and at the same time "another soldier came in with a hand grenade, 'looking for guerrillas,' " the missionaries took immediate action. "Dr. Burkwall insisted on taking the grenade away from him but said it would be returned when an officer came with him to claim it. Soon three officers (two Japanese and one Chinese) and a number of soldiers appeared at the front gate [which] I unlocked...at once. The three officers and the grenade soldier came in. We sent for Mr. Melrose and Dr. Burkwall, and of course gave back the grenade."[58]

The officers obviously had concerns more serious than the recovery of a grenade. They "asked us if the guerrillas had not used our compound as a passageway to enter the market for the attack. We said that to the best of our knowledge and belief they hadn't. We weren't up until the heavy firing began but our night watchmen were on duty as usual and would have called us if any armed men attempted to enter. And any considerable number of men crawling over a wall and crossing the Chinese gardens in the lower or western end of the compound would surely have left traces. The Japanese obviously do not know how the men got into the market and still think they came through here and that soldiers are hidden in here. We asked them several times to come and search, but this they refuse to do."[59]

Small Subterfuges

Margaret knew that under the circumstances it was wise not to write all her thoughts. Nevertheless, to her family she did write, "There are lots of things we would like to say about the recent events, but probably discretion is the better part of valor still. We do know that this place is supposed to be a black-cat, spill-the-salt, break-a-mirror, walk-under-a-ladder spot for officers of northern climes. Five have been in charge. Number one departed from the land of the living in a scrap just north of this market. Number two followed him at Long Meadow, not over fifteen miles from here....Number three got a head wound just outside the market here and departed for the port for treatment. Number four led an expedition out for help and literally lost his head. Number five [just departed]. We have it on good authority that losses on the local side only come to X as against a Y equivalent to almost XD, if you remember your Roman numerals and your algebra."[60]

From time to time planes interrupted life at the mission compound, sometimes on bombing and sometimes only on reconnaissance flights. "Yesterday we had some leaden rain [during]...choir practice....Two scout planes buzzed around, and fired two volleys of machine gun fire apiece but there were no casualties as everybody had run for cover at the first sounds of the planes. The firing was not in the direction of the compound at all. This morning we heard planes again and saw three off in the distance but they didn't even come over the compound."[61]

The missionaries at Hoihow/Kiungchow were still worried about the situation at the interior stations and did what they could to assist their friends. Dr. Morse wrote her sister, "Each week I send parcels of food stuffs to Miss Moninger. Since no freight can go in by road we try to keep a few essentials and occasional luxuries going in by post. But no parcel may be over a pound in weight, so you can imagine what a lot of wrapping of tins or parcels is necessary to get things in properly. I have sent in forty-three parcels during this month so far and will get off another six or eight before the month ends. This takes considerable time but I really enjoy it and it does make life more enjoyable for the folks cooped up in there, I believe."[62]

Leaving Nodoa

In August 1939 Margaret asked the Japanese for permission to leave Nodoa with the people from Hoihow who had accompanied the school when it moved, but she received no reply. Finally, in March 1940 Margaret and the others were permitted to leave. Margaret's account of their departure stated that while they were going about their daily routine one morning, "here came Mr. Steiner up the front walk with his bicycle, a small U.S. flag stuck on it and a big flag around him." Paul Melrose commented that "Steiner evidently placed a lot of faith in the American flag."[63]

The Reverend Mr. Steiner had arrived to evacuate Margaret, Mrs. Burkwall and her daughter, and any others the Japanese would allow out. Twenty-two people, including an elderly woman who rode in a ricksha, left the compound in midafternoon. It was "about fifty miles to the place where we could get cars. We walked six miles the first afternoon and spent the night in the evangelist's house....The next day we did eighteen miles, over a road where the ricksha had to be carried over rocky parts of the way, and we ducked under bushes when planes came. The next day...we did twenty-one miles, and spent the night in a big village on the edge of No-man's land. Carriers from there only dared take us three miles further." Margaret went on to relate that "Mr. Steiner, who had made arrangements with the military on his way in, went ahead with his bicycle and reported our arrival and carriers from within occupied territory took our loads on in." The group then met cars that had come from Hoihow, which were traveling "in convoy, armed guards on each, keeping always within sight of each other." The trip was slow, as the group had ten flat tires in fifty miles, but they finally reached Hoihow at dark. Margaret reported that she "couldn't bring all my baggage out from Nodoa, but I...got out most of what I really valued, including my dictionary, and my typewriter. It doesn't follow that I won't get the rest eventually. Mr. Melrose and Dr. Burkwall are still there....Mr. Steiner is an excellent organizer for such a trip, and very considerate of us all on the road."[64]

Vacationing in Hong Kong

Margaret was able to leave the island to go to Hong Kong on vacation shortly after she was evacuated from Nodoa. Dr. Morse had been in Yunnan attending a medical meeting, but later she joined Margaret in Hong Kong. To her family, the doctor reported, "Miss M. has a really thrilling tale to tell of the occupation days....There were many very anxious days, naturally, and some days of possible danger but most of the things she can tell are the sort of things one cannot write home, certainly not from Hainan. Suffice it to say that the [Japanese] left Nodoa in December because the guerrillas had made the place untenable. The [Japanese] are back in again, but whereas formerly the area around Nodoa in which all villages had been vacated and fields deserted was three miles in diameter now the area is eight miles across in either direction."[65]

From Hong Kong, Margaret told her family, "The Japanese re-occupied Nodoa the day after we left, but letters from Mr. Melrose and Dr. Burkwall said they were all right and no soldiers were occupying the compound." On a lighter note, she added that it was rainy and it was Easter, but "I haven't any new Easter bonnet even if [the sun] *does* come out! Am wearing a hat belonging to Mrs. [Paul] Melrose, which Mrs. [David] Tappan wore up Christmas time, and now I'm taking my turn at it." The next week she wrote, "The *President Taft* is leaving for U.S.A. today but this letter will not get on her, it isn't proper nowadays to mail letters on steamers or to have others take letters abroad to mail, so I'll just put it in the post office to catch the next boat out." It was on this trip that Margaret "smuggled...out to Hong Kong" and mailed home her account "Somewhere in Occupied Territory, 1938-1940," detailing the events that had occurred in Hainan.[66]

Despite the situation in Nodoa, there is no indication that Margaret or any of the other missionaries ever attempted to inform American consular personnel of their circumstances. Certainly the neutrality of the Americans was violated during the months they were virtual prisoners in Nodoa, but they probably feared that informing consular officials would have resulted in the immediate evacuation of all Americans from Hainan.

Margaret's sojourn in Hong Kong that summer was similar to many others she had made. She visited friends and former students from Hainan and saw the latest movies, including *Naughty Marietta!* "And I'd hate to confess how many times I've had ice cream. That, and a morning paper everyday, have been special extravagances I felt justified in having."[67]

Living at Kiungchow

Margaret returned to Hainan, but not to the interior. She spent the rest of her time at Kiungchow, where she served as mission agent, a job that became quite trying as the Japanese tightened their control over the island. The Japanese army of occupation issued its own currency, making Margaret's bookkeeping tasks even more difficult. She noted, "We rarely have such a complicated set of accounts as we have this year because we are dealing with two currencies all the time—Chinese national dollars and Army of Occupation certificates, usually referred to as 'Soldier Certificates' in local dialects, or, loosely, among ourselves, as yen though they are not regular yen. Exchange has been fluctuating for a long time, but steadily decreasing the value of the Chinese dollar, till now ten dollars Chinese brings about four thirty-three yen. Our accounts must all be reduced to Chinese dollars in the last analysis, as our appropriations come in that currency, though in daily practice we use both currencies, and in changing from one to the other at a variable rate it is hard for me to know how to figure with much accuracy. If I buy a hundred yen one day at 2.03 (one yen equals 2.03 Chinese) and use two-thirds of it, but buy two hundred yen in a few days at 2.20, and use about all I have on hand, and then buy more at 2.35, and have a certain amount left in the safe at the end of the month, how can I convert it into dollars in figuring my cash balance and be absolutely accurate?" If that were not complicated enough, "To add to the fun, I draw my current funds in Chinese dollars by selling Hong Kong checks, and that rate of exchange varies also! I carry a discount and premium account which serves as a dump heap—Hong Kong premium on checks varies from 4.00 and 4.10. When I get weary of that a steamer comes along with freight for us and I take a turn at changing Hong Kong or Shanghai values to Customs gold units for the customs declarations. I am having a perfectly good time at it, and enjoying it very much."[68]

When she had applied to the Board of Foreign Missions in 1913, Margaret wrote that she had no training in bookkeeping, and even after keeping such complicated accounts she wrote home, "I'm no trained bookkeeper, as you know, and feel I'm lucky to have had so little difficulty as the treasurer's accounts involve about $115,000 Chinese currency for a year. It is a bit more difficult this year because we are dealing in two currencies all the time but make all our reports in one only." Then she added, probably tongue-in-cheek, "I want some expert training in such matters when I go home, but doubt if the Central Iowa Business College carries such courses."[69]

The social life of the missionaries at the port continued and now seemed to include the Customs men and the diplomatic personnel more than in previous years. On Halloween 1940 Alice Skinner and Margaret entertained the son of the commissioner of the Customs, who was American, and the daughters of the harbormaster, who were British. For Christmas Margaret "fixed a little book about our days at home on the farm for Arthur and Gordon French, because they were always asking about things on the farm." She was already thinking of writing such an account for her nieces, and she reworked the story several times until it became the memoir of her childhood, "Cedarcroft."[70]

Margaret's association with the British in Kiungchow caused her to write home once that the office was "terribly draughty (see how *English* I'm getting to write draughty instead of drafty!)....Talking about *English* English—we are all smiling to ourselves over a recent expression the harbormaster used. In Hoihow the garbage wagons are small open carts hauled by one water buffalo and smelling to high heaven. Mr. Flynn speaks of them as 'offal carts'—and we all thought he said 'awful carts,' which would be quite true."[71]

By October 1940 the American diplomats and the Presbyterian China Council were becoming increasingly concerned about the Japanese presence in China and "suggested" that "so far as is practicable American citizens, particularly women and children and men whose presence is not urgently needed, withdraw to the United States." Margaret noted the China Council was authorizing the "return to America of the Frenches, the Seatons, [Miss] McCreery, and [Miss] Skinner." She added that that "would leave a 'skeleton force' in each station, only Dr. Morse, Dr. Bercovitz, and I certainly can't qualify as skeletons!"[72]

In America, Margaret's brother, John, decided either from her letters or from the general news he got about China that he wanted her to come home. She was due for a furlough, but because of the shortage of workers in Hainan, she decided to postpone it. In a letter to her brother in March 1941 Margaret discussed her postponed furlough and wrote, "If at any time you have any reason to think I should *hurry* home, a cable direct to Hoihow would be possible now, I think,...but no coding allowed....I am anticipating a year with Dad and all of you." This letter produced a cable from her brother informing her that her father, who was nearly eighty, had pernicious anemia and a limited life expectancy.

She responded to her brother on 30 May, writing that the mission was extremely shorthanded even though she felt "no one was indispensable in any set-up." She continued, "In some way I can't really think straight about the matter—and would always feel very, very badly if I did not get home in time to see him, and yet right now it does seem as if I were needed here until re-enforcements come....please do not think that the Board or the field authorities have hindered my leaving—I myself knew I should offer to stay and did so of my own free will, though I said at the time that father was the only factor that was concerning me in the decision....please let me know by air mail or wireless if anything more definitely serious or affecting the limit of time develops, because I care."[73]

Margaret continued to serve as the mission agent, and her position became more and more difficult with the passage of time. The Reverend John Steiner was sent by the Hainan missionaries to represent them at the China Council meetings in Shanghai in 1940, and apparently at the insistence of the Japanese, who thought he was a spy, his return to Hainan was blocked. Unable to leave Hong Kong, his location there was advantageous to those still in Hainan, as he aided them by sending much-needed food and medical supplies. In January 1941 he forwarded to the Hainan missionaries seventy-three cases of freight via Canton. When Margaret, as mission agent, went to the Customs building to clear the items, she found that only seventy-one had arrived, "one drum of hospital freight and a trunk...containing mail, U.S. packages, Hong Kong purchases, etc., being missing and presumably overcarried to Siam. The gendarmerie seemed certain Mr. Steiner was attempting to smuggle arms, ammunition, information or something into Hainan. They insisted on opening practically every case." The missionaries had nicknamed one of the Japanese officers, a Mr. Takada, "Bullethead," and it was he who sought the contraband. According to Margaret, he "opened sealed flour tins and poked his stick through them, sugar tins ditto, a twenty-five pound tin of powdered milk the same way. Apparently he didn't know cornstarch—split open a package, felt the powder he poured out on his palm, smelled it, tasted it. A tin of condensed milk rattled when he shook it—he grabbed a knife, opened the tin in spite of my attempt to show him the solder on the outside, poured out the contents and examined the little pellet of solder. He felt it, shook it, stepped on it, did all he could to discover what it was, and finally carried it off in his pocket, presumably as *Exhibit A*. I could *feel* the sympathy of the whole Customs staff—the examiners had always been most courteous to me—and Mr. Flynn and Mr. Hoshi, the harbormasters, were boiling when they came in and saw what was going on—but they too were helpless. So it went on for two hours....Altogether it was an experience I don't care to repeat and it was a providential thing the trunk was missing at the time." The missing trunk of letters and packages had been sent to the Japanese consulate and was returned to the Customs office on 28 February. Margaret cleared the items and left the Customs House "about five minutes before 'Bullethead' appeared, as Mr. Flynn told me later." [74]

Other aspects of life went on as usual. On Easter Sunday Margaret wrote, "We had our English Easter service in Hoihow....The Customs foreigners and quite a number of English-speaking Chinese were there....Mrs. Cheung, who studied piano in New York...for two years played a solo. Her husband, who has a fine baritone voice, sang two selections from 'The Messiah.' There were two numbers by a quintette, one of the Chinese nurses singing soprano, Mrs. Cheung alto, a Customs Chinese the high tenor (he has a lovely voice), Dr. Bercovitz second tenor and Dr. Cheung baritone. Since Dr. Bercovitz is the only missionary man in the station he led the service and gave a very good talk, too, better than I thought he could give. The house was decorated with big bowls of snapdragons and delphiniums." [75]

In June Alice Skinner celebrated her sixty-ninth birthday. As Margaret wrote later, it was "not really her 'big' birthday, but the Chinese gave her a wonderful celebration....With an almost uncanny prescience the Chinese had asked her if they might consider this as her 'big' birthday, and celebrate accordingly, and with later developments as they were, we are all so glad that these meetings were held at that time." Margaret had invited the other foreigners for a surprise tea on the afternoon of 23 June to celebrate the birthday. "Mr. and Mrs. Flynn and family, Mr. Cuthbert and Mr. Ambrose [came] up to Kiungchow....The Customs car came up bringing all the non-missionary friends except Mr. Flynn, and the hospital car brought the others. It was just after the rumor had come that America had entered the war, and the Hoihow and Kiungchow gendarmes had brisk telephone conversations as to why all the foreigners had gone to Kiungchow, although we knew nothing of it at the time." [76]

It was also during this time that Margaret had more contact with the Roman Catholic missionaries, who ran an orphanage. While shopping in Hoihow, she met "one of the French Catholic sisters on the street. I said 'Good Morning' to her in French, that being mighty near all the French I know. The sister turned and grabbed my hand and asked in French, in pathetic eagerness, if I spoke French. I hated to tell her I didn't, she seemed so anxious to hear her own tongue again. She said she only knew 'good morning' in English." From the French sister, Margaret learned that "the war in Europe has pretty much cut off all the contacts for the French priests and sisters here. They still have some contact with the French in Haiphong, the bishop went there not long ago, but steamers between here and Haiphong are very few and far between."[77]

The war was never far from Margaret's mind. Once she rather casually informed her father, "Planes are droning around overhead these few days. One evening last week they were using the landing lights, the first time I had seen the field lit up, and planes with their navigating lights on."[78] Apparently Margaret did not realize that it was such knowledge, which all the missionaries had acquired, if only by accident, that made their continued presence in Hainan very complicated.

Margaret suffered several health problems during these years. After returning from Hong Kong she had "an elevated blood pressure," which Dr. Morse treated with "a blood-pressure-reducing drug." Then in October 1941 Margaret wrote to Paul Melrose, "You may remember that in July 1938 while I was out here on summer vacation Dr. Bercovitz took a small mole or something of the sort off my nose with the electric cautery. The last two or three weeks the edge of the scar has begun to kick up a bit and the doctor says radium is needed to lay the ghost once and for all. So probably I'll be leaving by next steamer up unless monkey wrenches appear."[79] Monkey wrenches, of course, did appear, and Margaret was not allowed to leave Hainan, although Dr. Bercovitz indicated the urgency of her problem when he recommended that she return to the United States "by clipper," since the missionaries never crossed the Pacific by air, using instead the cheaper ships. Dr. Bercovitz finally operated on Margaret's nose on 2 January 1942, having obtained the permission of the Japanese to do so.[80]

House Arrest, July 1941

Station prayers had again become a routine part of the missionaries' lives. On 24 July 1941, when Alice Skinner and Margaret went to Hoihow for the prayers, they "found that the doctor was being obliged to turn over all the hospital account books to the Japanese authorities. Full lists of our property and the values were also being demanded. Mr. Mok of the Standard Oil was also obliged to turn over his books." Only later would the foreigners learn that the Japanese were preparing to freeze their assets. "July 27 the blow fell. About 9:00 A.M. a motorcycle with sidecar appeared at the auto gate and the soldiers demanded admittance. I opened the gate and found French-speaking Japanese who said they had come ashore from a boat from Haiphong, and were hunting the Catholic mission. I presume that was true, as they could have taken a wrong road out of Hoihow and not gone past the Catholic property. As soon as they left Mr. Iap hurried over to the house to see me and said that morning the local paper had announced the freezing of Chinese and Japanese credits in the United States and he was afraid there would be trouble."[81]

As it was Sunday, those at Kiungchow "had our usual church services," and then Margaret took a nap. "When I heard a commotion downstairs [I] hastily slipped on a dress and went down. Lt. Nakamura, Mr. Matsuzaki, several other officers and men were there. They told me credits were frozen, insisted that I open the safe and all locked drawers, sealed the safe, the drawers, the piano, the organ, my typewriter, and almost everything else. Lt. Nakamura put my partially-used Hongkong [and] Shanghai Banking Corporation checkbook and a brand new one in his pocket, allowed me about one hundred military yen which he said would have to do me two months, went all through the house upstairs and down, told me I could use two rooms and have three dresses to wear, etc. By about 4:00 they were through with me, and told me all Chinese must be off the compound by 6:00 or they would not be permitted to leave." Margaret was allowed one woman servant "but could continue to eat with Miss Skinner as I had been doing since my cook left about two weeks before."[82]

Margaret had learned that Lieutenant Nakamura, whom she called Lieutenant Nakamura the First, had been born in the United States. His family owned "two hundred acres of grape land near Sacramento. His uncle was the pastor of a Japanese church in the U.S., but he had given up his American citizenship to return to Japan and join the Japanese army." Mr. Matsuzaki, whom Margaret characterized as "really very friendly," was a Christian from the Congregational church in Formosa.[83]

Mr. Matsuzaki was sent to "freeze" Alice Skinner, whom he permitted "to take out from the safe a good deal of money belonging to various Chinese before he sealed it." All afternoon the Chinese who had lived and worked on the mission compound left in haste. "The next morning the military arrived, with some consular police, and proceeded to list all property and seal all buildings....It was a hot day, and a long one....Tuesday morning, July 29, Lt. Maruyama, the lieutenant stationed in Kiungchow City and directly in charge of us, arrived, and said to me, very deliberately, 'Your life is in my hands.' I didn't know what might be coming, so didn't dispute the matter, and was relieved to hear him lapse into pidgin English and say, 'I think more better you live with Skinner' and so it was arranged."[84]

Despite Margaret's pleas that caretakers be left on the compound across the street, where she had been living, the Japanese only locked it up. The women were guarded day and night by three or four men "who liv[ed] in the gatehouse, and tramp[ed] into the house any hour of the day, regularly inspecting the various seals. Weather without and cockroaches within were no respecters of the Imperial Japanese Army seals—but we really were." Margaret reported only one "really unpleasant experience with the sentries...when a soldier chased A-siu around the compound with a bayonet. We complained to the sergeant in charge, who looked at the man and then at us, and tapped his forehead significantly. Evidently the sergeant reported to...headquarters in Kiungchow, as Lt. Maruyama appeared a little later in the afternoon, asked us if we had had any 'unpleasant experiences,' and assured us they would take more care in the future. And evidently they did because thereafter in general our guards were very careful, though they did tramp all through the house, sit and smoke in our bedrooms, etc."[85]

Although all the missionaries at Hoihow and Kiungchow, as well as other foreigners in both locations, were placed under house arrest at the time the United States and Japan froze each other's assets in their countries, there is no indication that any of them ever attempted to contact their consular personnel, even though their treatment was tantamount to an act of war on the part of the Japanese. Such notification would not have been impossible. There was still a British consul on the island, living adjacent to the Hoihow compound, and ships bound for Haiphong and Hong Kong still called at the port. Instead, the missionaries, who had lived under various restrictions imposed by the Japanese in the previous two years, accepted their house arrest in silence. In the months that followed "some of the guards told [the women] they were Christians, many expressed their sorrow over the existing circumstances, but always said, 'It is the Imperial will,' or 'We have no choice but to obey orders,' which of course we knew."[86]

For Margaret, 9 August was an important day. "Miss Skinner and I were playing Anagrams, just at dusk, when the postman surprised us with quite a bagful of local and home mail. He looked harassed and weary, and said he had had to go to several different places to get permits to bring our precious letters to us after they had been released at the Hoihow post office. He certainly did all he could for us in every way he could."[87]

On 12 August Dr. Bercovitz visited Alice Skinner and Margaret, bringing them quinine, which he thought they might need, and a freezer of ice cream. As he was leaving, Margaret later wrote, "our guards suddenly told us they were 'going home' and left us." After waiting in the house for two days, the women sent for Lieutenant Maruyama. When he arrived, he "said that though the guards had been removed there was no change in our status. On the 16th he told us that we had our liberty but that no seals could be removed. We actually took a little walk out of the compound, and a longer one the next afternoon, though we were very careful not to involve our Chinese friends by entering their homes." Sentries came from time to time to inspect the seals, and "later we heard that the freezing in Hainan should all have been done by the navy, but that Lt. Nakamura had really 'jumped the gun' in our cases, and certainly gone far beyond the proper limits." The missionaries in Kachek and Nodoa had merely been asked to report to the military headquarters, where they were told they could not dispose of any property.[88]

Alice Skinner and Margaret spent their time cleaning up the compound, reading and writing, working puzzles, and "reading the Bible together in Chinese, four chapters each morning and four each afternoon."[89] By September they were "nearly half through the Bible. I have been afraid that when we came to the poetical books there would be a lot of characters I wouldn't know, and was surprised while reading Job that there were so few after all though more than in the historical books. Proverbs both Miss Skinner and I will have to work at." A month later she could report that they were "in Jeremiah now. We really are surprised to see how few characters we have to look up in the dictionaries, but disgusted at ourselves when we have to look the same character up over and over again. Miss Skinner writes the Romanized in her Bible when she comes to a character she doesn't know, and then when we come to it again we forget where it was before so she's no better off than I, who do not write in my characters. And it is a very good drill for both of us. Takes us about an hour morning and afternoon."[90]

As their sentries eased up on surveillance, the women were allowed to go to Hoihow, and the missionaries living there sometimes journeyed to Kiungchow. They did have some contact with the outside world and learned in September that the Reverend David Tappan was in Canton seeking passage for Hainan. One of the missionaries under house arrest at Kiungchow, Margaret Burkwall, had a birthday on 19 September, and Margaret Moninger's was the 23rd, so the others planned a party for them. "At noon Dr. and Mrs. Bercovitz brought me up in the car, first time Mrs. [Bercovitz] had been up since the chilly weather [the freezing of the missionaries' assets] set in the last of July....It was a *real* party, our first meal together as a station in over two months." [91]

Lieutenant Nakamura the Second

The situation for the missionaries improved markedly once Lieutenant Nakamura the First departed. Ironically, a second Lieutenant Nakamura then assumed responsibility for the Americans. Years later Margaret Burkwall described this man as "one of the nicest men I ever met." Margaret Moninger said that the second Lieutenant Nakamura was "a man of very different type. He was a graduate in jurisprudence from the Imperial University in Tokyo, and had been a practicing lawyer in Osaka before he was drafted for army service. His wife was a graduate from the Women's Christian College in Kobe, with a major in English literature. The fact that this man was over us made subsequent events much easier for us than they otherwise would have been." [92]

Eventually Margaret's typewriter was returned to her, and she used her time in literary pursuits. She wrote "Cedarcroft," and she "managed to type the rest of the English-Hainanese vocabulary for Mr. French, and...Mr. Matsuzaki asked me to translate into English and type out for him Book I of Caesar's Gallic War! He had borrowed a copy of the Latin text from Father Disperban, the French Catholic 'Apostolic Prefect' or Bishop of Hainan. It took me almost four days of steady work." [93]

Margaret continued to hope that she would be allowed to leave the island, but the steamer of 7 November took only the Customs Service personnel, the Flynns, and Mr. Ambrose. Despite the difficult situation for those remaining behind, there were some humorous moments. On 25 November "an officer of considerable rank (two gold bars and two gold stars), waterproof cape, spurs, etc. and his personal servant came in. He saw coconuts on one of the tall old trees, and asked in sign language if he might have them. We said no way to get them. He sent his man up—a rather short, heavy-set fellow. The man went up about half way to the top, gripping with his arms and knees, shook his head, puffed and panted and perspired, and came down. The officer grinned, removed his uniform and boots, and went up monkey fashion, got the two ripe nuts and came down—the best lark he'd had in a blue moon, apparently. Properly attired again, he offered to pay us, which we did not accept, and left us with many bows and a hearty handclasp."[94]

Life After Pearl Harbor

The missionaries had some freedom of movement between Hoihow and Kiungchow, but on Sunday, 7 December 1941, Margaret Burkwall failed to make an afternoon visit to Margaret Moninger and Alice Skinner. The telephone service between the two mission compounds had been restored, but when Margaret Moninger called Dr. Bercovitz "about 6:00 in the evening...I knew from the way he spoke something was wrong, though he could only say that their guards were back on duty, after an interval of about ten days without them." The following morning, "some officers called about 10 A.M. to tell us war had been declared, and to re-seal the rooms which had gradually been opened. The whole affair was rather weird and unsettled—the officers and especially the long-legged gawky kid of a gendarme did not seem to know quite what to do about it all. Heavy guards were posted and left in charge. In the afternoon Mr. Yamaguchi from the Hoihow headquarters office came and told us we were to be moved to Hoihow the next day. I was already packed, having long been ready to leave for furlough, but Miss Skinner had to break up the home she had occupied for more than thirty years and it was far from easy, especially as there were so many things she wanted to give to the Chinese, particularly Tai-mui," her amah.[95]

The women spent the next day packing, "with sentries constantly coming in." Alice Skinner and Margaret left late in the afternoon, taking everything they wanted. "However the officers and men appropriated several articles of furniture, dishes, and other things we had left behind, and much of the material destined for Tai-mui. They also took from our scanty store of food supplies a whole case of Carnation milk, several large tins of butter, and tins of coffee and fruit. We were told we were to be at the doctor's house, and after a slight delay at headquarters we were taken to the compound." Held with the missionaries were the Irish businessman Mr. Cuthbert and his Chinese wife, who had lived in Hoihow for many years. The missionaries were permitted several servants, including a "fourteen-year-old orphan boy, A-heng, [who]...begged and pleaded that he had nowhere else to go." [96]

The missionaries shared their food supply and worked out a schedule for cooking and housework and for their daily affairs. Much later, on her way home, Margaret wrote to her brother, "Remember the seeds you [sent] me in 1940 for Christmas? I got them in February 1941, too late to plant till fall. Miss Skinner and I planted half in Kiungchow, and they were coming beautifully when we were interned in Hoihow. The half I gave Hoihow people—none of us had any other home seeds—grew *gloriously* and our gardens certainly saved our diet from unbearable monotony." [97]

The missionaries, of course, held a regular Sunday worship service, and on 14 December, Margaret noted, six people attended. She wrote, "Mr. Cuthbert was there, somewhat under protest, I fancy, though he was a good sport about all the things that came to his hand to do." The missionaries also were making preparations for Christmas, when on the eighteenth "the Cuthberts were suddenly taken back to their own home, although we had made no request for such a change and they had cooperated in every way with us." At the same time Alice Skinner and Margaret were allowed to return to the Kiungchow compound to bring back some things. "Thieves had been busy in the Pitkin House, and it was a desolate mess." As Christmas approached, Mrs. Bercovitz trimmed the Christmas tree, which was "the top of a 'horsetail pine' from near the Manse." The missionaries exchanged presents at breakfast on Christmas and then in the afternoon "had invited official guests for tea." In attendance were "Colonel Matsuo, the commander-in-chief of military forces in Hainan; Lieutenant Nakamura, directly in charge of us; the Japanese consul in Hoihow, who did not appear because of too much sake previously imbibed; and Mr. Yamaguchi as interpreter....They seemed to enjoy themselves and unbent most decidedly. Their photographer and Mr. Inazu came and photographed the group in front of the tree, and outside against a background of coconut palms. The pictures were very good, and the indoor group at least was published in the Japanese papers of course as propaganda. We had boxes of candy for the officers to take away with them, paper bags of candy also for the non-coms, and a special box for Mr. Otsuke, who did not get in on the party. Fortunately, the headquarters people were above the gendarmerie, at least in their relations with us."[98]

Christmas was not the only time the missionaries entertained the Japanese military. On 19 January 1942 they gave "a farewell tea for three of the headquarters men who had been very friendly with us, and as helpful as possible under the circumstances—Messrs. Inazu, Yamaguchi and Setsani. They were being transferred to Manila we are quite sure, though military discipline did not allow them to say so....It was Mr. Yamaguchi who had asked me if I were the mission 'counter,' meaning cashier or treasurer." Ironically, at nearly the same moment the missionaries were entertaining the Japanese, their families in the United States were reading in newspapers that the Japanese had massacred all the Hainan missionaries. The story, which originated with a Nationalist Chinese communiqué from Chungking, Szechwan, headlined that the Hainan missionaries were "Missing in China" and "Slain by the Japanese."[99] The Moninger family did not believe Margaret was dead, but they still preserved the stories of her death from newspapers as far afield as Los Angeles and Washington, Pennsylvania, birthplace of her grandparents.

The whereabouts of the Hainan missionaries in the days after the United States and Japan declared war was the subject of much speculation. An official of the Presbyterian Board of Foreign Missions wrote to Margaret's brother on 30 December, saying that Margaret and the Melroses had been due to arrive in Canton in mid-November, but the Board could not confirm her presence in that city. After the newspapers published the stories of the missionaries' deaths, John Moninger informed one of his colleagues that the communiqué had only mentioned the Reverend and Mrs. David Thomas and Margaret Burkwall by name as being killed. By February 1942 the Board was able to confirm that Margaret and the Melroses had not left Hainan in November but could not say exactly where they were.[100]

Meanwhile, John had learned of the death of two French Catholic missionaries in Hainan and was urging the Presbyterian Board to get in touch with the Order of the Sacred Heart at the Catholic University of America to ask them to try to contact someone in Hainan concerning the Presbyterian missionaries. It was May before definite confirmation came, via a letter written by David Tappan in Canton and transmitted by carrier to Chungking, where it was mailed. The Reverend Mr. Tappan indicated that all the Hainan missionaries were still on the island and still occupying all three of the mission stations.[101]

Repatriation

Even though their families were uncertain of their whereabouts, life for the missionaries continued much the same during the early months of 1942. Then, early in May, Margaret reported that they "began cleaning out files and destroying old records, etc., and making out complete inventories of our baggage....we were told we were to sail from Shanghai for Lourenco Marques June 12 by the *Conte Verde*. An item we had seen in the Chinese newspaper a few weeks previously had more or less prepared us for the possibility of the African trip." Lieutenant Nakamura arranged for Alice Skinner and Margaret to visit the Kiungchow compound one afternoon, and they "were able to see a number of Chinese friends, and I in particular was very lucky because in all the mess of looted things in the house I found the papers necessary to complete my year's report to the Associated Mission Treasurers. The poor compound was a sight indeed, rapidly becoming a wilderness of grass and weeds." The possessions the missionaries could not take with them were sold at auction, with only the Japanese allowed to bid. "The funds received were to go towards making up the M¥1100.00 each one of us was to be allowed to take with us, and the proceeds above that amount were to be deposited in the Yokohama Specie Bank 'until after the war.' " [102]

Mary Taylor arrived from Nodoa on 19 May, and the Melroses and Mr. Sands, the British keeper of the Limko lighthouse who was employed by the Customs Service and had been interned at Nodoa with the missionaries, arrived three days later. "Our baggage was very cursorily inspected by Lt. Nakamura and sealed by the military....Lt. Nakamura said we were to travel to Shanghai by the *Menado Maru,* a coast steamer on which we had often made trips to and from Hong Kong in bygone days. He also said that the captain said he did not have a very good supply of food so we should take plenty." [103]

Leaving Hainan was not easy for the missionaries, particularly for Alice Skinner, who, because of her age, was due to retire in 1942. The others, of course, had no way of knowing if they would ever see the island again. Margaret was among those who would not. The Japanese eased the pain of departure for the missionary women, at least, by allowing Chinese women into the compound to say their good-by. "Those were hectic days, those last few in Hainan. There were so many things to do. A good many women friends came to tell Alice Skinner and others good-by, and the guards allowed them to come inside the gate and sit on benches there to talk with us. Miss Skinner obtained official permission at long last to give Tai-mui her sewing machine, and...various articles of bedding, clothing, etc. were hustled out as best we could by night or by day." [104]

On 23 May 1942, the missionaries' last morning in Hainan, Alice Skinner's amah, Tai-mui, whom Margaret had first mentioned in a 1915 letter written just a month after she arrived on the island, was permitted by the guards to enter the compound early and was cooking breakfast for the missionaries. "She scrambled eggs for us,...wiping away her tears as she did so, and made the coffee. I stepped out to the kitchen for something, and when she saw me she dropped her egg spoon, turned around and took me by the shoulders, almost shaking me in the excess of her emotion, and said, 'Miss Moninger, you take care of Miss Skinner until she reaches her own sister's hands.' " The missionaries went to the army headquarters, where "Colonel Matsuo wished us a safe journey and bade us a friendly good-by. Mr. Takada, resplendent in full uniform, and Mr. Ouija of the consular police, also in full regalia, joined the party and we drove on out from Hoihow to the new pier near the lighthouse....Lt. Nakamura himself came to the pier and waved us off....So we left the pier about 11:00 A.M., were soon on the *Menado,* and sailed away about 12:15....The *Menado* had huge white crosses painted on her battle ship grey hull, to show beyond doubt that she was a refugee-repatriate ship." Margaret reported that aboard the *Menado* the missionaries "saw our first Japanese war posters, and it was very noticeable that they used the characters 'holy war' or crusade, a very proper designation for the fanatical spirit in which they carry on." They anchored off Keelung, Formosa, but "as this was a fortified zone, we were not allowed outside the cabins." [105]

The group arrived in Shanghai on 31 May at about 1:00 in the afternoon and were met by "Swiss representatives [who] told us they had not even known we were being evacuated until about 11:00 that morning, when they had been told we would arrive shortly." Margaret later wrote her father, "And we hadn't moved off the dock at Shanghai before the workmen had the crosses on the *Menado* painted out." After being housed temporarily at the Shanghai American School, the missionaries moved to the Columbia Country Club, where the swimming pool was filled with water and inhabited by "millions, billions, and trillions of voracious mosquitoes!" Of the Americans at the country club, Margaret noted that "fully 80 per cent were between the ages of forty-five and fifty-five. Children were not numerous, and were limited to a few families. Single women, and men going home to join their families who had preceded them, were the rule." One of Margaret's classmates from Grinnell and another Grinnell graduate were among those going home.[106]

When they arrived in Shanghai, the missionaries were cautioned not to use either the telephone or the post office for important communications, but Margaret was "quietly told one day to be at a certain office in the Missions Building at a certain time, and was very happy to be present with about fifty others at a meeting of the National Christian Council." Margaret later wrote her family that "it wasn't until we reached Shanghai that we heard of the assassination rumor you people heard from Hainan. I don't think we were actually ever in any danger of losing our lives at any time."[107]

Of the Presbyterian missions in China, only the Hainan mission was being entirely vacated. The Reverend David Tappan, who was still in Canton, was the only member of the Hainan mission not being repatriated. (He would return to the United States in the second exchange of noncombatants.) While still in Shanghai, the missionaries celebrated Alice Skinner's seventieth birthday and the Bercovitzes' wedding anniversary.

In preparation for the ocean voyage home, mission doctors "secured two full cases of [powdered milk] (for $700, I believe) in five-pound tins for use of children and invalids on the steamer. In order to prevent difficulty with the Customs the boxes were opened and the tins distributed among any of the passengers who could carry a tin or two in their baggage, to be turned over to the doctors on the steamer." Then on 27 June the missionaries left on the Italian luxury liner the *Conte Verde,* pulling away from the dock at noon with "no 'sadness of farewell,' and no confetti, streamers of paper, flowers or waving friends, only a crowd of rain-soaked coolies leaving the sheds, a few Japanese officers and newspaper men watching us leave. We went down river and anchored at the bar to wait for the tide. So we left China—'thrust out,' verily, but in our cases at least feeling that for the time being our presence was more a liability than an asset for our Chinese Christians."[108]

Margaret reported that "there were seventy-eight adults and seven children of our Presbyterian missions on [the *Conte Verde*], by far the largest group of any one mission." After boarding the SS *Gripsholm* in Africa, she counted "144 adult Presbyterians...plus quite a number of children." On the trip from Africa Margaret met some Presbyterians from the Yunnan mission who told her they had friends in Scranton, Pennsylvania, named Mildred and Bill Moninger. "I said they surely must be distant relatives of ours, and that William was one of the family names."[109]

On the way to Africa, the *Conte Verde* was joined at Singapore by a sister ship, the *Asama Maru*. Margaret wrote to her father and her sister Helen that the two ships steamed "steadily along about half a mile...[apart], and both boats are well marked with huge white crosses" that were lit up at night. She later recalled that on "the morning of July 22 we awoke to see the shore of Africa and were soon steaming up the Limpopo River to the Lourenco Marques docks. As we passed the steamers anchored in the river the British and American boats shrieked out the Morse dot-dot-dot dash V for Victory on their whistles, and the crews cheered lustily. Those stained and faded and tattered Stars and Stripes at the mastheads of freighters and tankers looked mighty good to us, and most of us were wiping our eyes. We tied up at the big modern dock,...head up to the *Gripsholm,* and the *Asama Maru* anchored beyond her, three big liners in a row, making history, perhaps."[110] The Reverend John Steiner was repatriated from Hong Kong on the *Asama Maru* and rejoined the Hainan missionaries when they all boarded the *Gripsholm.*

In Lourenco Marques, Margaret received two air mail letters from her family and sent several home. The repatriates journeyed across the South Atlantic and stopped for a few days in Rio de Janeiro. After the *Gripsholm* left Rio "everybody took to writing in serious earnestness. We were asked to prepare data for Consul Myers of Canton on economic and industrial aspects of the occupation of Hainan; and very particularly to report on the treatment of Americans and status of American property after the freezing and up to the declaration of war; and also after war was declared. Our situation in Hoihow and Kiungchow was at the time of freezing the worst in all China—we got then what other places did not get until December 8th when war was declared."[111]

Aboard the *Gripsholm* E. Mowbray Tate of the Presbyterian mission in Thailand and Margaret decided to try to find out how many Phi Beta Kappa members were on board. Eventually forty people signed up, "twenty-seven men and thirteen women, representing thirty-three colleges and universities." The list included twenty-nine missionaries; eight consuls and embassy clerks; one Japanese woman, presumably American-born, who had been teaching in a government school in Japan; a university professor from California; an employee of the Chinese Customs Service; and one businessman.[112]

It was on the *Gripsholm* that the Hainan missionaries "first saw a copy of the *Reader's Digest*...article entitled, 'Prelude to Treachery,'...which should be read by every one interested in Hainan. It shows clearly several reasons why our communications were so cut off, and why any suspicious actions on the part of any foreigner on the island were immediately invested with significance of serious and sinister import."[113] The article detailed the Japanese use of Hainan as a staging area for their invasion of Southeast Asia.

Finally, on 25 August 1942 the Hainan missionaries and their shipmates "passed the Statue of Liberty just at 8:00 A.M....Groups on deck were singing, *The Star-Spangled Banner* and *America* as we steamed slowly in, and anchored at Jersey City." It was 27 August before Margaret was taken for questioning by the army and the F.B.I., along with Dr. Morse and the Melroses and others whose surnames started with *M*. "My questioning proceeded quietly and uneventfully except that the men questioned my statements as to the date of our internment in July, 1941, thinking of course it should be December, after war was declared....As I was signing for my letters...people said some one at the barrier was calling me, I looked around, and there was John!" Her brother had driven to Pittsburgh on a business trip and then had taken the train to New York to meet Margaret. She briefly visited the offices of the Board of Foreign Missions the next day, and then she and John took the train to Pittsburgh. Driving westward, they stopped to see the Arthur French family in Ohio and spent the night with John's family near Chicago. On 30 August they arrived in Marshalltown, where Margaret found "Dad well and happy." At the family home were her sisters, Dorothy, Helen, and Louise. Dorothy was joined by her husband and their four girls. It was the first time Margaret had been with all her siblings since she had departed for China at the end of her second furlough in 1929.[114]

Conclusion

WHEN MARGARET ARRIVED home that summer day in 1942, her life changed as drastically as it had the summer day in 1915 when she first departed for China. Her father, to whose home she returned, had given up the family farm and moved to Marshalltown shortly after his wife died in 1928. Margaret had been to the house in town on her furlough in 1935, but now it would be her home. Her youngest sister, Louise, also lived there, acting as housekeeper for their father. Margaret celebrated her fifty-first birthday a month after her return. She would live another seven and a half years. World War II, which had so disrupted Margaret's life in Hainan, still raged but little touched the family in Iowa. Margaret resumed teaching at Buffalo Center, Iowa, but a stroke in February 1944 ended her career. She went to stay temporarily with her sister Dorothy and her family in Strawberry Point, Iowa. Later that year three naval officers visited Margaret, talking in private with her for several hours. Most likely she drew them maps of Hainan and discussed with them the various peoples who inhabited the island.[1]

Margaret undoubtedly had great difficulty adjusting to her new life in Iowa. After the initial excitement of returning home and a round of talks at the local churches about mission work and the coming of the Japanese to Hainan, she really had no one with whom to discuss the life she had lived. When she wrote her lengthy manuscript "Hainan Was My Home," she dedicated it to "the Rev. and Mrs. C. Wayne Overholser, with deep appreciation for their sympathetic understanding, encouragement and counsel."[2] It is likely that they were the ones who suggested she write the account, which allowed her to come to grips with the life she had chosen for herself.

Certainly, one of the aspects of her life that gave her reason for reflection was the nature of the work she had done in China. In Shanghai awaiting repatriation in 1942, Margaret noted that the overwhelming majority of those sharing her plight were her contemporaries; indeed, one was a classmate from Grinnell. The Social Gospel had altered American Protestantism in the years just before Margaret joined the mission, and Grinnell College, to which she had gone in 1909, had a strong tradition of service. A member of the generation of American college students who had been swept up in the Student Volunteer Movement for Foreign Missions, Margaret, like many of her brightest contemporaries, believed in the slogan of the organization, "The Evangelization of the World in This Generation."

Although she had joined the SVMFM while in college, at the time Margaret applied to the Presbyterian Board of Foreign Missions in 1913 she had difficulty answering the questions about religious activities. Despite the Social Gospel's influence on American Protestantism, the application to become a Presbyterian missionary still indicated that a religious commitment was necessary. In answering the questions, Margaret clearly expressed her desire to "serve," but she could name no one she personally had led to Christ. Undoubtedly she had heard or read of missionaries who had experienced a call to the mission field, but clearly she had none. Perhaps thinking this would exclude her, she wrote the Board a letter trying to explain more fully her religious life. She even wrote that she would give up China if she were needed elsewhere.[3]

If she had no religious call, the question must be asked why Margaret decided to become a missionary. The answer lies as much in the American society that produced Margaret as in her desire to "serve." Although she graduated Phi Beta Kappa from college, American society offered few opportunities to challenge brilliant women like Margaret. America in 1913 still denied women the right to vote. Careers open to college-educated women of the day were teaching, nursing, and, for a few, medicine. There is no indication in any of Margaret's writing that she ever considered medicine. Margaret's mother, herself a college graduate, had taught only briefly before she became a full-time homemaker. Margaret's aunt Harriette, who had been a teacher, worked as an assistant at the Botany Department at Iowa State College but only obtained that position after her hearing failed, making teaching no longer possible. Margaret, faced with the choice of teaching in the small schools of rural Iowa or teaching in mission schools in China, opted for the latter. She indicated she was influenced in her decision by her conversations with a missionary to Turkey who was spending his furlough year at Grinnell, and she was likely influenced by some earlier vision of Romanticism that had prevailed among missionaries in the nineteenth century.

Margaret was typical of the women sent by the mainstream Protestant churches as missionaries in the early twentieth century, in that virtually every one was a college graduate. In the period before World War I, becoming a missionary was a respectable career choice that afforded Protestant women the opportunities to head schools, manage finances, and run hospitals, which some of their Roman Catholic sisters found by joining religious orders. Margaret had no religious call to China; rather, her call was to serve and to live a life that offered travel and more excitement than the one she would have had at home. She went to China as a teacher for the mission schools, although she did work as an itinerating missionary from time to time.

Leaving for China in 1915 with the SVMFM's goal in mind, Margaret must have realized within a short time after her arrival in Hainan how impossible it would be to carry out the Movement's motto. Certainly she was not the only missionary to face the reality of the Chinese situation, namely a culture far different from that of the West and one whose people showed little interest in the religion of the foreigners. Margaret revealed in her letters to her family and friends a China she found interesting and exotic. She wrote nothing to them about the futility of the SVMFM's slogan. Near the end of her first year in China, Margaret, suffering severe eye trouble, mentioned just once that she had suffered an attack of nerves. Many missionaries became ill in China and used their illnesses as a reason to return home quickly. Unfortunately, few left any records that might suggest that their illnesses were produced either by culture shock or by the realization that China would never be a Christian nation. Yet many missionaries, Margaret among them, recovered their health and came to terms with themselves and exactly what they could contribute to China. Margaret's intellectual strengths were in mathematics and Latin, but she abandoned both to teach at the elementary level in the mission schools, with only an occasional stint at teaching mathematics at the mission high school.

Margaret arrived at the Hainan mission at a time when foreigners still controlled all the money and made all the decisions. True, the mission had already ordained several Chinese pastors, but they were paid small salaries compared with the foreigners and had no say in the business of the mission. Even as growing Chinese nationalism and its attendant anti-Christian sentiment made it necessary for the missionaries to appoint Chinese to head their schools and to include Chinese Christians in their decision making, no Chinese ever attended the annual mission meetings. Intellectually, Margaret knew that according to Christian doctrine those Chinese who were Christians would share eternity with her, but she still had difficulty sharing her worldly life with them. As her housemate Esther Morse observed, Margaret enjoyed entertaining Chinese in their home, but she had trouble giving up her job as church organist to a Chinese schoolgirl whom she had taught to play the organ. Like many of her contemporaries who joined the mission in the early 1900s, Margaret did not question the superiority of American culture and wanted only to pass it on to the Chinese. Learning from the Chinese was not necessarily part of her desired experiences.

Yet Margaret did learn from the Chinese, and she came to enjoy some facets of Chinese culture. Soon after arriving in Hainan, she tried to discern the meanings of the figures she saw displayed in a Chinese temple, but she did so by comparing them with aspects of Western culture with which she was familiar. Her two-volume dictionary contains a long list of Chinese proverbs with English equivalents. Thus China was understandable to Margaret if translated into Western modes. But after she had been in China a number of years, she began to enjoy some aspects of Chinese culture on its own terms. Now she viewed the village dragon dance for the pure enjoyment of it. Kite flying in Kachek she compared with kite flying in Kiungchow, not with an American version of the pastime.

Margaret found in China an ambiguity that she expressed over the years in the letters she wrote. As a Christian, and especially as a missionary, Margaret had to deal with the Christian teaching of the equality of all in the sight of God. Yet daily in China she saw people who did not share that vision and were totally convinced of the superiority of their philosophical systems. She realized that many of the Chinese who came to the mission compound came not because of an interest in Christianity but because of a desire to see the foreigners—to see what their church was like, to see what their houses were like, and, particularly, to get a firsthand, close-up view of the curious-looking people. Indeed, she once wrote home that she felt it was impossible to discuss the Gospel with such huge crowds of people, noting that she had been stared at so much that she felt like a circus elephant. Margaret had no illusions that her visitors were interested in Christianity; they were simply curious about her. Somehow Margaret never attributed the same motive to the Miao people, whom she thought were genuinely interested in Christianity, even while she acknowledged that they came in great numbers to see her and the other foreigners who journeyed into their villages.

Margaret also found in China a country that little valued education for women. Even after several years in China, Margaret still found it unusual to talk about matters of importance only with men. As a Christian she found it difficult to resolve the dilemma presented by the fact that many Chinese women thought religion was a concern for men and that they, as women, were unimportant beings.

In the years Margaret was in China, the society was in turmoil in the aftermath of the collapse of the Ch'ing dynasty. Margaret witnessed the comings and goings of armies under the control of various Chinese political factions and the chaos they brought to the residents of Hainan, most of whom were simply trying to eke out a living for their families. Margaret longed for the order of American political life transported in toto to China. She wanted to teach the Chinese true patriotism. Yet Margaret's idea of patriotism included heavy doses of American Protestant Christianity. She, like many missionaries, became cynical about China's political problems, writing that she had observed that those who were seized by hostile political forces were frequently those who were able to pay the required ransoms. Describing one such situation, she wrote, "I do not especially care to be a Chinese citizen."[4]

As the work of the mission in Hainan became more and more the focus of Margaret's life, she personally became more interested in religion. Esther Morse, writing to her own family, found Margaret's interest in religion overwhelming and noted that Margaret enjoyed preaching, even if her fellow missionaries did not enjoy being the congregation. The Reverend Henry Bucher recalled that Margaret was more knowledgeable about the Bible than any of the ordained men of the mission and, indeed, was so capable that she intimidated all her male colleagues. Margaret's junior colleague Evelyn French remembered Margaret as one of the missionaries who she felt had definitely had a call to missionary service.[5] Yet both the Reverend Mr. Bucher and Mrs. French first met Margaret when she was close to forty and had been a missionary for fifteen years, so the Margaret they knew had certainly reconciled herself to the conditions of the life she had chosen for herself and was far different from the college undergraduate who had decided to become a missionary.

Margaret revealed little in her letters to suggest that she felt the will of God in her actions. Few of the letters she wrote mention a divine presence in her decisions and work. A rare reference appeared in a letter to the Board of Foreign Missions written on Christmas Day 1917, just a little over two years after Margaret arrived in Hainan. And at home between 1927 and 1929 partly because of the political turmoil in China, Margaret wrote to the Board, "I am not at all pessimistic, personally, over the *ultimate* triumph of Christianity in China, however dark the situation may seem at times."[6] In all of her other letters in those two years she made only one other reference to God's will, being concerned instead with the political conditions in China, her financial status particularly with regard to her pension, her teaching, and the courses she was taking at the State University of Iowa. Perhaps most telling, of the hundreds of Margaret's letters that survive, only the Christmas 1917 letter to the Board of Foreign Missions is signed "Yours in His Service." Her other letters to the Board and supporters at home end with "Very sincerely yours." To friends she occasionally used "Cordially," and to her family she closed with "Lovingly," "Love," or "As ever."

Margaret displayed an irrepressible sense of humor, which sustained her throughout her years in China. When her older colleague Katherine Schaeffer, who was thin and wiry, fell through the bamboo bed in the Chinese inn, she and Margaret laughed until they cried, and Margaret remarked she could not understand why it had not been her. Knowing she would be the center of attention on her trips to the Miao country and would have no privacy, Margaret took along the foamiest toothpaste she had so that she would provide a good show as she brushed her teeth before the crowd who had never before seen such a ritual. And even when the Japanese had her under house arrest, she could enjoy the sight of an Imperial Japanese Army officer, stripped of his finery, climbing a palm on the mission compound to obtain prized coconuts.

Living in retirement, Margaret could only think back over the life she had chosen for herself. In honesty, she would admit, after twenty-three years in China as a missionary, she had personally led very few Chinese to Christ, and probably none had made that decision solely through her efforts. Even her beloved Chinese teacher, Li Hai-so, was as much influenced by the Reverend David Tappan as he was by Margaret. Throughout the war years she corresponded with her fellow workers from the Hainan mission, most of whom were in the United States awaiting return to China. Her stroke in 1944 ensured that she would not accompany them, but now she used the same determination with which she had learned Chinese to recover her health.

After returning to Marshalltown, she became the financial secretary of the First Presbyterian Church there, a task that must have seemed easy after the bookkeeping she had done in the many currencies in use in China. Another stroke hospitalized Margaret in 1948, but again she recovered and took up her new hobby of following baseball games on the radio. A devoted fan, she knew the statistics of her favorite players and teams.[7] Margaret lived to see the Communists gain control of China in 1949 and begin to try to create order out of the chaos that had plagued the country for half a century.

It was not a religious call to mission that Margaret heard in 1913, but rather a call to service and a call to live a life of fun and excitement, not the mundane life she faced on the prairies of America. Margaret, who survived the mayhem of early twentieth-century China, traveled to the Miao country fulfilling her stated ambition of going "where no white woman has ever been," fled Hainan twice on orders from diplomatic personnel, lived under house arrest by the Japanese both before and after Pearl Harbor, and was repatriated from Asia via Africa and South America during World War II on ships brilliantly emblazoned night and day for protection, died quietly at the age of fifty-eight on 21 March 1950 at her Iowa home just a few miles from the house in which she was born. Her call had been answered; her life had not been dull.

Notes

Abbreviations

BFM   Board of Foreign Missions
DC   Dodson Collection
MMM   Mary Margaret Moninger
MP   Mary Margaret Moninger Papers
PHS   Presbyterian Historical Society

Introduction

1. For statistics on women college graduates, see Nancy Woloch, *Women and the American Experience* (New York: Knopf, 1984), 543.

2. The SVMFM forwarded the names of those who signed their pledge to the mission boards of the various churches to which the volunteers belonged, and the churches in turn recruited them as missionaries. For a discussion of the SVMFM, see Kenneth S. Latourette, *History of Christian Missions in China* (New York: MacMillan, 1929), 358, 535.

3. The estimate of 50,000 is mine, based on my previous work; see Kathleen L. Lodwick, *The Chinese Recorder Index: A Guide to Christian Missions in Asia, 1867-1941* (Wilmington, Del.: Scholarly Resources, 1986). About 50,000 individual names appeared in *The Chinese Recorder* during its seventy-two-year run, although many fewer appear in the published index owing to space restrictions. (The unpublished data are deposited at the Day Missions Library, Yale Univ. Divinity School.) Not everyone whose name appeared in *The Chinese Recorder* was a missionary, and not every missionary was included, but even considering these factors I believe 50,000 is a good estimate for the total number of people in China as missionaries between 1809 and 1949. The figure 6,500 is from Latourette, *History of Christian Missions in China*, 822; Latourette gives that number for 1 January 1927, citing the *Bulletin of the National Christian Council*. Most mission agencies working in China were American, and they were also the largest in number of

personnel. The single largest group, the China Inland Mission, however, recruited internationally. Perhaps 70 percent of the missionaries were Americans. Women constituted about 60 percent of the missionary force; one-third of them were single. Thus in 1927 about 4,550 American missionaries were working in China, of whom 2,730 were women; 910 of those women were single.

4. I am indeted to Frederick Heuser, director of the Presbyterian Historical Society, who has done research on Presbyterian women missionaries, for his views on this topic. We agree that there is no evidence that applicants were rejected on any grounds except that of health and that there was a distinct change in the qualifications for missionaries in the mid-1890s, as the Board sought better educated individuals. Applications on file at the Society bear a strong resemblance to one another. After the organization of the SVMFM, most applications came via that route. Letters of reference, generally written by clergymen, college professors, and longtime family friends, uniformly attest to the good character of the applicant and to the applicant's church membership and activities. See Frederick Heuser, "Culture, Feminism and the Gospel: American Presbyterian Women and Foreign Missions, 1870-1923" (Ph.D. diss., Temple University, 1991).

5. Evelyn French, telephone conversation, 17 May 1992. (Those individuals who went to China as independent, faith missionaries, that is, trusting God, not a mission board of a mainstream church at home, to support them, likely still attributed their actions to "a call.")

6. Jane Hunter, *The Gospel of Gentility: American Women Missionaries in Turn-of-the-Century China* (New Haven, Conn.: Yale Univ. Press, 1984).

7. After visiting Hainan in 1881, the Reverend B.C. Henry of the Canton mission wrote the Board of Foreign Missions in New York that the aborigines "have very little worship of their own...and are free from most of the prejudices and superstitions that are such a barrier among the Chinese....the disposition of the Lois is such that we may reasonably hope for ready acceptance of the gospel among them." B.C. Henry to Robert Ellinwood, 2 Jan. 1882, Canton, Presbyterian Church in the U.S.A., Board of Foreign Missions Papers, Record Group 82, Presbyterian Historical Society; hereinafter PCUSA, BFM Papers.

8. [Mary Margaret Moninger], ed., *Isle of Palms: Sketches of Hainan* (Shanghai: Commercial, 1919; rpt. New York: Garland, 1980), 58-74, 115, 116. In subsequent citations, Moninger will be referred to as MMM.

9. Evelyn French, telephone conversation, 17 May 1992.

10. MMM to Folks, 28 Nov. 1937, Nodoa, Mary Margaret Moninger Papers, Record Group 39, Presbyterian Historical Society; hereinafter cited as MP, PHS. Esther Morse to Ruth, 28 June 1931, Kachek, Esther Morse Papers, Special Collections, Univ. of Oregon; hereinafter cited as Morse Papers. The typewriter referred to was probably the one the Reverend Frank P. Gilman had used, which had remained in the possession of various missionaries after his death in 1918.

11. MMM to Auntie, 19 Aug. 1915, Yokohama, Japan, MP, PHS.

12. Edward H. Schafer, *Shore of Pearls* (Berkeley: Univ. of California Press, 1970), covers Hainan from ancient times to the end of the Sung dynasty, and although he mentions Carl C. Jeremiassen and B.C. Henry, who collected plants on the island, curiously Schafer does not mention Margaret. He also wrongly states

that the interior of the island was not known to Europeans until a series of scientific expeditions in the 1920s, overlooking the many published accounts of the numerous journeys Margaret and her colleagues, Frank P. Gilman, Henrietta Montgomery, Katherine Schaeffer, and George D. Byers, as well as Jeremiassen, had made into the region.

13. MMM, "Hainan Was My Home," 57, Margaret Moninger Papers, private collection of Susannah Moninger Dodson; hereinafter cited as MP, DC. It is unclear who the woman was. Dr. Morse seems the most likely possibility, but since she had served no other station before arriving in Hainan, the reference to familiarity with the situation at other stations seems to rule her out. Margaret Burkwall, a nurse, grew up in a mission in Canton, so she might be the person Margaret refers to here.

14. I am indebted to both Frederick Heuser and Kristen Gleeson at the Presbyterian Historical Society for sharing their views on this interpretation of the motivations of women missionaries. Gleeson is currently writing a dissertation on women medical doctors who became missionaries. We all agree that the career opportunities afforded women on the mission fields, compared to the limited ones at home, were strong attractions for very capable and ambitious women.

15. MMM, "An Excursion Trip," 22 June 1917, Kachek, MP, PHS. The Miao region was in the mountains to the south and west of the town of Kachek. Margaret reported that "one old-young woman told me she had moved *twelve* times in her life of forty-odd years." MMM, "The Hainanese Miao," *Journal of the North China Branch of the Royal Asiatic Society* 52 (1921):46.

16. John S. Service, ed., *Golden Inches: The China Memoir of Grace Service* (Berkeley: Univ. of California Press, 1989).

17. *Los Angeles Times, Washington (Pa.) Observer,* and *Marshalltown (Iowa) Times-Republican,* 17 and 18 Jan. 1942.

1. Joining the Hainan Mission, 1915

1. MMM to Dot, 29 Sept. 1918, Kachek, MP, PHS; MMM, "Hainan Was My Home," 1-2, MP, DC.

2. MMM to People, 14 Oct. 1917, Kachek, MP, PHS.

3. MMM, "Cedarcroft," unpublished typescript, Hainan, 1941-42, and Marshalltown, Iowa, 1943, 7-8, MP, DC. Margaret rarely used her full name, but she did on this typescript.

4. *Atlas of Marshall County, Iowa* (Des Moines: G.W. Anderson, 1924), 14. See also MMM, "Cedarcroft," MP, DC.

5. William R. Moninger, "Diary, 1891, Galvin, Iowa," MP, DC.

6. MMM, "Cedarcroft," 14, 26, MP, DC.

7. MMM to People, 23 Sept. 1915, Kachek, MP, PHS.

8. MMM, "Cedarcroft," 20, MP, DC.

9. Ibid., 32.

10. Ibid., 48.

11. Ibid., 47.

12. Ibid., 35.

13. MMM to John, 23 June 1940, Kiungchow, MP, PHS.
14. MMM, "Cedarcroft," 45, MP, DC. After returning home from China in 1942, Margaret wrote, "From high school days it seemed to me foreign missions was my lot," but she did not elaborate. MMM, "Hainan Was My Home," 1, MP, DC.
15. MMM, "Cedarcroft," 5, MP, DC.
16. MMM, scrapbook, MP, DC; *Grinnell College Scarlet and Black,* 5 March 1913, 1. Margaret's name appears third in the list of students, but there is no indication whether that was her rank in the class. Just before graduation in June 1913, five others were named to Phi Beta Kappa.
17. *Grinnell College Scarlet and Black,* 11 June 1913, 8.
18. MMM, Application, Student Volunteer Movement for Foreign Missions Collection, Yale Univ. Divinity School; hereinafter cited as SVMFM application. See also *Grinnell College Scarlet and Black,* 17 Nov. 1909, 2.
19. *Grinnell College Scarlet and Black,* 12 Jan. 1910; 7 Feb. 1912; 6, 9, 12, 16, 19, and 20 March 1912; 7 Dec. 1912; 15 and 25 Jan. 1913; 16, 23, and 30 April 1913; and 11 June 1913.
20. *Grinnell College Cyclone,* vol. 20, May 1912.
21. MMM, SVMFM application.
22. Ibid. The classmate was Jiro Imada of Hiroshima. There was also one African American in the class, J. Owen Redmon of Colfax, Iowa. *Grinnell College Cyclone,* vol. 20, May 1912.
23. *Grinnell College Cyclone,* vol. 20, May 1912.
24. MMM, "Cedarcroft," 50, MP, DC.
25. MMM, BFM application, MP, PHS.
26. Ibid.
27. Ibid. Margaret was a founding member of a Christian Endeavor group at the Hartland church, near her home, in 1908 and served as the group's vice president. She also belonged to Christian Endeavor while in college. MMM, scrapbook, private collection of Dorothy Gill Barnes; hereinafter cited as MP, Barnes collection.
28. Ibid.
29. Ibid.
30. Dorothy Gill Barnes, interviews by author, 11 Dec. 1989 and 5 June 1990.
31. MMM to John, 30 May 1941, Kiungchow, MP, DC.
32. MMM to John, 17 Aug. 1941, Kiungchow, MP, DC.
33. MMM to People, Monday [1915], someplace in Nevada, MP, PHS. Margaret apparently had an agreement or wager with some of her friends or family that she would not marry. In a letter to her mother's college friend Mary Munnell, called Aunt Tot, she wrote, "The contract shows no sign of even cracking yet although one young gentleman 'hangs around' quite a little bit. But he's just a kid, so don't worry." MMM to Aunt Tot, 14 Aug. 1915, SS *Manchuria.* Later from Hong Kong she mentioned to her grandmother that "a very interesting young gentleman of the [American Board of Commissioners for Foreign Missions], going out to India,...is at our table at the hotel. He is a Mr. Lundstrum from Minne-

sota, and we have had some very pleasant conversations, but the contract is O.K. as yet." MMM to Grandma, 4 Sept. 1915, Hong Kong, both in MP, PHS.

34. MMM to People, Monday [2 Aug. 1915], [SS *Manchuria*], MP, PHS. Margaret meant "pidgin" English, but she would acquire the patois of the China coast later.

35. MMM to Grandma, 5 Aug. 1915, [SS *Manchuria*], MMM to Girls, 11 Aug. 1915, [SS *Manchuria*], MMM to People, Monday [2 Aug. 1915], [SS *Manchuria*], all in MP, PHS.

36. MMM to Dad, 19 Aug. 1915, Yokohama, Japan, MP, PHS.

37. Ibid.

38. MMM to People, 31 Aug. 1915, Manila, Philippines, MP, PHS.

39. Margaret had probably heard the story of the Kellys' courtship from others of the Hainan mission, because within two days of meeting them she wrote home that "Dr. Kelly met Mrs. K. on a steamer and married her five days afterward. What about that for hustling?" MMM to Grandma, 4 Sept. 1915, Hong Kong, MP, PHS.

40. Ibid.; MMM, "Hainan Was My Home," 6, MP, DC.

41. MMM to People, 10 Sept. 1915, Kiungchow, MP, PHS. Margaret's journey from Hong Kong compared with one she later reported that Mrs. McCandliss, Ruth and Charles, and Dr. and Mrs. Bercovitz had. "They all had ptomaine poisoning, the ship's machinery was disabled for a while and they drifted for four hours, then came through the dangerous Hainan straits at night. To cap the climax, their cargo of live pigs got loose. So they are rather tired." MMM to Auntie, 14 Nov. 1915, Kiungchow, MP, PHS.

42. MMM, "Hainan Was My Home," 7, MP, DC. Margaret did not say who the missionary was.

43. MMM to People, 10 Sept. 1915, Kiungchow, MP, PHS.

44. MMM, "Hainan Was My Home," 7, MP, DC.

45. MMM to People, 10 Sept. 1915, Kiungchow, MP, PHS.

46. MMM to Helen, 26 Sept. 1915, Kachek, MP, PHS.

47. MMM to People, 10 Sept. 1915, Kiungchow, MP, PHS.

48. MMM, "Hainan Was My Home," 11, MP, DC.

49. MMM to Dot, 27 Sept. 1915, Kachek, MP, PHS.

50. MMM to People, 3 Oct. 1915, Kiungchow, MP, PHS.

51. MMM to People, 23 Sept. 1915, Kachek; MMM to Helen, 26 Sept. 1915, Kachek; both in MP, PHS.

52. MMM to People, 10 Sept. 1915, Kiungchow, MP, PHS.

53. MMM to People, 7 Nov. 1915, Kiungchow, MP, PHS.

54. MMM to Dot, 21 Nov. 1915, Kiungchow, MP, PHS.

55. MMM, "Hainan Was My Home," 16-17, MP, DC.

56. Ibid., 17.

57. MMM to Auntie, 26 Dec. 1915, Kiungchow, MP, PHS.

58. MMM to Daddy, 4 Jan. 1916, Hoihow; MMM to People, 9 Jan. 1916, Kiungchow, both in MP, PHS.

59. MMM to People, 26 Feb. 1916, Kachek, MP, PHS.

60. MMM to People, 15 April 1916, Kachek, MP, PHS.

61. Ibid.
62. MMM to Dot, 29 April 1916, Kachek, MP, PHS.
63. MMM to People, [13 Aug. 1916], Hong Kong, MP, PHS.
64. MMM to Girls, 26 Nov. 1916, Kachek, MP, PHS.
65. MMM to Dot, 21 Nov. 1915, Kiungchow, MP, PHS.
66. Ibid.
67. MMM to People, 9 Jan. 1916, Kiungchow, MP, PHS.
68. MMM to Auntie, 26 Dec. 1915, Kiungchow, MP, PHS.
69. MMM to Louise, 8 March 1916, Kachek, MP, PHS.
70. MMM to People, 1 Nov. 1915, Kiungchow, MP, PHS. Margaret's family published many of her letters in the *Marshalltown (Iowa) Times-Republican* in the years between 1915 and 1942, and articles appeared from time to time in other Iowa newspapers.
71. MMM to People, 10 Oct. 1915, Kiungchow; MMM to Auntie, 5 Dec. 1915, Kiungchow, both in MP, PHS.
72. MMM to People, 10 Oct. 1915, Kiungchow, MP, PHS.
73. MMM to Auntie Parks, 11 Oct. 1915, Kiungchow, MP, PHS. There were, in fact, two missionaries buried at Kiungchow at the time: Carl C. Jeremiassen, the founder of the mission, who had been in the Chinese Imperial Maritime Customs Service, who died from illness in 1901, and the Reverend John C. Melrose, who had joined the mission in 1890, who died from illness in 1897. Several missionary children, including Melrose's daughter, who died the same week he did, were also buried in the cemetery. (Margaret Melrose was John's widow.)
74. MMM to Helen, 24 Oct. 1915, Kiungchow; see also MMM to Auntie, 25 Oct. 1915, Kiungchow, both in MP, PHS; and [MMM], *Isle of Palms*. 47-50.
75. MMM to Auntie Parks, 11 Oct. 1915, Kiungchow, MP, PHS.
76. MMM to People, 10 Oct. 1915, Kiungchow, MP, PHS.
77. MMM to Auntie, 25 Oct. 1915, Kiungchow, MP, PHS.
78. MMM to People, 10 Oct. 1915, Kiungchow, MP, PHS.
79. MMM to Helen, 18 Jan. 1916, Kiungchow, MP, PHS.
80. MMM to People, 26 Jan. 1916, Kachek, MP, PHS.
81. MMM to People, 21 Dec. 1915, Kiungchow, MP, PHS.
82. MMM to People, 29 April 1916, Kachek, MP, PHS.
83. MMM to People, 7 May 1916, Kachek, MP, PHS.
84. MMM to People, 28 May 1916, Kachek, MP, PHS.
85. MMM to Girls, 16 July 1916, Kiungchow, MP, PHS.
86. MMM to Grandma, 6 Aug. 1916, Kiungchow, MP, PHS.
87. MMM to People, 10 Sept. 1915, Kiungchow; MMM to Auntie, 25 Oct. 1915, Kiungchow, both in MP, PHS.
88. MMM to People, 9 July 1916, Kiungchow, MP, PHS. See also *Grinnell College Bulletin* 8, no. 1 (March-May 1910).
89. MMM to People, 27 May 1917, Kachek, MP, PHS. Mrs. Kelly had been a Methodist missionary in India before her marriage. Margaret had regular correspondence with E.D. Merrill at the Manila Bureau of Science about the plants she was collecting, some of which are now a part of the permanent collection of the Philippine National Herbarium in Manila.

90. MMM to People, 1 Nov. 1915, Kiungchow, MP, PHS.
91. MMM, "Hainan Was My Home," 14, MP, DC.
92. Ibid.
93. MMM to People, 10 Oct. 1915, Kiungchow, MP, PHS.
94. MMM to People, 1 April 1916, Kachek, MP, PHS.
95. MMM to Helen, 24 Oct. 1915, Kiungchow, MP, PHS.
96. Katherine Schaeffer to Stanley White, 20 March 1915, Kachek, PCUSA, BFM Papers. The woman educator for Kachek was number seven on the list of personnel of the China Council. Schaeffer wrote, "I feel the importance of this lady's being sent out this year so keenly, that I want to be responsible for $275....deduct that amount yearly from my salary; please take all my salary month by month until the amount is paid, do not trouble to take a part and send a part." Schaeffer's salary was about $800 a year in 1915. She asked that her contribution be credited to "the China Campaign Fund...from the Synodical Society of Wisconsin as from a Wisconsin missionary."
97. MMM to Girls, 18 June 1916, Dengang Chapel; MMM to People, 9 July 1916, Kiungchow, both in MP, PHS. Evelyn French remembers that in the 1930s the missionaries customarily made a small contribution to the local church but reserved the larger part of their donations to aid the hospitals or needy students in the schools. French, telephone conversation with author, 19 Oct. 1991.
98. MMM to Helen, 26 Dec. 1915, Kiungchow; MMM to People, 26 Dec. 1915, Kiungchow, both in MP, PHS.
99. MMM to People, 17 Jan. 1916, Kiungchow, MP, PHS.
100. MMM to People, 26 Dec. 1915, Kiungchow, MP, PHS.
101. MMM to People, 19 Dec. 1915, Kiungchow, MP, PHS.
102. MMM to People, 23 Sept. 1915, Kachek, MP, PHS. Curiously, the following year Margaret arrived in Kachek just a few days before her twenty-fifth birthday, which she told her family passed quietly. "No one even knew it was my birthday." MMM to People, 24 Sept. 1916, Kachek, MP, PHS.
103. MMM to Auntie, 17 Jan. 1916, Kiungchow, MP, PHS. For a discussion of the problems of missionaries in alien environments, see Mary Taylor Huber, *The Bishop's Progress: A Historical Ethnography of Catholic Missionary Experience on the Sepik Frontier* (Washington, D.C.: Smithsonian Institution Press, 1988).
104. MMM to Dot, 6 Feb. 1916, Kachek; MMM to Auntie, 6 Feb. 1916, Kachek; both in MP, PHS.
105. MMM to People, 13 Feb. 1916, Kachek, MP, PHS.
106. MMM to People, 9 Jan. 1916, Kiungchow, MP, PHS.
107. MMM to People, 17 Jan. 1916, Kiungchow, MP, PHS; MMM, "Hainan Was My Home," 61, MP, DC.
108. MMM to People, 13 Feb. 1916, Kachek; MMM to People, 29 April 1916, Kachek, both in MP, PHS.
109. MMM to People, 30 July 1916, Kiungchow, MP, PHS. MMM to Dorothy, 13 May 1917, Kachek, MP, Barnes collection. MMM to Jack, 8 Aug. 1917, Hoihow, MP, PHS.
110. MMM to People, 21 Oct. 1917, Kachek, MP, PHS. Lung was a Yunnanese and a supporter of Yuan Shih-k'ai. After the death of Yuan in 1916,

Lung was made commissioner of mining development in Hainan and took control of the island with his army. In December 1917 the Peking government appointed him inspector general for Kwangtung and Kwangsi, and he moved his army across the straits to the Luichow Peninsula, where his army attacked the troops loyal to Sun Yat-sen. Lung's army was defeated, and he moved north in 1918. Shortly thereafter he retired, and he died in Shanghai in 1921. See Boorman, *Biographical Dictionary of Republican China* (New York: Columbia Univ. Press, 1968), 2: 455-57.

111. MMM to Grandma, 28 Oct. 1917, Kachek; MMM to People, 11 Nov. 1917, Kachek; MMM to People, 25 Nov. 1917, Kachek, all in MP, PHS.

112. U.S. consular officials often recommended that Americans include guns among their possessions when arriving in China to set up housekeeping. Robert Thomas, interview by author, 20 May 1987.

113. MMM to Helen, 12 March 1916, Kachek; MMM to Helen, 22 April 1916, Kachek, both in MP, PHS. Margaret either had not heard her colleagues' stories about pirate attacks or she wanted to keep the truth from her family. Many of the missionaries had been victims of pirates, particularly when they crossed the straits to the Luichow Peninsula.

114. MMM to Daddy, 4 Jan. 1916, Hoihow, MP, PHS.
115. MMM to People, 7 May 1916, Kachek, MP, PHS.
116. MMM to Girls, 18 June 1916, Dengang Chapel, MP, PHS.
117. Ibid.; MMM to People, 25 June 1916, Nodoa, MP, PHS.
118. MMM to People, 25 June 1916, Nodoa, MP, PHS.
119. MMM, "Report, 1916," PCUSA, BFM Papers.
120. MMM to People, 9 July 1916, Kiungchow; MMM to People, [13 Aug. 1916], Hong Kong, both in MP, PHS.
121. MMM to People, 25 June 1916, Nodoa, MP, PHS.

2: The Young Missionary, 1916-1921

1. MMM to People, 17 Nov. 1918, Kachek, MP, PHS.

2. This indifference to warfare among the Chinese was apparently widespread among missionaries in China. Eva Jane Price wrote from Shansi in the 1890s that the hostilities among the Chinese did not threaten foreigners. She, her family, and others of the mission steadfastly remained at their stations until all were killed during the Boxer Rebellion. See Eva Jane Price, *China Journal, 1889-1900: An American Missionary Family during the Boxer Rebellion* (New York: Scribner's, 1989).

3. MMM to People, 17 June 1917, Kachek, MP, PHS.
4. MMM to People, 15 July 1917, Kachek; MMM to Jimmie [Helen], 13 July 1917, Kachek, both in MP, PHS.
5. MMM to Mrs. Cummins, 20 Sept. 1917, Kachek, MP, PHS.
6. MMM to People, 18 Feb. 1918, Kachek, MP, PHS.
7. MMM to People, 4 Aug. 1918, Hong Kong; MMM to People, 29 Sept. 1918, Kachek, both in MP, PHS.
8. MMM to People, 27 Oct. 1918, Kachek, MP, PHS.

9. MMM to People, 3 Nov. 1918, Kachek, MP, PHS. Margaret was not the only foreign woman in Hainan to order Chinese troops around successfully. When Chinese soldiers entered the mission compound at Hoihow, they were disarmed by Olivia Kerr McCandliss. See Kathleen L. Lodwick, "Women at the Hainan Presbyterian Mission: Ministry and Diversion," *American Presbyterians: The Journal of Presbyterian History* 65 (Spring 1987): 19-28.

10. For a general discussion of nationalism, see Boyd Shafer, *Faces of Nationalism* (New York: Harcourt, 1972). One of the ironies of anti-foreign nationalism in China was that the concept of nationalism was itself borrowed from the West. See Jerome Grieder, *Intellectuals and the State in Modern China: A Narrative History* (New York: Free Press, 1981), 197-98; and Jessie G. Lutz, *China and the Christian Colleges* (Ithaca, N.Y.: Cornell Univ. Press, 1971), 207-8.

11. MMM to People, 15 Oct. 1916, Kachek, MP, PHS.

12. MMM to Friends of the Westminster Guild, 11 Oct. 1917, Kachek, MP, PHS.

13. MMM to Mother, 10 Oct. 1920, Kachek; MMM to Mother, 17 Oct. 1920, Kachek, both in MP, PHS.

14. MMM to People, 24 Nov. 1918, Kachek. See also Station Letter, Second Quarter 1919, to PCUSA, BFM, 6 Jan. 1919, Kachek, both in MP, PHS.

15. MMM to People, 25 May 1919, Kachek; MMM to Mother, 10 Oct. 1920, Kachek, both in MP, PHS.

16. MMM to People, 3 Jan. 1920, Kiungchow; MMM to Mother, 27 June 1920, Kiungchow, both in MP, PHS. For an account of the May Fourth movement, see Chow Tse-tsung, *The May Fourth Movement: Intellectual Revolution in Modern China* (Cambridge, Mass.: Harvard Univ. Press, 1960).

17. MMM to Mother, 8 June 1919, Kachek; MMM to People, 15 June 1919, Kachek; MMM to Mother, 2 Nov. 1919, Kiungchow, all in MP, PHS.

18. MMM to Daddy, 18 April 1920, Kiungchow, MP, PHS.

19. MMM to Mother, 2 May 1920, Kiungchow, MP, PHS.

20. The Senior [Katherine Schaeffer] to Emsie [MMM], 11 April 1920, Kachek, MP, PHS.

21. MMM to Mother, 12 Sept. 1920, Kiungchow, MP, PHS.

22. MMM to Jimmie [Helen], 13 July 1917, Kachek, MP, PHS.

23. MMM, "Hainan Was My Home," 38-39, MP, DC.

24. MMM to People, 10 March 1918, Kachek, MP, PHS.

25. Henry Bucher, interview by author, 3 July 1987.

26. MMM to People, 25 Aug. 1918, Kachek, MP, PHS.

27. MMM to Mother, 6 May 1919, Kachek, MP, PHS.

28. MMM to People, 28 Oct. 1916, Kachek, MP, PHS.

29. MMM to People, 28 April 1918, Kachek, MP, PHS.

30. MMM to People, 30 March 1919, Kachek, MP, PHS.

31. MMM to People, 12 May 1918, Kachek, MP, PHS.

32. MMM to People, 1 April 1917, Kachek, MP, PHS.

33. MMM to People, 28 Oct. 1916, Kachek, MP, PHS.

34. MMM to People, 16 Dec. 1917, Kachek; MMM to People, 25 Aug. 1918, Kachek; MMM to People, 8 Sept. 1918, Kachek, all in MP, PHS.

35. MMM to Mother, 27 July 1919, Kachek, MP, PHS.
36. MMM to Mother, 10 Aug. 1919, Kachek; MMM to Auntie Parks, 13 March 1920, Kiungchow, both in MP, PHS.
37. MMM to Mother, 3 April 1921, Kachek, MP, PHS.
38. MMM to People, 12 May 1918, Kachek; MMM to Mother, 1 June 1919, Kachek, both in MP, PHS.
39. MMM to Stanley White, 25 Dec. 1917, Kachek, PCUSA, BFM Papers.
40. MMM to Mother, 28 Jan. 1918, Kachek, MP, PHS.
41. MMM to Mother, 12 Sept. 1920, Kiungchow, MP, PHS.
42. MMM to Mother, 16 May 1920, Kiungchow, MP, PHS.
43. MMM to People, 8 Sept. 1918, Kachek, MP, PHS.
44. MMM to People, 18 Feb. 1917, Kachek, MP, PHS.
45. MMM to People, 13 Oct. 1918, Kachek, MP, PHS; MMM, "The Husband of One Wife," Moninger Papers, Special Collections, Univ. of Oregon Library; hereinafter cited as MP, Oregon.
46. MMM to People, 23 March 1918, Kachek; MMM to People, 31 March 1918, Kachek; MMM to People, 7 April 1918, Kachek, all in MP, PHS.
47. MMM to Mother, 24 Feb. 1918, Kachek, MP, PHS.
48. MMM to People, 6 Jan. 1918, Kachek, MP, PHS.
49. MMM to Grandma, 9 June 1918, Kachek; MMM to People, 18 Feb. 1918, Kachek, both in MP, PHS.
50. MMM to People, 27 May 1917, Kachek, MP, PHS.
51. MMM to Mother, 10 March 1918, Kachek; MMM to People, 22 Dec. 1918, Kachek, both in MP, PHS.
52. MMM to Grandma, 8 Dec. 1918, Kachek; MMM to Louise, 12 March 1921, Kachek, both in MP, PHS.
53. MMM to Mother, 30 Jan. 1921, Hoihow; MMM to John, 17 Feb. 1921, Kachek, both in MP, PHS.
54. MMM to Mother, 19 June 1921, Kachek, MP, PHS.
55. MMM to Mother, 10 April 1921, Kachek, MP, PHS.
56. MMM to Auntie Parks, 13 March 1920, Kiungchow; MMM to Mother, 14 March 1920, Kiungchow; MMM to Mother, 21 March 1920, Kiungchow, all in MP, PHS.
57. MMM to Auntie Parks, 20 Jan. 1920, Kiungchow, MP, PHS.
58. MMM to Mother, 13 Feb. 1921, Kachek, MP, PHS.
59. MMM to People, 19 Aug. 1917, Kiungchow; MMM to People, 26 Aug. 1917, Kachek, both in MP, PHS.
60. MMM to Helen, 30 Sept. 1917, Kachek, MP, PHS.
61. MMM to People, 30 March 1919, Kachek, MP, PHS.
62. MMM to Mother, 27 July 1919, Kachek, MP, PHS.
63. MMM to Mother, 29 Feb. 1920, Kachek; MMM to Mother, 14 March 1920, Kiungchow; MMM to Mother, 28 March 1920, Kiungchow; MMM to Mother, 25 April 1920, Kiungchow; all in MP, PHS; [MMM], ed., *Isle of Palms*. The handbook was part of the effort to professionalize foreign missions and increase the intellectual level of discussions at local missionary society meetings in the United States. For an examination of this type of effort as it related to women,

see Patricia Hill, *The World Their Household: The American Woman's Foreign Mission Movement and Cultural Transformation, 1870-1920* (Ann Arbor: Univ. of Michigan Press, 1980), and R. Pierce Beaver, *All Loves Excelling: American Protestant Women in World Mission* (Grand Rapids, Mich.: Eerdmans, 1968).

64. A.W. Halsey to MMM, 4 Nov. 1920, New York, MP, PHS. Halsey's comment that he knew of no other such work was prophetic. In 1980 Margaret's *Isle of Palms* was reprinted as part of the Hoover Institution's series on the economy of modern China. It was the only work in the series originally published by a mission to publicize its work.

65. MMM to People, 17 March 1918, Kachek, MP, PHS; MMM, "Picturesque Hainan," *Forward* (21 Jan. 1928:18; 28 Jan. 1922:26; 4 Feb. 1923:34).

66. MMM to People, 5 Aug. 1917, Hoihow; MMM to Helen, 30 Sept. 1917, Kachek; MMM to People, 25 Nov. 1917, Kachek; MMM to People, 17 March 1918, Kachek, all in MP, PHS.

67. MMM to Friends of the Westminster Guild, 11 Oct. 1917, Kachek; MMM to People, 14 Oct. 1917, Kachek, both in MP, PHS.

68. MMM to People, 13 Jan. 1918, Kachek; MMM to People, 6 Oct. 1918, Kachek; MMM to Mother, 25 April 1920, Kiungchow, all in MP, PHS.

69. MMM to Mother, 19 Dec. 1920, Kachek, MP, PHS; Iap Hi-soang and MMM, "Hainanese Colloquial Dictionary" (Romanized-Character-English), 2 vols., 1061pp., manuscript, 1933-35, MP, Oregon. Margaret wrote that her first language teacher had helped her with the dictionary but that another man, Iap Hi-soang, did the last draft. She did not give the name of the first teacher. See MMM, "Hainan Was My Home," 18, 33, MP, DC.

70. MMM to People, 8 Sept. 1918, Kachek; MMM to Mother, 29 May 1921, Kachek, both in MP, PHS.

71. MMM to Mother, 17 Oct. 1920, Kachek, MP, PHS.

72. MMM to Mother, 7 March 1920, Kiungchow, MP, PHS.

73. MMM to People, 23 June 1918, Kachek, MP, PHS.

74. MMM to Mother, 20 June 1920, Kiungchow, MP, PHS.

75. MMM to People, 3 June 1917, Kachek, MP, PHS.

76. MMM to People, 18 Feb. 1917, Kachek, MP, PHS. Margaret was mistaken in her belief that the Miao of Hainan were related to the Miao of the mainland, as she would later learn.

77. Ibid.

78. MMM to People, 16 Sept. 1917, Kachek, MP, PHS.

79. MMM to Grandma and All the Rest, 20 April 1918, Tinsui village, Miao country; MMM to People, 28 April 1918, Kachek, both in MP, PHS.

80. MMM to People, 5 May 1918, Kachek; MMM to Grandma, 9 June 1918, Kachek, both in MP, PHS.

81. MMM to People, 4 May 1919, Mokdo, MP, PHS.

82. MMM to Mother, 1 Feb. 1920, Kalai village, Miao country, MP, PHS.

83. Ibid.

84. MMM to Mother, 8 Feb. 1920, Mokdo village, Miao country, MP, PHS. Evelyn French, who arrived in Hainan in 1931, remembers several itinerating trips she made with Margaret Moninger and says Margaret emphasized the supernatu-

ral when talking about Christianity to the Miao. French, interview by author, 21 May 1987. It is likely that the Reverend George Byers, who was specifically assigned to work among the aborigines from the Kachek station, also discussed this aspect of Christianity. It is obvious from this account of Margaret's that the chief was acquainted with Christian eschatology.

85. Ibid.
86. MMM, "Hainan Was My Home," 39, MP, DC.
87. MMM to Mother, 8 Feb. 1920, Mokdo village, Miao country, MP, PHS.
88. MMM, "Hainan Was My Home," 40, MP, DC.
89. Katherine Schaeffer to Emsie [MMM], 20 Nov. 1920, Bakfo, MP, PHS.
90. MMM, "Hainan Was My Home," 36, MP, DC.
91. MMM to Mother, Sunday afternoon [9 Jan. 1921?], Tinsui village, Miao country, MP, PHS.
92. MMM to Mother, 16 Jan. 1921, Baklia Chapel, MP, PHS.
93. MMM to Mother, 25 July 1920, Hong Kong, MP, PHS.
94. MMM, "The Hainanese Miao," 40-50.
95. Ibid., 40.
96. Ibid., 41. See also S. Robert Ramsey, *The Languages of China* (Princeton, N.J.: Princeton Univ. Press, 1987), 280-86. Ramsey identifies the Hainan Miao as Yao brought by Chinese to Hainan from the mainland in the sixteenth century.
97. MMM, "The Hainanese Miao," 45.
98. Ibid., 44, 48.
99. MMM to People, 5 Feb. 1917, Kachek, MP, PHS.
100. MMM, "An Excursion Trip," 22 June 1917, Kachek, MP, PHS.
101. Ibid.
102. Ibid.; MMM to Grandma, 18 Nov. 1917, Kachek, MP, PHS.
103. MMM to Grandma and All the Rest, 20 April 1918, Tinsui village, Miao country; MMM to Grandma, 9 June 1918, Kachek; MMM to Mother, 24 April 1921, Kachek, all in MP, PHS.
104. MMM to People, 17 June 1917, Kachek, MP, PHS.
105. MMM to People, 3 June 1917, Kachek, MP, PHS.
106. MMM to People, 31 March 1918, Kachek, MP, PHS. Ivory Soap advertisement, *Ladies' Home Journal,* Jan. 1921; and *American Magazine* 91 (Jan. 1921). MMM to Mother, 20 March 1921, Kachek; MMM to Mother, 1 May 1921, Kachek, both in MP, PHS.
107. MMM to Mother, 10 Aug. 1919, Kachek, MP, PHS.
108. MMM to Mother, 28 Sept. 1920, Kachek, MP, PHS.
109. MMM to Jimmie [Helen], 8 Nov. 1920, Kachek; Katherine Schaeffer to Emsie [MMM], 10 Dec. 1920, Loikifo in Vongkoai, both in MP, PHS.
110. MMM to Mother, 23 May 1920, Kiungchow, MP, PHS.
111. MMM to People, 30 Dec. 1917, Kachek, MP, PHS.
112. MMM to Grandma, 23 Dec. 1917, Kachek; MMM to Mother, 1 Dec. 1918, Kachek; MMM to People, 10 Feb. 1918, Kachek; MMM to People, 31 March 1918, Kachek, all in MP, PHS.
113. MMM to Grandma, 14 April 1918, Kachek, MP, PHS.
114. MMM to Mother, 21 March 1920, Kiungchow, MP, PHS.

115. MMM to Mother, 7 March 1920, Kiungchow; MMM to Louise, 29 Dec. 1918, Kachek; MMM to Jimmie [Helen], 8 Nov. 1920, Kachek, all in MP, PHS.

116. MMM to Auntie Parks, 4 Jan. 1920, Kiungchow; MMM to Mother, 11 Jan. 1920, Kiungchow; MMM to Mother, 5 Dec. 1920, Kachek; MMM to Mother, 29 Nov. 1920, Kachek, all in MP, PHS.

117. MMM to Mother, 29 May 1921, Kachek, MP, PHS.

118. MMM to People, 25 Nov. 1917, Kachek; MMM to Grandma, 18 Nov. 1917, Kachek, both in MP, PHS. In her memoir of her life in Hainan, Margaret wrote that their cooks placed coals under and over the oven. The missionaries discovered they could not do as well when they did their own cooking when under house arrest by the Japanese. See MMM, "Hainan Was My Home," 58, MP, DC.

119. MMM to Mother, 11 July 1920, Hong Kong, MP, PHS.

120. MMM to Mother, 25 July 1920, Hong Kong, MP, PHS.

121. MMM to People, 8 Sept. 1918, Kachek, MP, PHS.

122. MMM to Mother, 20 Sept. 1920, Kiungchow; MMM to Mother, 24 Oct. 1920, Kachek; MMM to Mother, 12 Dec. 1920, Kachek, all in MP, PHS.

123. MMM to Mother, 16 May 1920, Kiungchow, MP, PHS.

124. MMM to Mother, 12 Dec. 1920, Kiungchow; MMM to Mother, 27 March 1921, Kachek, both in MP, PHS.

125. MMM to Mother, 15 May 1921, Kachek; MMM to Mother, 6 Feb. 1921, Kiungchow, both in MP, PHS.

126. MMM to Mother, 24 April 1921, Kachek; MMM to Mother, 3 July 1921, Tunngai; MMM to Mother, 10 July 1921, SS *Hanoi*, all in MP, PHS.

127. MMM to Committee on Furlough Study, 12 March 1927, Kachek; MMM, "Personal Record Blank of Furloughed Missionaries," 30 July 1927, both in PCUSA, BFM Papers.

3: *Turmoil and Flight, 1922-1927*

1. MMM to [Mother?], 27 Aug. 1922, Hong Kong; MMM to Mother, 29 Aug. 1922, Hong Kong, both in MP, PHS.

2. MMM to Mother, 9 Sept. 1922, Kachek, MP, PHS.

3. MMM to Mother, 24 Sept. 1922, Kachek, MP, PHS.

4. MMM to Folks, 17 Sept. 1922, Kachek, MP, PHS.

5. MMM to Mother, 5 Nov. 1922, Kachek; MMM to Mother, 12 Nov. 1922, Kachek; MMM to Mother, 23 Sept. 1923, Kachek; MMM to Mother, 15 June 1924, Kachek, all in MP, PHS. Margaret and some of the other missionaries occasionally worked in the government-run schools. After proctoring a government school examination in 1923, Margaret reported, "The boys think it quite all right to cheat and did aplenty--I knew the papers were copied....Our standards are much different from theirs. I have told the [mission school] boys repeatedly that daily work counted and that written work must be handed in, but boys who never handed in papers thought if they could get 100 per cent in examinations that would stand as their grade. Of course Chinese teachers grade only on the examination papers." See MMM to Mother, 20 Jan. 1923, Kachek, MP, PHS.

6. MMM to Auntie Parks, 23 Sept. 1923, Kachek, MP, PHS. A few years later she reported, "The principal of the government school for girls, where I go on Saturday afternoons,...[is the girl that] Mrs. Campbell...raised. Her sister-in-law is the Chinese doctor who graduated here and then from the Hackett Medical College in Canton, and is now making a hospital for women and children out of a nunnery here just near our compound." MMM to Mother, 14 Feb. 1926, Kiungchow, MP, PHS.

7. MMM to Mother, 16 Dec. 1923, Kachek, MP, PHS.

8. MMM to Jack, 22 March 1925, Kiungchow; MMM to Mother, 18 Oct. 1925, Kiungchow, both in MP, PHS.

9. MMM to Mother, 21 Oct. 1923, Kachek, MP, PHS.

10. MMM to Mother, 8 Oct. 1922, Kachek, MP, PHS.

11. MMM to Folks, 17 Sept. 1922, Kachek; MMM to Mother, 22 Oct. 1922, Kachek; MMM to Mother, 12 Nov. 1922, Kachek, all in MP, PHS.

12. MMM to Mother, 20 Jan. 1923, Kachek, MP, PHS.

13. MMM to Auntie Parks, 27 Sept. 1923, Kachek, MP, PHS.

14. MMM to Mother, 19 Aug. 1923, Miao country; MMM to Mother, 25 Aug. 1923, Kachek, both in MP, PHS.

15. MMM to Mother and Daddy, 30 Dec. 1923, Kachek, MP, PHS.

16. MMM to Mother, 18 Feb. 1923, Kachek, MP, PHS; MMM to Dorothy Dot, 4 March 1923, Kachek, MP, Barnes collection.

17. MMM to Mother, 1 April 1923, Kachek; MMM to Daddy and Mother, 30 Dec. 1923, Kachek; MMM to Mother, 7 Jan. 1924, Kachek, all in MP, PHS.

18. MMM to Mother, 1 March 1925, Kiungchow, MP, PHS.

19. MMM to Mother, 28 Sept. 1924, Shanghai, MP, PHS.

20. MMM to Women of the South China, Yunnan, and Hainan Missions, 27 Sept. 1924, Shanghai, PCUSA, BFM Papers.

21. MMM to Mother, 5 Oct. 1924, Shanghai, MP, PHS.

22. MMM to Mother, 12 Oct. 1924, Shanghai, MP, PHS; MMM to Women of the South China, Yunnan, and Hainan Missions, 21 Oct. 1924, Shanghai, PCUSA, BFM Papers.

23. MMM to Mother, 19 Oct. 1924, Shanghai; MMM to Mother, 26 Oct. 1924, en route from Shanghai to Hong Kong aboard the SS *Sicilia*, both in MP, PHS.

24. MMM to Mother, 26 Oct. 1924, en route from Shanghai to Hong Kong aboard the SS *Sicilia*; MMM to Mother, 1 Nov. 1924, en route from Hong Kong to Hoihow aboard the SS *Taming*, both in MP, PHS.

25. MMM to Mother, 6 Jan. 1924, Kachek, MP, PHS.

26. MMM to Mother, 7 Dec. 1924, Kiungchow, MP, PHS.

27. MMM, "Hainan Alphabet for New Recruits" (handwritten booklet), MP, PHS.

28. MMM to Mother, 4 Feb. 1923, Kachek, MP, PHS.

29. MMM to Mother, 24 Dec. 1922, Kachek, MP, PHS.

30. MMM to Jack, 22 July 1923, Canton, MP, PHS.

31. MMM to Mother, 23 Sept. 1923, Kiungchow; MMM to Mother, 13 Jan. 1924, Kiungchow, both in MP, PHS. This was not the first time Margaret had

experienced a school strike. There had been one at Grinnell College when she was an undergraduate. That strike began when students celebrating an upcoming football game cut classes after chapel one Friday morning. As a result, the faculty canceled the game, and the students went on strike to protest. The matter was resolved when it was decided that the team members would be allowed to play the game but Grinnell students could not attend. *Grinnell College Scarlet and Black*, 25 Nov. 1911, 1. It seems unlikely that the scholarly Margaret would have participated in the strike.

32. MMM to Papa Daddy, 31 Aug. 1924, Kiungchow; MMM to Mother, 14 Sept. 1924, en route to Hong Kong; MMM to Mother, 19 Oct. 1924, Shanghai, all in MP, PHS.

33. MMM to Mother, 25 Jan. 1925, Kiungchow, MP, PHS.

34. In addition to Jeremiassen and Melrose (see Chapter 1, note 73), the Reverend Frank P. Gilman, the first Presbyterian clergyman to reside on Hainan, was buried at Kiungchow. He died in 1918, presumably from a blood clot, three days after he jumped from the compound wall and injured his knee.

35. MMM to Daddy and Mother, 30 June 1924, Kiungchow; George T. Scott, PCUSA, BFM, to Relatives and Friends of Our Kachek Missionaries, 30 June 1924, New York; Mabel M. Roys, foreign executive secretary, BFM, to Mr. and Mrs. W.R. Moninger, 30 June 1924, New York, all in MP, PHS.

36. MMM to Mother, 6 July 1924, Hoihow; MMM to Mother, 11 Jan. 1925, Kiungchow, both in MP, PHS.

37. MMM to Papa Daddy, 31 Aug. 1924, Kiungchow; MMM to Mother, 7 Dec. 1924, Kiungchow, both in MP, PHS.

38. MMM to Mother, 11 Jan. 1925, Kiungchow; MMM to Mother, 18 Jan. 1925, Kiungchow; MMM to Mother, 16 Nov. 1924, Kiungchow; MMM to Mother, 8 March 1925, Kiungchow, all in MP, PHS.

39. MMM to Mother, 19 Oct. 1924, Shanghai, MP, PHS.

40. MMM to Mother, 15 Feb. 1925, Kiungchow; MMM to Mother, 1 March 1925, Kiungchow, both in MP, PHS.

41. MMM to Mother, 22 March 1925, Kiungchow; MMM to Daddy, 29 March 1925, Kiungchow, both in MP, PHS.

42. MMM to Mother, 22 March 1925, Kiungchow; MMM to Mother, 5 April 1925, Kiungchow, both in MP, PHS. Margaret had expressed similar sentiments in her 4 January 1925 letter to her mother.

43. MMM to Mother, 26 April 1925, Kiungchow; MMM to Mother, 24 May 1925, Kiungchow, both in MP, PHS.

44. MMM to Mother, 3 May 1925, Kiungchow, MP, PHS.

45. MMM to Mother, 7 June 1925, Kiungchow, MP, PHS. For a discussion of the May Thirtieth Incident, see James E. Sheridan, *China in Disintegration: The Republican Era in Chinese History, 1912-1949* (New York: Free Press, 1975). For a detailed description of the impact of the incident and the influence it had on anti-Christian activities, see Jessie G. Lutz, *Chinese Politics and Christian Missions: The Anti-Christian Movements of 1920-1928* (Notre Dame, Ind.: Cross Cultural Publication, 1988).

46. MMM to Mother, 20 June 1925, Kiungchow, MP, PHS.

47. Frances Graham to Relatives of Our Hainan Missionaries, 11 July 1925, New York, MP, PHS.
48. MMM to Mother, 28 June 1925, Pakhoi, MP, PHS.
49. Ibid.
50. MMM to Jack, 30 June 1925, Haiphong, MP, PHS. If Margaret's family saved her French newspaper clippings, they were later lost, as they are not among her many papers that survive.
51. *The Refugee Rampage,* typewritten newsletter by MMM, Myrle Seaton Papers, private collection of Stuart Seaton.
52. MMM to Jimmie Helen, 12 July 1925, Haiphong, MP, PHS.
53. MMM to Mother, 4 July 1925, Haiphong, MP, PHS; MMM, "Hainan Was My Home," 80, MP, DC.
54. MMM, "Hainan Was My Home," 80, MP, DC; MMM to Mother, 2 Aug. 1925, Haiphong, MP, PHS.
55. MMM to Mother, 2 Aug. 1925, Haiphong, MP, PHS.
56. MMM to Mother, 12 July 1925, Haiphong; MMM to Jack, 26 July 1925, Haiphong, both in MP, PHS.
57. MMM to Mother, 26 July 1925, Haiphong; MMM to Mother, 13 March 1927, Hoihow, MP, PHS. See also F.M. Savina, *Histoire des Miao* (Hong Kong: Société des Missions-Etrangères, 1924). Savina was partially correct: the Hainan Miao are now thought to be related to the Yao of the mainland. See Chapter 2, note 96.
58. MMM to Mother, 2 Aug. 1925, Haiphong, MP, PHS.
59. Ibid.; MMM to Mother, 9 Aug. 1925, Kiungchow, MP, PHS.
60. MMM to Mother, 9 Aug. 1925, Kiungchow, MP, PHS.
61. Ibid.
62. MMM to Mother, 16 Aug. 1925, Kiungchow, MP, PHS.
63. MMM to Mother, 30 Aug. 1925, Kiungchow; MMM to Mother, 6 Sept. 1925, Kiungchow, both in MP, PHS.
64. MMM to Mother, 15 Nov. 1925, Kiungchow, MP, PHS.
65. MMM to Mother, 22 Nov. 1925, Kiungchow, MP, PHS.
66. MMM to Jack, 22 Nov. 1925, Kiungchow, MP, PHS.
67. MMM to Daddy, 29 Nov. 1925, Kiungchow, MP, PHS. Despite their own financial difficulties, the Hainan missionaries frequently acted as bankers for the people of the island, particularly as the unrest increased. Margaret mentioned that in one day in Hoihow she had done the treasurer's business and took "in over $2,000 in silver dollars for treasurer's orders. It is not very often that I handle so much money in one day." MMM to Mother, 27 June 1926, Kiungchow, MP, PHS.
68. MMM to Mother, 6 Dec. 1925, Kiungchow, MP, PHS.
69. MMM to Mother, 13 Dec. 1925, Kiungchow, MP, PHS. Margaret is referring to items in the *Chinese Recorder* 56 (Nov. 1925): an editorial, [Frank Rawlinson?], "What Shall We Do with the 'Toleration Clauses,'" 697-703; and three articles, A.L. Warnshuis, "Christian Missions and Treaties with China," 705-15; [Frank Rawlinson?], "Treaty Toleration of Christianity (Excerpts from Various Treaties)," 716-19; and Frank Rawlinson, "The Evolution of 'Christian' Treaty 'Rights' in China," 719-28.

70. MMM to Mother, 22 Feb. 1925, Kiungchow; MMM to Mother, 11 Oct. 1925, Kiungchow, both in MP, PHS.
71. MMM to Mother, 3 Jan. 1926, Kiungchow, MP, PHS.
72. MMM to Mother, 17 Jan. 1926, Kiungchow; MMM to Mother, 14 Feb. 1926, Kiungchow, both in MP, PHS.
73. MMM to Mother, 21 Feb. 1926, Kiungchow, MP, PHS.
74. MMM to Mother, 16 Dec. 1923, Kachek; MMM to Jimmie Helen, 14 March 1926, Kiungchow, both in MP, PHS.
75. MMM to Mother, 28 Feb. 1926, Kiungchow; MMM to Jimmie Helen, 14 March 1926, Kiungchow, both in MP, PHS.
76. MMM to Jimmie Helen, 14 March 1926, Kiungchow, MP, PHS.
77. MMM to Mother, 21 March 1926, Kiungchow, MP, PHS.
78. MMM to Mother, 28 March 1926, Kiungchow, MP, PHS.
79. Ibid. See also MMM to Daddy, 18 April 1926, Kiungchow, MP, PHS.
80. MMM to Mother, 4 April 1926, Kiungchow; MMM to Mother, 9 May 1926, Kiungchow, both in MP, PHS.
81. MMM to Mother, 11 April 1926, Kiungchow, MP, PHS.
82. MMM to Louise, 19 April 1926, Kiungchow; MMM to Mother, 25 April 1926, Kiungchow, both in MP, PHS.
83. MMM to Mother, 16 May 1926, Kiungchow, MP, PHS.
84. Ibid.; MMM to Daddy, 30 May 1926, Kiungchow, MP, PHS.
85. MMM to Mother, 6 June 1926, Kiungchow; MMM to Daddy, 30 May 1926, Kiungchow; MMM to Mother, 27 June 1926, Kiungchow, all in MP, PHS.
86. MMM to Mother, 6 June 1926, Kiungchow, MP, PHS.
87. MMM to Mother, 13 June 1926, Kiungchow, MP, PHS.
88. MMM to Jack, 27 June 1926, Kiungchow, MP, PHS.
89. Ibid.
90. MMM to Mother, 15 Aug. 1926, Hoihow; MMM to Daddy, 29 Aug. 1926, Kiungchow; MMM to Mother, 5 Sept. 1926, Kiungchow, all in MP, PHS.
91. MMM to Mother, 2 May 1926, Kiungchow, MP, PHS.
92. MMM to Mother, 12 Sept. 1926, Kiungchow, MP, PHS.
93. Ibid.
94. MMM to Mother, 10 Oct. 1926, Hong Kong, MP, PHS.
95. MMM to Mother, 17 Oct. 1926, Shanghai; MMM to Mother, 21 Nov. 1926, Shanghai; MMM to Mother, 17 Oct. 1926, Shanghai, all in MP, PHS.
96. MMM to Mother, 24 Oct. 1926, Nanking, MP, PHS.
97. MMM to Mother, 16 Nov. 1924, Kiungchow, MP, PHS.
98. MMM to Mother, 24 Oct. 1926, Nanking, MP, PHS.
99. Ibid. Previously, Margaret had only heard of Sarah Liang, who was in the United States in 1915 when Margaret arrived in Hainan.
100. MMM to Louise, 21 Nov. 1926, Shanghai; MMM to Mother, 12 Dec. 1926, en route from Shanghai to Hong Kong aboard the SS *City of Tokio,* both in MP, PHS.
101. MMM to Mother, 19 Dec. 1926, Hoihow, MP, PHS.
102. MMM to Mother, 26 Dec. 1926, Hoihow, MP, PHS.

103. MMM to Mother, 13 Feb. 1927, Hoihow, MP, PHS.
104. Ibid.
105. MMM to Mother, 20 Feb. 1927, Hoihow, MP, PHS.
106. Ibid.
107. MMM to Mother, 9 Jan. 1927, Hoihow, MP, PHS. The reasons the Hainan girls gave were the same ones given elsewhere in China.
108. MMM to Mother, 20 Feb. 1927, Hoihow, MP, PHS.
109. Ibid.
110. MMM to Mother, 27 Feb. 1927, Hoihow; MMM to Mother, 6 March 1927, Hoihow, both in MP, PHS.
111. MMM to Mother, 6 March 1927, Hoihow; MMM to Mother, 13 March 1927, Hoihow, both in MP, PHS.
112. MMM to Mother, 14 Feb. 1926, Kiungchow, MP, PHS.
113. MMM to Mother, 3 April 1927, Hoihow, MP, PHS.
114. Cable from MMM to L.C. Moninger, 13 April 1927, Hong Kong; George T. Scott and Ruth Elliott, BFM, to Moningers, April 1927, New York, both in MP, PHS.
115. MMM to Dorothy Dot, 5 May 1927, SS *President Taft,* MP, PHS.
116. Telegram from MMM to W.R. Moninger, 9 May 1927, Seattle, MP, PHS.

4: Come Rejoicing, 1928-1935

1. MMM to Committee on Furlough Study, 12 March 1927, Hoihow; Orville Reed to MMM, 26 April 1927, New York, both in PCUSA, BFM Papers.
2. MMM to George T. Scott, 20 May 1927, Marshalltown, Iowa, PCUSA, BFM Papers.
3. [Frances Graham] to MMM, 11 Feb. 1928, New York; MMM to Frances Graham, 14 Feb. 1928, Washington, Iowa; MMM to Frances Graham, 21 Feb. 1928, Washington, Iowa; [Frances Graham] to MMM, 29 Feb. 1928, New York, all in PCUSA, BFM Papers.
4. MMM to George T. Scott, 9 Nov. 1927, Washington, Iowa; MMM to George T. Scott, 13 Jan. 1928, Washington, Iowa, both in PCUSA, BFM Papers. The Reverend Henry Bucher made the remark about Margaret's being the mission historian. Bucher, interview by author, 3 July 1987.
5. MMM to Mrs. Charles K. Roys, 31 March 1928, Washington, Iowa; MMM to George T. Scott, 13 Jan. 1928, Washington, Iowa, both in PCUSA, BFM Papers.
6. Esther Morse to Dad, 17 May 1931, Kachek, Morse Papers. Morse wrote that she did not know to which sibling Margaret wrote when a fifth Sunday occurred in the month.
7. Esther Morse, Diary, 12 Sept. 1930; Morse to Folks, 15 Sept. 1930, Hong Kong; Morse to Folks, 20 Oct. 1930, Kachek; Morse to Folks, 4 Jan. 1931, Kachek, all in Morse Papers.
8. MMM to Folks, 1 Sept. 1929, Nodoa, MP, PHS.
9. MMM to Daddy and Louise, 8 Sept. 1929, Nodoa; MMM to Louise, 8

Dec. 1929, Nodoa; MMM to Daddy, 12 Jan. 1930, Nodoa; MMM to Louise, 27 July 1930, Nodoa, all in MP, PHS.

10. MMM to Louise, 8 Dec. 1929, Nodoa; MMM to Daddy, 12 Jan. 1930, Nodoa, both in MP, PHS. Morse to Alice and family, 9 Nov. 1930, Kachek, Morse Papers.

11. Morse to Edna, 27 Sept. 1931, Kachek, Morse Papers.

12. MMM to Louise, 21 Oct. 1929, Nodoa, MP, PHS.

13. MMM to Daddy, 15 Dec. 1929, Nodoa; MMM to Louise, 26 Jan. 1930, Nodoa, both in MP, PHS.

14. MMM to Dad, 4 May 1930, Nodoa, MP, PHS; MMM to [Frances] Graham, 21 Aug. 1931, Kachek, PCUSA, BFM Papers.

15. MMM to Daddy, 3 July 1932, Kachek, MP, PHS; Morse to A.C. and Dad, 1 and 2 July 1932, [Kachek], Morse Papers.

16. Morse to Ruth, 15 July 1932, [Kachek], Morse Papers.

17. MMM to Daddy, 3 July 1932, Kachek, MP, PHS.

18. MMM to Louise, 10 July [1932], Hoihow harbor, SS *Kiungyuan*, MP,PHS.

19. MMM to Louise, 10 Dec. 1933, Kachek, MP, PHS.

20. MMM to Daddy, 3 July 1932, Kachek, MP, PHS.

21. MMM to Daddy, 17 Feb. 1935, Bakfo market, MP, PHS.

22. MMM to Daddy, 6 Jan. 1935, Kachek, MP, PHS.

23. MMM to Daddy, 17 March 1935, Kachek, MP, PHS.

24. MMM to Daddy, 15 Dec. 1929, Nodoa, MP, PHS.

25. MMM to Louise, 23 April 1933, Doaloa Chapel, MP, PHS.

26. MMM, "Hainan Was My Home," 44-45, MP, DC.

27. MMM to Daddy, 7 Jan. 1934, Kachek; MMM to Louise, 26 Aug. 1934, Kachek, both in MP, PHS.

28. MMM to Daddy, 31 June 1934, Fongmui village; MMM to Daddy, 20 May 1934, Kachek, both in MP, PHS. MMM, "Salt Making in Khengdong District, Island of Hainan," *Lingnan Science Journal* 13(1934): 697-98.

29. MMM to Daddy, 31 June 1934, Fongmui village, MP, PHS.

30. MMM to Daddy, 20 Aug. 1934, Kachek, MP, PHS.

31. MMM to Daddy, 1 April 1934, Kachek, MP, PHS.

32. MMM to Louise, 11 Feb. 1934, Kiungchow, MP, PHS.

33. MMM to Daddy, 4, 11, and 19 March 1934, Tinsui village, Miao country, both in MP, PHS. Margaret continued this letter to her father for several weeks until she reached a post office where she could mail it.

34. Ibid.

35. Ibid.

36. Ibid.

37. MMM to Louise, 13 May 1933, Liangsit Chapel, MP, PHS.

38. MMM to Louise, 23 Feb. 1930, Nodoa; MMM to Daddy, 18 June 1933, Kachek, both in MP, PHS.

39. MMM to Dad, 4 May 1930, Nodoa, MP, PHS.

40. MMM to Dad, 4 Feb. 1934, Kachek, MP, PHS.

41. MMM to Louise, 26 June 1933, Kachek, MP, PHS.

42. MMM to Daddy, 2 June 1935, Kiungchow, MP, PHS.
43. MMM to Folks, 15 May 1938, Nodoa, MP, PHS.
44. MMM to Louise, 19 March 1933, Kachek; MMM to Daddy, 16 April 1933, Kachek, both in MP, PHS.
45. Morse to Papa, 15 Oct. 1933, [Kachek], Morse Papers; MMM to Daddy, 22 Oct. 1933, Amoy, MP, PHS.
46. MMM to Louise, 23 April 1933, Doaloa Chapel; MMM to Louise, 13 May 1933, Liangsit Chapel, both in MP, PHS.
47. MMM, "Hainan Was My Home," 22, MP, DC.
48. MMM to Louise, 10 July [1932], Hoihow harbor, SS *Kiungyuan,* MP, PHS.
49. Morse to Dad, 11 Jan. 1931, Kachek; Morse to Alice, 29 Nov. 1931, Kachek, both in Morse Papers. Margaret also mentioned the cards in her memoir; see MMM, "Hainan Was My Home," 36, MP, DC.
50. MMM to Dad, 4 Feb. 1934, Kachek, MP, PHS.
51. Morse to Clayton, 2 April 1933, [Kachek], Morse Papers. Esther Morse was also single, but she didn't suggest how she dealt with her own physical desires.
52. Morse to Clayton, 22 Oct. 1933, [Kachek?], Morse Papers.
53. Ibid.; Morse to Alice, 11 Jan. 1931, Kachek, Morse Papers.
54. Morse to Papa, 7 Feb. 1932, [Kachek?], Morse Papers.
55. MMM to Daddy, 3 July 1932, Kachek, MP, PHS.
56. Ibid.
57. MMM to Louise, 26 Aug. 1934, Kachek, MP, PHS.
58. MMM to Daddy, 3 June 1934, Kachek, MP, PHS; MMM, "Hainan Was My Home," 53, MP, DC; Morse to Ruth, 15 July 1932, [Kachek], Morse Papers.
59. MMM to Louise, 23 Feb. 1930, Nodoa, MP, PHS. Morse to Folks, 4 Jan. 1931, Kachek; Morse to Ruth, 24 Jan. 1931, Kachek, both in Morse Papers.
60. MMM, "Advance Information for Furlough Study Committee," 1935, PCUSA, BFM Papers. Morse to Dad, 1 March 1931, Kachek; Morse to Dad, 4 July 1931, Kachek, both in Morse Papers.
61. Morse to Papa and Clayton, 25 Nov. 1933, [Kachek]; Morse to Folks, 6 Aug. 1938, Nodoa, both in Morse Papers.
62. Morse to Ruth, 15 July 1932, [Kachek], Morse Papers.
63. Morse to Papa, 9 March 1932, Kachek; Morse to Ruth, 3 April 1932, [Kachek], both in Morse Papers.
64. Morse to Family, 18 May 1935, [Kachek], Morse Papers.
65. Morse to Folks, 28 May 1933, [Kachek]; Morse to Papa, 4 June 1933, [Kachek], both in Morse Papers.
66. Morse to Alice, 5 May 1931, Kachek, Morse Papers.
67. Morse to Folks, 21 May 1931, Kachek, Morse Papers.
68. Morse to Folks, 20 March 1932, Kachek, Morse Papers.
69. Morse to Ruth, 20 Nov. 1934, [Kachek], Morse Papers.
70. MMM to Daddy, 3 Sept. 1933, Kachek, MP, PHS.
71. Morse to Polly, 15 Feb. 1931, Kachek, Morse Papers.

72. Morse to Dad, 29 Nov. 1931, [Kachek], Morse Papers.
73. Morse to Ruth, 5 Feb. 1933, [Kachek]; Morse to Clayton and Papa, 28 Dec. 1935, [Kachek], both in Morse Papers.
74. Morse to Ruth, 7 Nov. 1931, [Kachek]; Morse to A.C., 13 Dec. 1931, [Kachek], both in Morse Papers.
75. MMM to Louise, 14 Jan. 1934, Kachek, MP, PHS.
76. Morse to Folks, 19 Nov. 1932, [Kachek], Morse Papers.
77. Morse to Papa and Clayton, 10 Nov. 1934, [Kachek], Morse Papers.
78. Margaret had written to her family, "We usually write Pastor Ngou's name Wu in the *News Letter* as that is the Mandarin romanized of it. In Cantonese it is plain Ng. This Chinese language is a mess." MMM to Dad, 1 Oct. 1933, Kachek, MP, PHS. Margaret had had six hundred pages of foolscap bound to use for her dictionary, and because of its size it was jokingly called Big Bertha. See MMM, "Hainan Was My Home," 48, MP, DC.
79. MMM to Daddy, 20 Aug. 1934, Kachek; MMM to Louise, 9 Sept. 1934, Kachek, both in MP, PHS.
80. MMM to Daddy, 16 Sept. 1934, Kachek, MP, PHS.
81. MMM to Daddy, 4 Nov. 1934, Kachek, MP, PHS.
82. In January 1935 the teacher was baptized. Margaret wrote, "We are very happy to have him make a public confession of faith, as he has been a believer for a long time." MMM to Daddy, 6 Jan. 1935, Kachek, MP, PHS.
83. MMM to Daddy, 20 Jan. 1935, Kachek; MMM to Louise, 27 Jan. 1935, Kachek, both in MP, PHS.
84. MMM to Daddy, 17 Feb. 1935, Bakfo market, MP, PHS.
85. MMM to Daddy, 31 March 1935, Kachek, MP, PHS.
86. Morse to Dad and A.C., 17 April 1933, [Kachek], Morse Papers.
87. MMM to Louise, 23 June 1935, Kiungchow, MP, PHS.
88. MMM to Daddy, 30 June 1935, en route to Hong Kong aboard the SS *Yochow*, MP, PHS.

5: Warfare, 1936-1942

1. MMM to Folks, 28 March 1937, Kiungchow, MP, PHS.
2. MMM to Dad, 23 May 1937, Kiungchow; MMM to Folks, 27 June 1937, Kiungchow; MMM to Folks, 29 Aug. 1937, [Kiungchow], all in MP, PHS.
3. MMM to Folks, 5 Sept. 1937, Kiungchow, MP, PHS.
4. MMM to Folks, 8 Aug. 1937, Hong Kong, MP, PHS.
5. MMM to Folks, 5 Sept. 1937, Kiungchow, MP, PHS.
6. For an account of the missionaries at all three Hainan stations during these years, see Kathleen L. Lodwick, "The Presbyterian Mission on Hainan Island under the Japanese, 1937-1941," *American Presbyterians: The Journal of Presbyterian History* 70 (Winter 1992): 247-58.
7. MMM to Folks, 12 Sept. 1937, Kiungchow, MP, PHS.
8. MMM to Daddy, 19 Sept. 1937, Kiungchow, MP, PHS.
9. Ibid.; MMM to Daddy, 26 Sept. 1937, Kiungchow, MP, PHS.
10. MMM to Folks, 3 Oct. 1937, Nodoa, MP, PHS.

11. MMM to Daddy, 10 Oct. 1937, Nodoa, MP, PHS.
12. MMM to Daddy and Helen, 31 Oct. 1937, Nodoa; MMM to Dad and Helen, 21 Nov. 1937, Nodoa, both in MP, PHS.
13. MMM to Folks, 28 Nov. 1937, Nodoa, MP, PHS.
14. MMM to Daddy and Helen, 31 Oct. 1937, Nodoa; MMM to Daddy and Helen, 7 Nov. 1937, Nodoa, both in MP, PHS.
15. MMM to Daddy, 10 Oct. 1937, Nodoa, MP, PHS.
16. MMM to Daddy and Helen, 31 Oct. 1937, Nodoa; MMM to Folks, 1 May 1938, Nodoa; MMM to Folks, 22 May 1938, Nodoa, all in MP, PHS.
17. MMM to Louise and Dad and Helen, 14 Nov. 1937, Nodoa; MMM to Daddy, 19 Dec. 1937, Nodoa; MMM to Dad and Helen, 3 April 1938, Nodoa; MMM to Folks, 25 Sept. 1938, Nodoa, all in MP, PHS.
18. MMM to Folks, 23 Oct. 1938, Nodoa; MMM to Helen and Dad, 6 Nov. 1938, Nodoa, both in MP, PHS.
19. MMM to Dad, 16 Oct. 1938, Nodoa, MP, PHS.
20. Morse to Folks, 20 Feb. 1938, Nodoa, Morse Papers.
21. MMM to Folks, 27 Feb. 1938, Nodoa, MP, PHS.
22. MMM to Louise, 16 Jan. 1938, Nodoa, MP, PHS.
23. MMM to Dad and Helen, 23 Jan. 1938, Kiungchow, MP, PHS.
24. MMM to Folks, 10 April 1938, Nodoa, MP, PHS.
25. MMM to Folks, 28 March 1937, Kiungchow; MMM to Folks, 18 July 1937, Kiungchow; MMM to Daddy, 21 Aug. 1938, Nodoa; MMM to Louise, 26 March 1939, Nodoa, all in MP, PHS.
26. MMM to Daddy, 2 April 1939, Nodoa; MMM to Daddy, 28 May 1939, Nodoa, both in MP, PHS. Margaret made frequent references to her dictionary between June 1939 and February 1940. See, for example, MMM to Daddy, 4 and 25 June, 20 Aug., 10 Sept., and 8 and 15 Oct. 1939, and 19 Feb. 1940, Nodoa, all in MP, PHS.
27. MMM to Chicago Family [the family of her brother, John], 14 Sept. 1939, Nodoa, MP, PHS.
28. Morse to Folks, 17 Dec. 1938, [Nodoa], Morse Papers; MMM to Folks, 26 Dec. 1938, Nodoa, MP, PHS.
29. MMM to Daddy, 11 Dec. 1938, Nodoa, MP, PHS. Alice Skinner, then living at Kiungchow, was the senior member of the mission on Hainan.
30. MMM to Daddy, 19 Dec. 1937, Nodoa; MMM to Dad and Helen, 30 Jan. 1938, Nodoa, both in MP, PHS.
31. MMM to Seattle Family [the family of her brother, John], 8 Jan. 1939, Nodoa, MP, PHS.
32. Ibid.
33. MMM to Folks, 20 March 1938, Nodoa; MMM to Helen and Dad, 18 Dec. 1938, Nodoa; MMM to Seattle Family [the family of her brother John], 8 Jan. 1939, Nodoa, all in MP, PHS.
34. MMM to Louise, 5 Feb. 1939, Nodoa, MP, PHS.
35. MMM to Dad and All of You, 12 and 26 Feb. and 18 March 1939, Nodoa, MP, PHS.
36. Ibid.

37. MMM to Folks, 20 Feb. 1939, Nodoa, MP, PHS.
38. MMM to Daddy, 2 April 1939, Nodoa, MP, PHS.
39. MMM to Louise, 23 April 1939, Nodoa; MMM to Daddy, 30 April 1939, Nodoa, both in MP, PHS.
40. MMM to Daddy, 9 May 1939, Nodoa, MP, PHS.
41. MMM to Daddy, 4 June 1939, Nodoa, MP, PHS.
42. MMM to Louise, 23 April 1939, Nodoa, MP, PHS.
43. MMM to Louise and All, 11 June 1939, Nodoa, MP, PHS.
44. Morse to Family, 14 June 1939, Hoihow, Morse Papers; MMM to Daddy, 25 June 1939, Nodoa, MP, PHS.
45. Morse to Ruth, 16 July 1939, Hoihow, Morse Papers.
46. MMM, "Somewhere in Occupied Territory: In China before Pearl Harbor," 11, unpublished typescript, MP, Oregon. Margaret revised and typed the manuscript she had mailed home in 1940, adding the names of people to whom she had referred by nicknames and changing the subtitle from "1938-1940."
47. Paul Melrose, "Great Is Thy Faithfulness," 10, 13, unpublished typescript, Paul Melrose Papers, Special Collections, Univ. of Oregon Library; hereinafter cited as Melrose Papers.
48. MMM to Daddy, 10 Sept. 1939, Nodoa, MP, PHS.
49. MMM to Chicago Family [the family of her brother John], 14 Sept. 1939, Nodoa, MP, PHS.
50. MMM to Daddy, 17 Sept. 1939, Nodoa, MP, PHS.
51. MMM to Louise, 24 Sept. 1939, Nodoa, MP, PHS.
52. MMM to Louise, 11 Nov. 1939, Nodoa, MP, PHS.
53. Ibid.
54. Ibid. See also MMM, "Somewhere in Occupied Territory," 25, MP, Oregon.
55. MMM to Daddy, 10 Dec. 1939, Nodoa, MP, PHS.
56. Ibid.
57. Ibid.
58. MMM to Daddy, 17 Dec. 1939, Nodoa, MP, PHS.
59. Ibid.
60. MMM to John and Sue, 24 Dec. 1939, Nodoa, MP, PHS. Margaret's writing in such codes at one time convinced her brother, John, that she was becoming mentally unbalanced as a result of the tension in her situation. When she returned to the United States in 1942 she was provoked that he had been unable to decipher her codes. Barnes, interview by author, 5 June 1990.
61. MMM to Daddy, 20 Jan. 1940, Nodoa, MP, PHS.
62. Morse to Ruth, 28 Jan. 1940, Hoihow, Morse Papers.
63. MMM to Daddy, 20 Aug. 1939, Nodoa; MMM to Daddy, 10 March 1940, Kiungchow, both in MP, PHS. Melrose, "Great Is Thy Faithfulness," 35, Melrose Papers.
64. MMM to Daddy, 10 March 1940, Kiungchow, MP, PHS.
65. Morse to Family, 21 April 1940, Hong Kong, Morse Papers.
66. MMM to Daddy, 24 March 1940, Hong Kong; MMM to Louise, 31

March 1940, Hong Kong, both in MP, PHS. MMM, "Hainan Was My Home," 83, MP, DC.

67. MMM to Dad, 28 April 1940, Hong Kong, MP, PHS.
68. MMM to John, 30 March 1941, Kiungchow, MP, PHS.
69. MMM to Dad, 13 April 1941, Kiungchow, MP, PHS.
70. MMM to Dad, 3 Nov. 1940, Kiungchow; MMM to Sue, 26 Jan. 1941, Kiungchow, both in MP, PHS.
71. MMM to Daddy, 2 Feb. 1941, Kiungchow, MP, PHS.
72. M.S. Myers, American consul general, to Hainan mission, 9 Oct. 1940, Canton; MMM to Daddy, 27 Oct. 1940, Kiungchow, both in MP, PHS. Alice Skinner did not return to the United States with the others, but the reason for her staying in Hainan is unclear. She was repatriated with the other members of the mission in 1942.
73. MMM to John, 30 March 1941, Kiungchow; MMM to John, 30 May 1941, Kiungchow, both in MP, PHS. John had warned Margaret that their father knew nothing of his illness. In fact, their father was not ill; this was only John's ruse to convince the Board of Foreign Missions to evacuate Margaret before more warfare ensued. The Board finally informed John that Margaret stayed in Hainan by her own choice. Margaret's father lived, not only to welcome her home in 1942, but for five years thereafter. Barnes, interview by author, 5 June 1990.
74. MMM, "Twenty-three Thousand Miles of Miracles," 4-5, 6, MP, DC. Esther Morse confirms Margaret's account in Morse to Family, 16 Feb. 1941, Hoihow, Morse Papers.
75. MMM to Dad, 13 April 1941, Kiungchow, MP, PHS.
76. MMM, "Twenty-three Thousand Miles of Miracles," 1, 7, MP, Barnescollection. See also MMM to John, 22 June 1941, Kiungchow, MP, PHS.
77. MMM to Daddy, 13 July 1941, Kiungchow, MP, PHS. Margaret had apparently forgotten French, which she had spoken with some success in Haiphong in 1925.
78. MMM to Dad, 11 May 1941, Kiungchow, MP, PHS.
79. Morse to Dad and A.C. and Ruth, 25 May 1940, Hoihow, Morse Papers; MMM to [Paul] Melrose, 5 Oct. 1941, [Kiungchow]; see also MMM to John, 5 Oct. 1941, Kiungchow, both in MP, PHS.
80. David S. Tappan to BFM, 13 Nov. 1941, Hoihow, Tappan Papers, Special Collections, Univ. of Oregon Library; MMM, "Twenty-three Thousand Miles of Miracles," 15, MP, DC.
81. MMM, "Twenty-three Thousand Miles of Miracles," 8-9, MP, DC.
82. Ibid.
83. Ibid.
84. Ibid.
85. Ibid.
86. Ibid.
87. Ibid.
88. Ibid., 10.
89. MMM to Daddy, 10 Aug. 1941, [Kiungchow], MP, PHS. Several words in this letter were blacked out by the censor.

90. MMM to Daddy, 30 Sept. 1941, Kiungchow; MMM to Louise, 20 Oct. 1941, Kiungchow, both in MP, PHS.
91. MMM to Daddy, 7 Sept. 1941, Kiungchow; MMM to Daddy, 30 Sept. 1941, Kiungchow, both in MP, PHS. Margaret Burkwall was the sister of Dr. Herman Burkwall.
92. Margaret Burkwall, interview by author, 19 May 1987; MMM, "Twenty-three Thousand Miles of Miracles," 11, MP, DC.
93. MMM, "Twenty-three Thousand Miles of Miracles," 12, MP, DC.
94. Ibid., 13.
95. Ibid.
96. Ibid., 13-14.
97. MMM to Chicago Family [the family of her brother John], 6 Aug. 1942, SS *Gripsholm,* rolling up to Rio [de Janeiro], MP, DC.
98. MMM, "Twenty-three Thousand Miles of Miracles," 14, MP, DC.
99. Ibid., 16; *Los Angeles Times, Washington (Pa.) Observer,* and *Marshalltown (Iowa) Times-Republican,* 17 and 18 Jan. 1942.
100. Lloyd S. Ruland, BFM, to J.H. Moninger, 30 Dec. 1941, New York; J.H. Moninger to Leo Holstad, 19 Jan. 1942, [Chicago?], both in MP, DC. Frances Graham to John Moninger, 6 Feb. 1942, New York, PCUSA, BFM Papers.
101. John H. Moninger to Frances Graham, 9 Feb. 1942, [Chicago?], MP, DC; Lloyd S. Ruland to Relatives and Friends of Our South China and Hainan Missionaries, 28 May 1942, New York, PCUSA, BFM Papers. Ruland's letter contained David Tappan's entire letter to his family dated 1 March 1942, written from the Hackett Compound, Canton.
102. MMM, "Twenty-three Thousand Miles of Miracles," 18-19, MP, DC.
103. Ibid., 19.
104. Ibid., 20.
105. Ibid.
106. Ibid.; MMM to Daddy, 5 Aug. 1942, SS *Gripsholm,* rolling up to Rio [de Janeiro], MP, DC; MMM, "Twenty-three Thousand Miles of Miracles," 22, 24, MP, DC.
107. MMM, "Twenty-three Thousand Miles of Miracles," 24, MP, DC; MMM toDaddy, 5 Aug. 1942, SS *Gripsholm,* rolling up to Rio [de Janeiro], MP, DC.
108. MMM, "Twenty-three Thousand Miles of Miracles," 24-25, MP, DC.
109. MMM to Daddy, 5 Aug. 1942, SS *Gripsholm,* rolling up to Rio [de Janeiro], MP, DC.
110. MMM to Chicago Family [the family of ther brother John], 6 Aug. 1942, SS *Gripsholm,* rolling up to Rio [de Janeiro]; MMM to Daddy and Helen, 22 July 1942, SS *Conte Verde,* Lourenco Marques, both in MP, DC. MMM, "Twenty-three Thousand Miles of Miracles," 30, MP, DC.
111. MMM, "Twenty-three Thousand Miles of Miracles," 35, MP, DC.
112. "*Gripsholm* Passengers," *Key Reporter* 7 (May 1942): 3.
113. Ibid., 37. See also Mark J. Gayn, "Prelude to Treachery," *Reader'sDigest* (April 1942): 5-12.
114. MMM, "Twenty-three Thousand Miles of Miracles," 37, MP, DC.

Conclusion

1. Barnes, interview by author, 5 June 1990.
2. MMM, "Hainan Was My Home," 1, MP, DC.
3. MMM, BFM application, MP, PHS.
4. MMM to Grandma, 8 April 1917, Kachek, MP, PHS.
5. Bucher, interview by author, 3 July 1987; French, telephone conversation with author, 14 Sept. 1992.
6. MMM to William P. Schell, 3 July 1927, Marshalltown, Iowa, PCUSA, BFM Papers.
7. First Presbyterian Church, Marshalltown, Iowa, *Centennial Observance, 1858-1958,* 22; Barnes, interview by author, 11 Dec. 1989.

Bibliography

Archival Holdings

Melrose, Esther, and Paul Melrose. Papers. Special Collections, Univ. of Oregon Library, Eugene, Oreg.
Moninger, Mary Margaret. Application. Student Volunteer Movement for Foreign Missions Collection, Yale Univ. Divinity School, New Haven, Conn.
———. Papers. Private collection of Dorothy Gill Barnes, Columbus, Ohio.
———. Papers. Private collection of Susannah Moninger Dodson, Excelsior, Minn.
———. Papers. Archives of Grinnell College, Grinnell, Iowa.
———. Papers. Record Group 39. Presbyterian Historical Society, Philadelphia, Pa.
———. Papers. Special Collections, Univ. of Oregon Library, Eugene, Oreg.
Morse, Esther. Papers. Special Collections, Univ. of Oregon Library, Eugene, Oreg.
Presbyterian Church in the U.S.A. Board of Foreign Missions. Papers. Record Group 82. Presbyterian Historical Society, Philadelphia, Pa.
Seaton, Myrle, and Stuart Seaton. Papers. Private collection of Stuart Seaton, Johnson City, Tenn.
Tappan, David, and Luella Tappan. Papers. Special Collections, Univ. of Oregon Library, Eugene, Oreg.

Interviews

Barnes, Dorothy Gill. Interviews by author, Columbus, Ohio, 11 Dec. 1989 and 5 June 1990.
Bucher, Henry. Interview by author, Santa Fe, N.Mex., 3 July 1987.
Burkwall, Margaret. Interview by author, Duarte, Calif., 19 May 1987.
French, Evelyn. Interview by author, Pasadena, Calif., 21 May 1987; telephone conversations with author, 19 Oct. 1991, 17 May 1992, and 14 Sept. 1992.
Seaton, Stuart. Interviews by author, Johnson City, Tenn., 18 Feb. and 11 Aug. 1987.
Thomas, Robert. Interview by author, Riverside, Calif., 20 May 1987.

Published Books and Articles

Atlas of Marshall County, Iowa. Des Moines: G. W. Anderson, 1924.
Beaver, R. Pierce. *All Loves Excelling: American Protestant Women in World Mission.* Grand Rapids, Mich.: Eerdmans, 1968.
Boorman, Howard L. *Biographical Dictionary of Republican China.* 5 vols. New York: Columbia Univ. Press, 1968.
Chow Tse-tsung. *The May Fourth Movement: Intellectual Revolution in Modern China.* Cambridge, Mass.: Harvard Univ. Press, 1960.
Gayn, Mark J. "Prelude to Treachery." *Reader's Digest* (April 1942): 5-12.
Grieder, Jerome. *Intellectuals and the State in Modern China: A Narrative History.* New York: Free Press, 1981.
"*Gripsholm* Passengers." *Key Reporter* 7 (May 1942):3.
Hill, Patricia R. *The World Their Household: The American Woman's Foreign Mission Movement and Cultural Transformation, 1870-1920.* Ann Arbor: Univ. of Michigan Press, 1980.
Huber, Mary Taylor. *The Bishop's Progress: A Historical Ethnography of Catholic Missionary Experience on the Sepik Frontier.* Washington, D.C.: Smithsonian Institution Press, 1988.
Hunter, Jane. *The Gospel of Gentility: American Women Missionaries in Turn-of-the-Century China.* New Haven, Conn.: Yale Univ. Press, 1984.
Latourette, Kenneth Scott. *A History of Christian Missions in China.* New York: Macmillan, 1929.
Lodwick, Kathleen L. *The Chinese Recorder Index: A Guide to Christian Missions in Asia, 1867-1941.* 2 vols. Wilmington, Del.: Scholarly Resources, 1986.
———. "The Presbyterian Mission on Hainan Island under the Japanese, 1937-1941." *American Presbyterians: The Journal of Presbyterian History* 70 (Winter 1992): 247-58.
———. "Women at the Hainan Presbyterian Mission: Ministry and Diversion." *American Presbyterians: The Journal of Presbyterian History* 65 (Spring 1987): 19-28.
Lutz, Jessie Gregory. *China and the Christian Colleges, 1850-1950.* Ithaca, N.Y.: Cornell Univ. Press, 1971
———. *Chinese Politics and Christian Missions: The Anti-Christian Movements of 1920-1928.* Notre Dame, Ind.: Cross Cultural Publications, 1988.
Moninger, M[ary] M[argaret]. "The Hainanese Miao." *Journal of the North China Branch of the Royal Asiatic Society* 52 (1921): 40-50.
———. "The Hainanese Miao and Their Food Supply." *Lingnan Science Journal* 11, 4 (1932): 512-526ff.
———. "Paper Making in Stone Bridge Village, Hainan Island." *Lingnan Science Journal* 12, 3 (1933): 441-44.
———. "Picturesque Hainan," *Forward* (21 Jan. 1922): 18; (28 Jan. 1922): 26; and (4 Feb. 1922): 34.
———. "Salt Making in Khengdong District, Island of Hainan." *Lingnan Science Journal* 13 (1934): 697-98.
———. Trees and Typhoons in Hainan." *Lingnan Science Journal* 13, 2 (1934): 323-25ff.

———. "Times of Testing in China." *Women and Missions* 4 (Jan. 1928): 384-85.
[———], ed. *Isle of Palms: Sketches of Hainan*. Shanghai: Commercial Press, 1919; rpt., New York: Garland, 1980.
Price, Eva Jane. *China Journal, 1889-1900: An American Missionary Family during the Boxer Rebellion*. New York: Scribner's, 1989.
Ramsey, S. Robert. *The Languages of China*. Princeton, N.J.: Princeton Univ. Press, 1987.
Savina, F.M. *Histoire des Miao*. Hong Kong: Société des Missions-Etrangères, 1924.
Schafer, Edward H. *Shore of Pearls*. Berkeley: Univ. of California Press, 1970.
Service, John S., ed. *Golden Inches: The China Memoir of Grace Service*. Berkeley: Univ. of California Press, 1989.
Shafer, Boyd C. *Faces of Nationalism*. New York: Harcourt, 1972.
Sheridan, James E. *China in Disintegration: The Republican Era in Chinese History, 1912-1949*. New York: Free Press, 1975.
Woloch, Nancy. *Women and the American Experience*. New York: Knopf, 1984.

Periodicals, Pamphlets, and Dissertations

American Magazine 91 (Jan. 1921).
Chinese Recorder. 1915-41.
First Presbyterian Church, Marshalltown, Iowa. *Centennial Observance, 1858-1958*. Privately printed.
Grinnell College Bulletin 8, no. 1 (March-May 1910).
Grinnell College Cyclone. Vol. 20. May 1912. Published by the Class of 1913.
Grinnell College Scarlet and Black. 1909-13.
Heuser, Frederick. *Culture, Feminism and the Gospel: American Presbyterian Women and Foreign Missions, 1870-1923*, Ph.D. diss., Temple Univ., 1991.
Ladies' Home Journal. Jan. 1921.
Los Angeles Times. 17 and 18 Jan. 1942.
Marshalltown (Iowa) Times-Republican. 1915-42, 1950.
Washington (Pa.) Observer. 17 and 18 Jan. 1942.
Woman's Work, 1915-24.

Index

Note: Numbers in italic denote pages of photo insert.

aborigines, 111, 219 n 7. *See also* Kak Miao; Loi; Miao; Yao
Aeneid (Virgil), 31
Africa, 17, 206, 208, 209, 217
agriculture, 147-48. *See also* Miao, agriculture
A-heng, 204
Ainu, 71
airplanes, 90, 145, 173, 174, 182, 183, 189, 191, 198
Albion (Iowa), 15, 19
Ambrose (Mr.), 197, 202
America, 7, 210
American Board of Commissioners for Foreign Missions, 221 n 33
American Dutch Reformed Church, 154
American Magazine, 86, 229 n 106
Ames (Iowa), 15
Amoy (Fukien), 154, 172
Anatolia College (Marsovan, Turkey) 16
Annam/Annamese, 115, 119
anti-Christian activities, 62, 97, 105-6, 111-12, 121-22, 123-29, 132-37, 151-53, 214, 232 n 45
anti-foreignism, 105-6, 111-12, 113, 121, 123, 129, 132-33, 135, 226 n 10
Appleton (Mr.), 165
Argentina, 138
Art of Thinking, The (Dimnet), 161
Asama Maru, SS, 209
Asiatic Petroleum Co., 32
A-siu, 200

athletics, 67, 147
automobiles, 140-41, 148-49, 178-79
Baller, 26
Bang (Elder), 61, 70
Bang Hin-zong, 61, 130-31
Bangkok (Siam), 118
Bank of China, 172
banks, 36, 73-74, 114, 120, 172. *See also names of specific banks*
Baptists, 3, 44, 54
Barnes, Dorothy Gill, 19
Bastille Day, 114
beggars, 23, 24
Benet, Stephen Vincent, 162
Bercovitz, Elizabeth, *97c*, 88
Bercovitz, Elva (Mrs. Nathaniel), *97c, 97h*, 24, 26, 38, 70, 72, 75, 202, 204, 208, 222 n 41
Bercovitz, Nathaniel (M.D.), *97c, 97h*, 24, 26, 38, 70, 72, 75, 100, 108, 140, 182, 195, 197, 198, 201, 202, 203, 208, 222 n 41
Bercovitz, Peter, *97c*
Bible studies, 57, 201
Bible women, 62-63, 65
Big Sundays, 55, 58
Board of Foreign Missions, 2-3, 4, 5, 6, 8, 9, 13, 17, 18, 19, 21, 44, 61, 70, 71, 100, 102, 108, 112, 113, 129, 137, 138, 139, 143, 153, 158, 159, 161, 163-64, 181, 194, 196, 205, 210, 212, 216, 219 n 7, 241 n 73
Bolshevists. *See* Communists

Book of Martyrs (Foxes), 31
Botany (Gray), 34
botany, 7, 15, 34-35, 46, 81, 83-85, 95, 100
Bousman, H.H. (Rev.), 126
Boxers, 106, 225 n 2
boycotts, 53-54, 116, 118-19, 123, 125, 127
Braden, Samuel (Rev.), 20
Braden (Mrs. Samuel), 20
brigandage, 55, 77, 95, 96, 98, 106-8, 110-11, 118-19, 120, 126, 128-29, 142-44, 178. *See also* pirates
Bringing in the Sheaves, 139
British, 22, 112, 118, 129
Brooks, Van Wyck, 161
Brown, 25
Bucher, Henry (Rev.), 7, 57, 182, 215, 235 n 4
Bucher, Louise (Mrs. Henry), 183
Buck, Pearl S., xi
Buddhism, 56-57, 100
Buffalo Center (Iowa), 211
Burkwall, Geneva (Mrs. Herman), *97c*, 183, 187, 188, 192
Burkwall, Herman (M.D.), *97c*, 166, 182, 183, 184, 185, 186, 187, 190, 192, 193, 242 n 91
Burkwall, Margaret, *97h*, 202, 203, 205, 220 n 13, 242 n 91
Burkwall, Yola, *97c*, 192
Byers, Bobby, 20, 22, 88
Byers, Clara (Mrs. George), 20, 22, 39, 50, 58, 60, 62, 70, 77, 107, 110
Byers, David, 88
Byers, George D. (Rev.), 5, 10, 20, 22, 24, 34, 39, 40, 44, 63, 75, 76, 77, 80, *97c*, 100, 219 n 12, 228 n 84; murder of, 95, 106-10, 111, 146-47

Caesar, 202
Campbell, Dwight, 24
Campbell, Gertrude, 24
Campbell, Inetta (Mrs. Wilbur), 21, 24, 38, 94, *97c*, 100, 231 n 6
Campbell, Wilbur (Rev.), 24, 38, 94, *97c*, 100, 132
Canton, 33, 37, 44, 74, 94, 104-6, 107, 111-12, 113, 116, 125, 129, 145, 146, 177, 181, 196, 202, 205
Canton Christian College, 94
Canton Union Normal School, 62
Catholic University of America (Washington, D.C.), 205
Chamberlain, C.B. (U.S. vice consul), 108
Champaign (Ill.), 29

Chapin, Mae, 21, 24, 26, 29, 30, 31, 35, 36, 37, 38, 39, 62, 86, 96, *97c*, 109, 114, 168
Chengtu (Szechwan), 183
Cheung (Dr.), 197
Cheung (Mrs.), 197
Chicago, (Ill.), 210
China Council, 3, 5, 20, 24, 95, 101-2, 108, 112, 117, 129, 136, 159, 164, 195, 196, 224 n 96
China Inland Mission, 218 n 3
Chinese customs and lifestyle, 23, 38, 58-60, 68-69, 86, 93, 97-98, 121, 145-47, 148, 165. *See also* funerals; weddings, Chinese
Chinese government officials, 104-6, 107, 110, 111, 124, 126, 127-28, 134, 160; officials' wives, 47, 65-66
Chinese Imperial Maritime Customs Service personnel, 100, 113, 132, 134, 165-66, 182, 195, 196-97, 202, 206
Chinese military, 41, 54-56, 79, 100, 107, 118-22, 123-24, 128, 142-43, 145, 150, 166, 178, 184, 188, 189
Chinese New Year, 39-40, 69, 79, 100, 121, 122, 123, 142, 178, 180, 181, 183
Chinese Recorder, 121, 218 n 3
Christian and Missionary Alliance, 114
Christian Endeavor Society, 18, 89, 142, 221 n 27
Christian Herald, 162
Christians, Chinese, 6, 48, 54, 127, 141, 154, 156, 197; control of mission, 122, 135, 153; decision to convert, 58-61, 63-64; weddings, 32, 136. *See also* weddings, Chinese
Christians, Japanese, 199, 200
Christian Scientists, 3
Christmas, 8, 37-38, 87, 88, *97h*, 100, 104, 132-33, 166, 180, 185, 187, 195, 204, 205, 216
Christo-paganism, 75-76, 80
Chungking (Szechwan), 12, 205
Church of Christ in China, 142, 153-54. *See also* MMM, Church of Christ in China delegate
Cimmaron (Ferber), 161
City of Tokio, SS, 132
Columbia Country Club (Shanghai), 207
communications, 91, 183
communists, 97, 116, 118, 119, 126, 128, 129, 143, 144-45, 146, 148, 151, 162, 166, 217
Conard, Henry Shoemaker, 35, 83, 84
Confucianism and Modern China (Johnston), 161

Confucius/Confucianism, 34, 48, 52
Congregationalists, 3, 15, 18, 108, 199
consuls, British, 49-50, 105, 107, 108, 113, 118-19, 120, 124, 125, 134, 200
consuls, French, 105, 113, 125, 134
consuls, U.S., 5, 105, 107, 108, 109, 112, 113, 120, 125, 159, 172, 177, 193, 195, 209, 225 n 112
Conte Verde, SS, 206, 208, 209
cross cultural exchanges, 6-7, 67-68, 89, 213, 214
cultural imperialism, x, 6-7, 46, 50-54, 67-68, 78, 86
currencies, 74, 141, 194
Cuthbert (Mr.), 197, 204

D.A.R., 14, 93
Damtsiu (Hainan), 58, 183
Dang, (Mr.), 25, 30
Dante, 31
Dealan (Hainan), 42
Deng Vun-in, 105
Dengang (Hainan), 43
Depression (1930s), 4, 153
de Rautenfeld (Mr.), 100
Des Moines (Iowa), 13
Dickinson, Emily (relative), 17
Dimnet, 161
diseases, 66-67, 106, 125-26
Disperban, Father, 202
Dong (General), 118, 119, 120, 121
Dong (Little), 118
Double Ten Day, 50-52, 64, 121, 142, 177. *See also* nationalism; Revolution of 1911

Easter, 193, 197
Emerging Christian Faith, An (Nixon), 161-62
Empress of Asia, SS, 93
England, 176
Ensign, S.J.R. (Rev.), 103, 115, 124
Ensign, (Mrs. S.J.R.), 103, 115, 124
Errand to the World (Hutchinson), xi
evangelists, 62-63
Exile, The (Buck), xi
extraterritoriality, 6, 10, 47, 107-10, 121, 124, 125, 126, 134

F.B.I., 26, 210
Fahhih (Hainan), 41, 43
fauna of Hainan, 81, 85, 90, 103, 151
Ferber, Edna, 161
festivals, Chinese, 145-46
Fighting Angel (Buck), xi

finances, mission, 73-75, 100-101, 120, 141, 153, 233 n 67. *See also* MMM, mission treasurer
finances, personal, 25, 36, 37, 65, 120, 171-72, 199, 206, 224 n 96
Fletcher (Mr.), 108
Flynn (Mr.), 195, 197, 202
Flynn (Mrs.), 197, 202
Foa, 72
Foochow (Fukien), 154
Foochow affair, 133-34
food, Chinese, 23, 32, 39, 63, 147, 182-83; Western, 8-9, 39, 87-88, 118, 132, 166, 185, 188, 191-92, 203, 208
Foreign Missionary (Brown), 25
Fort Bayard (Kwangtung), 133
Forty Winks, 129
Forward, 72, 89
Fourth of July, 44, 50, 108, 114
Foxes, 31
Frame, Margaret, 101, 102, 164
France, 176
French, Arthur (Rev.), 97c, 141, 146, 147, 149, 150, 157, 160, 168, 195, 202, 210
French, Arthur (son), 195
French, Evelyn (Mrs. Arthur), 7, 97g, 141, 160, 195, 210, 215, 224 n 97, 228 n 84
French, Gordon, 195
French missionaries in Hainan. *See* Roman Catholics
Friends, Society of, 15, 18, 108
funerals, 30, 107, 156

Gallic War (Caesar), 202
gambling, 65, 98, 119, 124
games, 67, 88, 157, 163, 166, 201
Gilman, Frank P. (Rev.), 24, 31, 32, 58, 75, 88, 97c, 219 n 10, 219 n 12, 232 n 34
Gilman, Janet, 4, 97c
Gilman, Marion M. (Mrs. Frank P.), 24, 75
Ginling College (Nanking), 130-31
Gleeson, Kristen, 220 n 14
Golden Inches: The China Memoir of Grace Service (Service), 11
Gospel of Gentility (Hunter), xi, 5
Graham, Frances, 138
Gray, 34
Grinnell (Iowa), 14, 16, 18, 154, 208, 212, 213
Grinnell College, 1, 2, 14, 16, 17, 19, 35, 37, 83, 94, 138, 231 n 31
Grinnell-in-China, 16
Gripsholm, SS, 5, 208, 209
Hackett Medical College (Canton), 231 n 6

Index

Hainan News Letter, 9, 69-70
Haiphong (French Indochina), 90, 96, 112-18, 127, 133, 137, 176, 198, 199, 200, 241 n 77
Hakka, 111, 141
Halloween, 195
Halsey, A.W., 71, 228 n 64
Hamilton, M.M. (U.S. consul), 108, 109
Hangchow Christian College, 60
Hankow (Hupei), 129
Hanoi, SS, 92, 93-94, 113, 114, 115, 127, 133
Hanoi (French Indochina), 133
Hanyang (Hunan), 129
Hartland (Iowa), 221 n 27
Harvard University, 35
Henry, B.C. (Rev.), 219 n 7, 219 n 12
Heuser, Frederick, 219 n 4, 220 n 14
history, Chinese, 7
History of the Miaos (Savina), 116
Hoihow (Hainan), 6, 8, 11, 12, 23, 26, 31, 35, 42, 44, 54, 55, 72, 74, 90, 91, 92, 93, 95, 96, 100, 101, 105, 106, 107, 108, 112, 113, 115, 118, 119, 120, 121, 125, 127, 128, 132, 133, 134, 135, 136, 142, 143, 145, 146, 153, 155, 157, 162, 172, 173, 174, 176, 178, 180, 182, 185, 188, 190, 191, 192, 195, 197, 198, 199, 200, 201, 202, 203, 204, 207, 209, 226 n 9
Hoiping, SS, 90
Hokkaido (Japan), 71
Hong Kong, 8, 21-22, 24, 28, 33, 34, 44, 48, 62, 75, 82, 87, 90, 91, 92, 93, 94, 96, 102-3, 104, 107, 108, 112, 113, 115, 116, 117, 118, 119, 120, 125, 127, 129-30, 133, 134, 136, 137, 155, 162, 164, 171, 176, 183, 190, 193, 196, 200, 206, 209, 222 n 41
Hongkong and Shanghai Bank, 108, 114, 199
Hoover Institution (Stanford Univ.), 228 n 64
horses, 15, 40-41, 43, 78, 82, 96
Hoshi (Mr.), 197
hospitals, mission, 6, 55, 160-61, 190
House of Exile (Waln), 161
Hunter, Jane, xi, 5
Hutchinson, William, xi
Hyatt, Irwin, xi

Iap (Mr.), 168, 174, 179, 199
Iap Hi-soang, 228 n 69
Imada, Jiro, 221 n 22
Imperial University (Tokyo), 202
Inazu (Mr.), 204, 205

Inferno (Dante), 31
Introduction to the Study of Chinese (Mateer), 25
Iowa, 57, 65, 72, 74, 87, 91, 94, 108, 139, 211, 217. *See also placenames*
Iowa State College, 14, 15, 35, 212
Isle of Palms, 6, 9, 70-71, 227 n 63, 228 n 64
Ivory soap advertisement, 86, 229 n 106

Jade, SS, 92
Japan, 8, 53, 115. *See also placenames*
Japanese, 16, 54, 111, 112, 115, 137
Japanese military in Hainan, 12, 19, 97b, 170, 172-74, 179-81, 182-207, 210, 238 n 6. *See also* World War II
Jeremiassen, Carl C., 147, 219 n 12, 223 n 73, 232 n 34
Jersey City (N.J.), 210
John Brown's Body (Benét), 162
Johnston, R.F., 161
Journal of the North China Branch of the Royal Asiatic Society, 9, 82
Juliet (Father), 134

Kachek (Hainan), 3, 6, 9, 11, 21, 24, 27, 33, 34, 39, 40, 41, 42, 43, 44, 46, 48, 50, 52, 54, 55, 58, 61, 62, 63, 64, 65, 66, 67, 70, 72, 73, 76, 77, 79, 80, 83, 86, 87, 90, 91, 93, 96, 100, 105, 106, 107, 108, 109, 110, 111, 113, 125, 126, 128, 131, 133, 135, 136, 139, 141, 145, 146, 148, 149, 152, 153, 156, 159, 160, 163, 164, 168, 170, 171, 177, 178, 182, 201, 224 n 96
Kahanamoku, Duke, 20
Kaifong, SS, 94
Kak Miao, 7, 99. *See also* Miao
Kansas City (Mo.), 13, 17
Karlsruhe (Germany), 14
Keelung (Formosa), 207
Kellogg, Hariette (aunt), 15, 35, 89, 212
Kellogg, Maria Parks (grandmother), 89, 97a, 154
Kelly, J. Franklin (M.D.), 9, 21, 22, 24, 33, 44, 70, 72, 222 n 39
Kelly, Lillian M. (Mrs. J. Franklin), 9, 21, 22, 24, 35, 66, 70, 72, 222 n 39, 223 n 89
Khengtoa (Hainan), 58
Kialiakha (Hainan), 80
Kia-sang, 24, 25, 40
kites, 97d, 146, 214
Kiungchow (Hainan), 6, 8, 21, 22-23, 24, 25, 27, 29-30, 34, 36, 37, 39, 40, 44, 46, 48, 50, 53, 54, 55, 61, 62, 63, 68, 73, 75, 86, 95, 101, 105, 108, 109, 112, 118, 121, 125,

Index

127, 128, 132, 134, 135, 136, 139, 142, 143, 145, 149, 152, 153, 157, 168, 169, 170, 171, 172, 173, 174, 177, 178, 179, 181, 185, 191, 194, 195, 197, 199, 200, 202, 203, 204, 206, 209, 232 n 34
Koan-sio, 36
Kobe (Japan), 93, 137, 202
Korea, 96
Kramer Girls, The (Suchow), 161
Kuala Lumpur (Malaya), 24
Kuomintang, 131
Kwangtung, 34, 123, 152
Kyoto (Japan), 56

Ladies' Home Journal, 86, 229 n 106
LaMoilie (Iowa), 15
Lasell, Syndey (M.D.), 87
Laura Haygood Memorial School (Soochow), 131
Ledeboer (Mrs.), 32
Legal system, Chinese, 30, 110
Lengtui (Hainan), 67, 104
lepers, 24, 168
Leverett, William (Rev.), 24, 100
Li (Elder), 34, 144
Li (Mr.), 76
Li (Mrs.), 168
Li A-seng, 168
Li A-voe, 168
Li Hai-so, 55, 59-61, 216
Liamui (Hainan), 79
Liang, Sarah, 131, 234 n 99
Life of Emerson (Brooks), 161
Lim-kit, 36
Limko, 58, 111, 141
Lincoln, Abraham, 52
Lingnan Branch School for Boys (Kiungchow, Hainan), 159
Lingnan Science Journal, 9, 148
Little French Girl, The (Sedwick), 161
Loi, 6, 58, 62, 67, 72, 76, 77, 79, 81, 82, 83, 97f, 97g, 166, 219 n 7
Long Meadow (Hainan), 191
Lorenco Marques (Africa), 206, 209
Los Angeles (Calif.), 12, 205
Luichow Peninsula (Kwangtung), 55, 225 n 113
Lundstrum (Mr.), 221 n 33
Lung Ci-koang (Lung Chi-kuang), 41, 47, 48, 49, 66, 224 n 110
Lutz, Grace Livingstone, 161
Macdonald, Grace, 96, 97c, 164, 181, 182
Malaya, 84. *See also placenames*

Manchuria, SS, 20, 21
Manila (Philippines), 21, 84, 90, 117, 183, 205
Manila Bureau of Science, 35, 83-85
Marshalltown (Iowa), 8, 13, 16, 92, 108, 114, 181, 210, 211, 217
Marshalltown (Iowa) Times-Republican, 71, 89, 223 n 70
Maruyama (Lt.), 200, 201
Mary Farnham School (Shanghai), 130
Maryland, 14
Mateer, 25
Matsuo (Lt. Col.), 97b, 204, 207
Matsuzaki (Mr.), 199, 202
May Fourth movement, 7, 52-53
May Thirtieth incident, 111, 126, 232 n 45
McCandliss, Charles, 24, 222 n 41
McCandliss, Henry M. (M.D.), 97c 26, 35, 36, 42, 44, 70, 71, 72, 113
McCandliss, Olivia Kerr (Mrs. Henry M.), 24, 32, 72, 97c, 222 n 41, 226 n 9
McCandliss, Ruth, 4, 24, 97c, 222 n 41
McClintock (Mrs. Paul), 20, 24,
McClintock, Paul (Rev.), 20, 24
McCormick School (Kachek, Hainan), 159
McCreery, Caroline, 97c, 103, 107, 108, 109, 111, 118, 164, 181, 195
Meacham, Frank, 17
Meier-Graefe, Julius, 161
Melrose, Esther (Mrs. Paul), 97c, 141, 180, 186, 193, 205, 206, 210
Melrose, Jack, 97c
Melrose, John (Rev.), 89, 223 n 73, 232 n 34
Melrose, Margaret ("Mother," Mrs. John), 20, 22, 41, 89, 91, 97c, 141, 162, 163, 180, 223 n 73
Melrose, Paul (Rev.), 8, 87, 97c, 138, 141, 162, 180, 185-86, 187, 188, 190, 192, 193, 198, 205, 206, 210
Melrose, Sylvia, 97c
Memory Palace of Matteo Ricci, The (Spence), xi
Menado Maru, SS, 206, 207
Merrill, E.D., 83, 84, 85, 223 n 89
Methodists, 3, 17, 54, 131, 138, 169
Miao, 5, 6, 11, 46, 57, 62, 66, 75-83, 87, 95, 97e, 99-100, 116, 149-51, 166, 215, 216, 217, 228 n 76, 228 n 84, 229 n 96, 233 n 57; agriculture, 82-83, 150-51; Christians, 75-76, 77, 79-80, 81, 97f, 99-100, 150-51; clothing, 76-77, 99; customs, 76-77, 82-83, 220 n 15; girls at mission school, 78; language, 80
Millican (Mrs. Frank R.), 154

252 Index

Mirtz, Orville ("Jimmie," Rev.), *97c*
mission, Canton (South China), 101, 109, 129
mission, Hainan: Chinese employees, 24, 40, 59, 60, 62, 63, 122, 160-61, 207; churches, 6, *97g*; history, 6, 11-12, 31, 106, 138-39, 208, 213-14, 219 n 7; statistics, 6
mission, Nanking, 131
mission, Soochow, 131
mission, Szechwan, 130
mission, Thailand, 209. *See also* Siam
mission meetings, 42-44, 69-70, *97c,* 100, 108-9, 163, 170, 179, 181
mission, Yunnan, 101, 129, 208
missionaries: lifestyle of, ix-xii, 4, 6-7, 8-9, 10, 34-45, 59, 72, 75, 85-92, 96, 102-4, 107-9, 111, 114-18, 123-24, 129-30, 131, 133, 136, 137, 140-42, 159-66, 168-69, 171, 180, 197, 208, 224 n 103, 225 n 2; qualifications of, 2-5, 56, 219 n 4; statistics, 2, 208, 218 n 3; women, 2, 3-4, 5, 10-11, 17, 100, 154, 218 n 3, 220 n 14, 226 n 9
Missionary Home (Shanghai), 131
Moji (Japan), 93
Mok (Mr.), 199
Moninger, Bill (distant relative?), 208
Moninger, Demas (grandfather), 14, 108
Moninger, Dorothy ("Dot," sister), 15, 39, 93, *97b,* 137, 210, 211
Moninger, Frank (uncle), 14
Moninger, Harold (uncle), 15
Moninger, Helen ("Jimmie," sister), 15, 25, 28, 87, 89, *97b,* 114, 158, 209, 210
Moninger, John ("Jack," brother), 13, 15, 19, *97b,* 181, 195, 205, 210, 240 n 60, 241 n 73
Moninger, John Howard (uncle), 14
Moninger, Louise (sister), 15, 67, *97b,* 139, 153, 154, 158, 161, 210, 211
Moninger, Margaret, *97a, 97b, 97c, 97h;* attitude toward Chinese, 23, 29, 48, 49, 50-52, 59, 60, 62, 67-69, 70-71, 97, 101, 104-6, 110, 111, 119-20, 122, 123, 124, 128, 130, 135, 143-44, 147, 153, 163, 167, 177-78, 213, 214, 215, 230 n 5; birthdays, 14-15, 38-39, 87, 188, 202, 224 n 102; books read, 161-62; "Cedarcroft," 15, 195; childhood, 1, 14-16, 19, 195; China Council member, 101-2, 129-32, 139, 140, 142; Church of Christ in China delegate, 139, 154; clothing, 8; death, 12, 217; death reported in error, 12, 205; decision to become a missionary, 1-2, 11, 13, 16, 17-19, 212-13, 215-16, 221 n 14; education, 1-2, 15-17, 94, 138, 216, 221 n 16; entertaining, 67-68, 87, 159, 164-66, 180, 195, 202, 204, 205; evaluation by colleagues, 1, 7, 9-10, 57, 71, 138-39, 140-42, 143-44, 156-58, 162-63; family, 13-16, 19, 57, 72, 87, 88-89, *97a, 97b,* 108, 114, 139, 158, 195-96, 210, 221 n 33; furloughs, 2, 92-94, 136-37, 138-39, 153-54, 161, 168, 169, 195; goals, 61-62, 78, 139, 217; Hainanese-English dictionary, 5, 9, 73, 167-68, 179-80, 188, 214, 228 n 69, 238 n 78, 239 n 26; house arrest, 12, 19, *97b,* 170, 198-207, 216, 217, 238 n 6; housekeeping, 39, 85-86, 91, 159-60, 230 n 118; illnesses, 9, 26-27, 28, 35-36, 166-67, 198, 211, 217; itinerating/evangelistic work, 11, 57, 58-59, 75-83, 139, 145-49, 158-59, 228 n 84; language lessons and ability, 5, 17, 19, 20, 25-28, 72-73, 80, 88, 99, 115, 141, 168, 238 n 78, 241 n 77; letters, ix, 7-8, 23, 29, 39-40, 46, 89-90, 95-96, 115, 116-17, 123, 127, 139, 151, 158, 162, 170, 176, 181, 183, 185, 190, 193, 201, 209, 235 n 6, 236 n 33; mission agent, 95, 141, 194-95, 196-97; mission secretary, 5, 70, 100, 107-8, 158-59, 181; mission treasurer, 5, 46, 74-75, 95, 100-101, 136, 141, 159, 171-72, 194-95, 206, 233 n 67; poetry, 9, 35, 44, 103-4; publications, 6, 9, 46, 69-72, 82, 103-4, 148, 159, 202, 227 n 63, 228 n 64; relations with colleagues, xi, 13, 20, 72, 102, 109, 138, 141-42, 156-58, 163, 164, 181, 191-92, 210; religious beliefs, x, 2, 5, 15, 16, 17, 18, 19, 56-57, 154-58, 212, 214-15, 216, 228 n 84; repatriation, 5, 12, 206-10; retirement, 211-17; sense of humor, 12, 20, 22, 26, 35-36, 37-38, 53, 67, 80-81, 103-4, 114, 131-32, 181, 187, 195, 202-3, 216; teaching career, 1-2, 5, 17, 46, 53, 57, 61-62, 64-65, 68-69, 73, 97-99, 121-22, 138, 139, 151-53, 159, 168, 170-71, 175, 178, 179, 211, 212, 213; vacations, 62, 91-92, 104-5, 107, 117, 171, 193
Moninger, Mary Helen Kellogg ("Minnie," mother), 14, 15, 19, *97a, 97b,* 139, 158
Moninger, Mary Ringland (grandmother), 14, 15, 19, 57
Moninger, Mildred (distant relative?), 208
Moninger, William R. (father), 1, 8, 14, 19, *97b,* 139, 185, 195, 210, 211, 241 n 73
Montgomery, Henrietta, 21, 24, 79, 219 n 12
Montgomery Ward, 38
morphine, 21
Morse, Esther (M.D.), x, xi, 1, 2, 8, 9, *97c,*

140, 141-42, 143, 144, 145, 154-67, 171, 177-78, 180, 181, 185, 191, 193, 195, 198, 210, 214, 215, 220 n 13, 237 n 51
Morton, Annie R., 130
Munnell, Mary ("Aunt Tot"), 108, 221 n 33
music, 23, 67-68, 197
Muslims, 147
Myers, (U. S. consul), 209
Myers, Ramon H., 9

Nagasaki (Japan), 93
Nakamura, Lt. (the first), 199, 201, 202
Nakamura, Lt. (the second), *97b,* 202, 204, 206, 207
Namfo (Hainan), 81
Namfong (Hainan), 182
Namhoang, SS, 90
Nanking (Kiangsu), 19, 130, 131
National Christian Council, 208
nationalism, Chinese, 7, 50-54, 105-6, 111-12, 115-16, 142, 153, 177, 214, 226 n 10
Naughty Marietta, 193
Navy, British, 113, 129
Navy, U.S., 108, 129, 211
neutrality of missionaries, 33, 116, 185-87
New Providence (Iowa), 1, 17, 19
newspapers, 9, 176, 233 n 50. *See also names of specific newspapers*
New Terms for New Ideas, 88
Newton, Clarence (Rev.), 49, *97c*
Newton (Mrs. Clarence), 24
New York (N.Y.), 13, 94, 112
Ngou (Elder), 122
Ngou (Mr.), 63-64,
Ngou (Pastor), 146, 238 n 78
Ngou Ngi-tin, 27
Ngou Ziau-hoa, 63-64
Nixon, Justin W., 161
Nodoa (Hainan), 6, 11, 34, 40, 41, 42, 43, 44, 45, 61, 73, 109, 111, 133, 135, 139, 140, 141, 142, 143, 151, 152, 157, 163, 164, 170, 171, 172, 174, 175, 176, 177, 179, 180, 181, 182, 183, 184, 185, 186, 187, 188, 189, 192, 193, 201, 206
North China Herald, 89, 90, 106
Northern Expedition, 133

Ong (Mr.), 33
opium 8, 23, 58, 124
Osaka (Japan), 202
Ostenso, Martha, 161
Otsuke (Mr.), 204
Ouija (Mr.), 207
Our Ordered Lives Confess (Hyatt), xi

Overholser, C. Wayne (Rev.), 211
Overholser (Mrs. C. Wayne), 211
Overseas Chinese, 115

pagoda, 38, *97d*
Pakhoi (Kwangtung), 113, 117, 118
Paris Peace Conference, 52. *See also* World War I
Parks, Auntie (aunt), 16, 30
Parks, Phoebe Farnham (great-grandmother), *97a*
Peking (Hopeh), 106, 111, 116, 117, 123
Peking Bureau of Education, 123
Peking Union Medical College, 167
Peking University, 52
Penang (Malaya), 24
Phi Beta Kappa, 1, 5, 16, 20, 209, 212, 221 n 16
Philippine National Herbarium (Manila), 223 n 89
Philippines, 12, 46, 84, 85, 176
Pilgrim's Progress (John Bunyan), 67
pirates, 42, 225 n 113
Pitkin School (Kiungchow, Hainan), *97e,* 152, 159, 170, 174-76, 179, 186, 187
Pittsburgh (Penn.), 210
politics, Chinese, 33-34, 47-50, 121, 123-24, 143, 215. *See also* Revolution of 1911
Presbyterian church, 2, 15, 18
Presbyterians, 44, 54, 71, 95, 96, 117, 122, 131, 133, 208
President Madison, SS, 96
President McKinley, SS, 131-32, 169
President Taft, SS, 137, 193
Price, Eva Jane, 225 n 2
Procter and Gamble, 86

Queen Victoria (Strachey), 161

Rawlinson, Frank, 233 n 69
Reader's Digest, 210
Recreation (Lutz), 161
Red Cross, 181-82
Redmon, J. Owen, 221 n 22
Red Star Over China (Snow), 162
refugees, 47, 55-56, 119-20, 182-83, 185, 188-92; missionaries as, 112-18, 135-37
religion, Chinese, 23, 31, 58-59
Religion in a Changing World (Silver), 161
Re-thinking Missions, 162
Revolution of 1911, 7, 33, 48, 105
Ricci, Matteo, xi
Ringland, Mary (great-grandmother), 15
Rio de Janeiro (Brazil), 209

Roman Catholics, 79, 199, 202, 205, 213; Hoihow orphanage, 32, 133-34, 197-98; Jesuits in 17th-century Hainan, 30. *See also* Ricci, Matteo
Royal Asiatic Society, 93
Russians, 117

Sacramento, SS, 108
St. Paul (Minn.), 13
Salsbury, Chalmers, *97c*
Salsbury, Clarence (M.D.), 24, 41, *97c*, 113
Salsbury, Cora (Mrs. Clarence), 24, *97c*
salt making, 148
Sands (Mr.), 206
San Francisco (Calif.), 20
Saturday Evening Post, 162
Savina, F.M. (Father), 116, 134, 233 n 57
schools, Chinese, 97, 109-110, 135, 151, 230 n 5, 231 n 6
schools, mission, 6, 28, 61, 62, 109-110, 125-27, 134, 139, 142-43, 173, 174-76, 178, 182; curricula, 67, 122; fees, 29, 175; female students, 28-29, 37, 47, 50, 52-53, 61-65, 68-69, 97-98, *97e*, 105, 119, 123, 124, 126-27, 130-31, 134-35, 151-52, 171, 173-76; male students, 37, 52-53, 67-68, 81, 97-98, 105, 152, 171, 173-76, 184; registration issue, 121-22, 123, 126, 135, 151-53, 175; relations with government officials, 65, 122, 126-27, 152-53, 175; student health, 66-67; teachers, 63, 68-69, 105, 131, 182. *See also names of specific schools*
Schaeffer, Katherine, 10, 21, 24, 25, 27, 33, 36, 37, 39, 40, 41, 43, 54, 55, 59, 60, 62-66, 70, 72, 73, 75, 79, 81-84, 87-88, 90, 91, 97, *97c*, 99, 101, 111, 125, 128, 163, 164, 216, 219 n 12, 224 n 96
Scranton (Penn.), 208
Search, The (Lutz), 161
Seaton, Myrle (Mrs. Stuart), *97c*, 103, 114, 116, 195
Seaton, Ronald, *97c*
Seaton, Stuart (M.D.), 7, *97c*, 103, 195
Seaton, Wallace, *97c*
Seattle (Wash.), 90, 137, 181
Sedgwick, Ann Douglass, 161
Service, Grace, 11
Setsani (Mr.), 205
Shameen Island (Kwangtung), 105
Shanghai (Baptist) College, 131
Shanghai (Kiangsu), 8, 33, 44, 70, 93, 95, 101-2, 106, 111, 112, 117, 125, 126, 129, 130, 131, 132, 136, 140, 142, 165, 172, 177, 206, 207-8, 212

Shanghai American School, 207
Shannon, Grace (Mrs. James), 38, 87, *97c*
Shannon, James (Rev.), 38, *97c*
Shannon, Mary Elizabeth, *97c*
Siam, 119, 196. *See also* mission, Thailand
Silver, Abba Hillel (Rabbi), 161
Sin Hau-koang, 166
Sin Si-ki, 54, 55
Singapore, 24, 64, 74, 118, 119, 147, 148, 209
Skinner, Alice, x, 20, 21, 24, 54, 62, 79, *97c*, *97h*, 147, 164, 171, 174, 181, 195, 197, 198-99, 200, 201, 203, 204, 206, 207, 208, 239 n 29, 241 n 72
Snow, Edgar, 162
Sokolsky, George, 162
Soochow (Kiangsu), 131
South America, 14, 217
Spence, Jonathan, xi
Standard Oil Co., 22, 114, 115, 199
Star-Spangled Banner, The, 210
State University of Iowa, 14, 216
Steiner, Elizabeth, *97c*
Steiner, Geneva, *97c*
Steiner, John (Rev.), 24, *97c*, 107, 113, 192, 196, 209
Steiner, Madeline (Mrs. John), 24, *97c*, 114, 116
Stinson, William (Rev.), 95, *97c*, 106, 132
Story of Philosophy, The, 161
Strachey, Lytton, 161
Strawberry Point (Iowa), 211
Street, Alfred (Mrs.), 24, 32
Street, Alfred (Rev.), 36, 42, 72
Street, Edith, 24
strikes (*see also* boycotts), 52-54, 105, 106, 111-12, 113, 123, 124, 125, 127-28
student demonstrations, 105, 111-12, 113, 115-16, 118-19, 127-28, 132, 231 n 31. *See also* anti-Christian activities; boycotts; May 4th movement; strikes
Student Volunteer Movement for Foreign Missions (SVMFM), 1-2, 13, 17, 18, 212, 213, 218 n 2, 219 n 4
Suchow, Ruth, 161
Su Dung-po, 168
Sui-moe, 183
Sunday, Billy, 16, 19
Sun Yat-sen, 105, 106, 109, 110, 118, 125, 136, 224 n 110
Swatow (Kwangtung), 172, 181
Swiss people, 207

Tai-mui, 36, 203, 207
Takada (Mr.), 196, 207

Talmage, Katherine M., 154
Tappan, David (Rev.), 24, 27, 39, 42, 44, 60, 61, 63, 64, 72, 73, 88, 97c, 105, 110, 113 121, 124, 154, 156, 163, 202, 205, 208, 216, 242 n 101
Tappan, David (son), 97c, 114
Tappan, Luella (Mrs. David), 97c, 114, 193
Tate, E. Mowbray, 209
Taylor, Mary, 97c, 112, 114, 181, 206
Thanksgiving, 8, 87, 88, 165
theater, 23
thievery, 30-31, 33, 41-42, 75, 79, 98-99, 128, 175, 204. See also brigandage
Thomas, Daniel, 165
Thomas, David (Rev.), 52, 74, 93, 97c, 109, 110, 126, 145, 146, 149, 157, 163, 165, 181, 205
Thomas, David, Jr., 165
Thomas, Jean, 97c
Thomas, Meta (Mrs. David), 97c, 165, 181, 205
Thomas, Richard, 97c
Thomas, Robert, 97c
Tientsin (Hopeh), 111
tin mines, 175-76
Tinderbox of Asia, The (Sokolsky), 162
Tinsui (Hainan), 79
Tintai (Hainan), 98
Tong (Dr.), 141
Tot, Aunt. *See* Munnell, Mary
travel by steamers, 9, 20-22, 91-94, 96, 113, 132, 137, 169, 206-10, 222 n 41
travel in Hainan, 8, 9, 22-23, 24-25, 31-32, 40-43, 73-74, 96, 140-41, 148-49, 151, 178-79, 181-82, 192, 216
travel in U.S., 13, 181, 210
treaty relations, U.S./China, 121
Tsingtao (Shangung), 111
Tu (Dr.), 131
Tunggnai (Hainan), 24

U.S.A., 176
Uidiok (Hainan), 24-25
Uihong (Hainan), 34, 44
University of Philippines (Manila), 83

Valentine's Day, 165
Vancouver (B.C.), 93, 96
Vangtsiu (Hainan), 55
Vantvort (Mr.), 165
Vautrin, Minnie, 131
Victoria (B.C.), 90

Vincent Van Gogh (Meier-Grafe), 161
Virgil, 31
Vunsio, Hainan, 143

Walker's Comprehensive Concordance, 57
Waln, Nora, 161
Warnshuis, A.L., 233 n 69
warfare, 33-34, 47-50, 54, 95, 105, 118, 120, 121, 142-46, 172, 180-81, 182-207
Washington, George 52
Washington (Iowa), 138
Washington (Penn.), 12, 14, 205
Waterloo (Iowa), 13
Waters under the Earth, The (Ostenko), 161
weddings, Chinese (non-Christian), 97-98, 97d. *See also* Chinese customs and lifestyle
Westerners (non-mission): in Hainan, 44, 113, 195, 204, 219 n 12; in Hong Kong, 22, 129-30
Whampoa (Kwangtung), 105
White, George E. 16
White, Stanley, 61, 70
Wisconsin, 94
Woman's Work, 9, 71
women, Chinese, 28-29, 39, 40, 61, 62, 63, 66, 206-7, 215, 231 n 6; concubines, 66, 69, 160; lifestyle, 134-35. *See also* Bible women; Christians, Chinese; schools, mission: female students
Women's Christian College (Kobe, Japan), 202
World War I, 22, 52, 72, 89. *See also* Paris Peace Conference
World War II, 12, 170, 172-74, 177, 180-81, 182-210, 211, 217. *See also* Japanese military in Hainan
Wuchang (Hupeh), 129
Wu Pei-fu, 121

YMCA, 16
YWCA, 16, 17, 18
Yale-in-China (Changsha), 106
Yamaguchi (Mr.), 204, 205
Yangtze River, 129
Yao, 7, 99, 229 n 96, 233 n 57
Yokohama (Japan), 17, 21 93
Yokohama Specie Bank, 206
Yuan Shih-k'ai, 33, 53, 224 n 110
Yunnan, 54, 117, 193

Zih-fong, 58
Zi-keng, 98
Zongsaubae (Hainan), 78

www.ingramcontent.com/pod-product-compliance
Lightning Source LLC
Chambersburg PA
CBHW021836220426
43663CB00005B/274